1999

)

00
2001

21 DEC 2001

BROKEN NUPTIALS IN SHAKE-SPEARE'S PLAYS

CAROL THOMAS NEELY

University of Illinois Press

Urbana and Chicago

Illini Books edition, 1993
© 1985 by Carol Thomas Neely
Manufactured in the United States of America
P 5 4 3 2 1

This book is printed on acid-free paper.

Library of Congress Cataloging-in-Publication Data

Neely, Carol Thomas, 1939–
    Broken nuptials in Shakespeare's plays / Carol Thomas Neely.
        p.   cm.
    "Illini books ed."—T.p. verso.
    Originally published: New Haven : Yale University Press, © 1985.
    Includes bibliographical references and index.
    ISBN 0-252-06362-7 (pbk. : alk. paper)
    1. Shakespeare, William, 1564–1616—Knowledge—Manners and
customs.   2. Man-woman relationships in literature.   3. Marriage in
literature.   4. Sex role in literature.   5. Love in literature.
I. Title.
PR3069.L6N44   1993
822.3'3—dc20   93-24730
                                                          CIP

Previously published in cloth (ISBN 0-300-03341-9)
by Yale University Press.

For

Sophia, Mark, and Juliet

now grown in grace / Equal with wond'ring

. . . wooing, wedding, and repenting·is as a Scotch jig, a measure, and a cinquepace. The first suit is hot and hasty like a Scotch jig (and full as fantastical); the wedding, mannerly modest, as a measure, full of state and ancientry; and then comes Repentance and with his bad legs falls into the cinquepace faster and faster till he sink into his grave.

—Beatrice, in *Much Ado About Nothing*

Contents

Preface

The manuscript of *Broken Nuptials in Shakespeare's Plays* was completed in 1983, midway between 1973, when I began writing it, and its reprinting now in 1993. The book grew out of theoretical movements and methods of the sixties and seventies: New Criticism, feminist criticism, and psychoanalytic criticism. It opens up into the developments of the eighties and nineties: New Historicism, feminist materialist criticism, and cultural studies.[1] The introduction and notes to *Broken Nuptials* record the critical dialogues I was engaged in while I was writing it. This preface puts the book into dialogue with approaches that have gained prominence in the field of Renaissance literary studies since it was written. I analyze how its extended interpretations of five Shakespeare plays, situated within their dramatic genres, provide material for thinking through questions that, when I wrote it, had not yet been formulated.

Since the late sixties, political, institutional, and theoretical movements influencing all academic fields have worked to dismantle in productive and unsettling ways the fixed assumptions I grew up with—assumptions of the unity, coherent identity, and autonomy of the author, the artwork, the self, and the history in which these are enveloped. Subsequently, gender, race, class, sexuality, and subjectivity—the critical categories that helped call into question older notions of unity, universality, and transcendence—were in their turn disunified, in part because of their shifting intersections with each other.[2] Women can be black or white, gay or straight; the lower ranks include men and women. History, once believed solid enough to provide answers to interpretive questions, in its turn came to be construed as multiple and unstable—a function of the fragmentary texts out of which it is read and the differing investments of those who do the reading.

In Renaissance studies, challenges to formalism's assumptions of the unity and autonomy of the artwork emerged in the seventies. Psychoanalytic critics uncovered the unconscious of the self and the text. Feminist critics sought to recover the hidden woman's part; in doing so they began to re-form the shape of texts and the literary canon. Continental theory (Derridean deconstruction, Lacanian psychoanalysis, and French feminism) theorized a self that was fractured at its origins by language's disjunction from reality and desire's division from its object. Feminism and psychoanalysis provided the context for *Broken Nuptials;* continental theory was less influential.

The theoretical movements emerging in the eighties, especially New Historicism and cultural materialism, renamed the field "early modern" in order to avoid the humanist, elitist, and validating implications of "Renaissance" and redirected its energies. In particular they explored the intersections of literary texts with new histories, with politics and culture, with ideology, a vexed term redefined to mean the economic and cultural forces that form individual subjects and inform their beliefs and actions. In 1985, the year *Broken Nuptials* was published, these new directions were consolidated by the appearance of three collections of essays on Shakespeare: *Political Shakespeare: New Essays on Cultural Materialism,* edited by Jonathan Dollimore and Alan Sinfield; *Alternative Shakespeares,* edited by John Drakakis; and *Shakespeare and the Question of Theory,* edited by Patricia Parker and Geoffrey Hartman. These books opened up Shakespeare plays to systematic theorizing, to persistent historicizing, to political analysis, and to deconstruction of the text and its ongoing cultural reproductions.[3] They dis-unified Shakespeare texts, seeing them as ideologically contradictory and structurally fractured. At the same time they re-placed the plays in contexts broader than those from which they had been extracted by New Critical practices. Rejecting notions of literary "foreground" and historical "background," critics stressed the fluid interactions of Shakespeare's plays with "history," nonliterary texts, and other Renaissance drama and literature.

Soon afterward more explicitly feminist collections appeared: *Rewriting the Renaissance: The Discourses of Sexual Difference in Early Modern Europe*, edited by Margaret Ferguson, Maureen Quilligan, and Nancy Vickers; and *Women in the Middle Ages and the Renaissance: Literary and Historical Perspectives*, edited by Mary Beth Rose. More extensively than the earlier collections, these included familial and political relations, feminist and materialist criticism, literature and history, and placed Shakespeare amidst other writers including women. They emphasized how gender difference inflects communities, artworks, and historical periods.[4] Since then, attention has continued to be focused on history and on difference: gender difference, sexual difference, ethnic difference. These developments have eroded further the once circumscribed human subject and the once sharply demarcated boundaries between literary and nonliterary texts. The titles of some recent books on Shakespeare signal these new assumptions of permeable boundaries and proliferating differences: *Shakespeare Reproduced: The Text in History and Ideology*, edited by Jean Howard and Marion O'Connor; *Shakespearean Negotiations: The Circulation of Social Energy in Renaissance England*, by Stephen Greenblatt; and *The Matter of Difference: Materialist Feminist Criticism of Shakespeare*, edited by Valerie Wayne. Some of these critical developments emerge in the introduction to *Broken Nuptials*; others shadow its margins. In the rest of this preface, I will explore how the book enters into dialogue with these reconfigured issues of history and ideology, of sexual and cultural difference.

MARRIAGE AND IDEOLOGICAL CONTRADICTIONS

My book's title signals its focus on disruption and on the social construction of women through the institution of marriage. It examines how marriage as a legal, religious, and social institution decisively shapes women's subjectivity, sexuality, and social roles in the plays. "Nuptials" are the series of ritualized contracts that together make a marriage: the betrothal, the wedding ceremony, and the sexual consummation. Nuptials or marriages in Shakespeare's plays are "broken"—are interrupted, irregular, or aborted. These interruptions, I show, enact the conflicting psychological needs marriage must satisfy and the competing ideologies it must serve in the period. The book's introduction examines some of the period's conceptions of marriage. More recent scholarship has broadened our understanding of women's marital roles, analyzing a wide range of period documents and providing new editions of them that help to situate the plays.[5] In particular this scholarship looks at how women are contradictorily seen as both equal to and subordinate to their husbands. Valerie Wayne's introduction to her edition of Edmund Tilney's *Flower of Friendship*, for example, extends and contextualizes the brief analysis of this work in my original introduction. She shows how its contradictory ideas of women's marital status have widespread roots: in humanist, Protestant, and puritan discourse, in English and continental handbooks, and in Elizabeth's attitudes toward marriage. The instances of broken nuptials I analyze reveal similar faultlines in the plays: in the weddings that cement misogyny and silence shrews in *Much Ado About Nothing* and *The Taming of the Shrew*, in the delusory sexual encounter required to complete sovereign-enforced cross-class marriage in *All's Well That Ends Well*, in the sundered or deferred cross-cultural unions of *Othello* and *Antony and Cleopatra*, and in the substitute asexual families required to reconstitute marriage in *The Winter's Tale*. Neither weddings nor marriages—in the plays discussed or in my interpretations of them—constitute straightforward happy endings; they are variously marked, as are all the discourses of marriage in the period, by disruption and gender trouble.

THE DISCOURSE OF MISOGYNY

Intersecting with the period's debates about marriage is the discourse of misogyny—of woman-hating—and the negative stereotypes of women that it promulgates. My book includes extensive analysis of the function of misogyny in particular characters, in the formation of male homosocial bonds, in the structure of plays, in the shaping of genres. Recent work has made it possible to theorize and historicize this discourse further by examining it in the light of its appearances in, for example, Castiglione's *The Courtier*, Tilney's *The Flower of Friendship*, the Women Controversy pamphlets, especially the responses by Ester Sowernam, Rachel Speght, and Constantia Munda to Joseph Swetnam's *Arraignment . . .* , and in other drama, such as Elizabeth Cary's *Tragedy of Mariam*.[6] The discourse has a comic, highly conventionalized rhetorical structure. Its satiric attacks produce a negative stereotype of women particular to the early modern period. Swetnam's title, for example, accuses women of being aggressively "lewd, idle, froward, and unconstant"; in contrast, Professor von X, the caricatured misogynist in Virginia Woolf's *A Room of One's Own*, attacks instead women's mental, moral, and physical inferiority. In early modern culture, misogyny is a recyclable discourse; it can be reproduced in unexpected places with unexpected results. Linda Woodbridge notes, in *Women and the English Renaissance*, that Renaissance misogynists represent aspects of women that their idealizing defenders suppress. Therefore Rosalind, in disguise, can use the discourse of misogyny to express and justify women's unruliness. In its historical development, in particular treatises, and in stage plays, the discourse often catalyzes the defense of women. *The Romance of the Rose* begets Christine de Pisan's *City of Ladies;* Gaspare's attack on women in *The Courtier* generates a defense of them in Book 3; dramatic misogynists, like Benedick in *Much Ado*, Enobarbus in *Antony and Cleopatra*, and Leontes in *The Winter's Tale*, characterized and rendered comic by their misogyny, convert to become defenders of women. But Iago instead converts Othello. My discussions of these misogynists provoke questions about the historical development and cultural and dramatic uses of this surprisingly fluid and unpredictable discourse.

THE GENDERING OF THE SUBJECT

Broken Nuptials analyzes how marriage constructs gendered selves, defining men by their public and institutional roles while shaping women within the private family roles of maid/wife/widow. Current criticism often terms these selves "subjects," to emphasize the ways in which division within or structures outside individuals shape their identity (or subjectivity).[7] It claims that, although human beings act as originators of their own desires and actions, they are also partially subjugated by forces, including language, that elude consciousness or control. And men and women are shaped differently. Jaques's well-known "Seven Ages of Man" speech in *As You Like It* is a telling example of how cultural discourses and institutions shape the human subject and define it as male, silently erasing women. Jaques begins his speech arguing that men and women both play prefabricated parts. But his depictions, between the first, pre-gendered state of infancy and the final, post-gendered state of senility, picture roles that only (upper-class) men could play: schoolboy, Petrarchan lover with mistress (as object of his love), soldier, judge, pantaloon. Even the biological markers of growth are signified by the exclusively male conditions of beardedness and voice change. Sexuality, marriage, and child rearing are excluded. In contrast, as my interpretations of the female characters reveal, even when they are rulers like Cleopatra or healers like Helena, they are characterized largely by their sexuality and their relation to male authority. The female selves that get represented in the plays are defined by their stages in the marriage paradigm—as unmarried virgins, married women, mothers, widows.

Because culture defines women as other and places contradictory demands on them, their representations are marked by division, disjunction, and disappearance.[8] As *Broken Nuptials* shows, when women characters move from maidenhood to marriage, the loss of family, name, and virginity attending this rite of passage is represented as a loss of identity and subjectivity, one marked by silence (of Helena and Hermia in *Midsummer Night's Dream*) or by disappearance and mock death (by Hero in *Much Ado About Nothing* and Helena in *All's Well That*

Ends Well). Married women characters who are mothers also disappear for reasons I explore in the last chapter of the book. They die or appear to die in childbirth; they too undergo mock deaths, and reappear suddenly and surprisingly, without accounting for their absence. These disjunctive representations of Shakespeare's women characters manifest how culture doles out roles to women in particular historical periods, shaping how they can be represented and how they see themselves.

SEXUALITY

Broken Nuptials spends a good deal of time exploring the different ways in which male and female sexuality are represented in particular plays and, especially, in different Shakespearean genres. It points toward current work, particularly in gay and lesbian studies, that historicizes sexuality, separates it from gender, and theorizes the multiple structures and representations of homosexual and heterosexual pleasures and desires.[9] Such work shows how sexuality, like subjectivity, is not monolithic and is shaped by ideological pressures. It clarifies for me how the plays participate in what Adrienne Rich calls "compulsory heterosexuality," steering characters into conventionally gendered heterosexual unions. My book also analyzes the cost of those unions, which suppress competing transgressive desires such as Titania's eroticized bonds with the Indian votress, with her changeling child, and with Bottom in A Midsummer Night's Dream, or Enobarbus's powerfully erotic bond with Antony, represented though his hyperbolic praise and degradation of Cleopatra, and through his death-ditch identification with her. While much of the work currently being done on desire and sexuality in the plays and period focuses on the disturbances generated by cross-dressing by actors and characters,[10] and on recovering the cultural signs and meanings of male homosexuality, my book implies other dissonant desires that disrupt normalized sexuality, gender relations, and marriage. Further examination of how they participate in marriage's regularization of the social order are called for. My analysis of bawdy imagery of penetration in Much Ado, of tumescence and detumescence in All's Well, of orgasmic foreplay at Cleopatra's death, of grotesque breeding in Autolycus's ballads can prompt readers to ask who is aroused by these images, how they are inflected by the bodies of boy actors, and how they intersect with social discourses of sexual regulation.

ETHNICITY, RACE, AND CLASS

Like much of the American psychoanalytic feminism of the early seventies, *Broken Nuptials* analyzes gender difference at the expense of other differences of race, class, and sexuality that intersect with and complicate gender construction.[11] This omission is most visible in my essay on *Othello,* written earliest. Rigorously supporting my claim that the male characters are all alike, as are the female characters, the chapter downplays the differences among them created by Othello's race, by Emilia's and Bianca's class, or by the homoerotic bonds and rivalries between Iago and Othello. Recent scholarship has begun to explore the effects of race in the play, to examine its treatment in the history of productions, and to retrieve the sixteenth-century history of Moors and of Africa. But explorations of racial difference sometimes subordinate gender or reduce Desdemona to her gender and Othello to his race, instead of examining the play's representations of the interlocking oppressions of race and gender.[12] Current discussions of "racism" or "colonialism" sometimes oversimplify or dehistoricize these categories, imposing nineteenth-century models on *Othello* rather than analyzing it in conjunction with other texts to uncover the period's still pre-unified constructs of race. My analysis of the part the Moorish handkerchief plays in the gender dynamics of the play provides one place to explore further the conflicts of this cross-cultural marriage, conflicts that I now see represented as well in Othello's and Desdemona's wedding night at the Inn of the Saggitary, a place of travelers, and their honeymoon on Cyprus, an island at the borderlands of Christian Europe, Islamic Asia Minor, and Africa.

My analysis of *Othello* in the book opens out toward all the prominent issues in Shakespeare studies that I have addressed in this preface. I examine conflicting attitudes toward marriage in the play and their resonance with those that emerge in early modern culture. I analyze how Iago's lethal use of misogynistic commonplaces catalyzes Othello's (partly racial) insecurities. I suggest the ways in which Othello and Desdemona are subjugated to different gender and cultural heritages. I explore the play's nuanced conceptions of male and female sexuality and the ways these are disrupted by homosocial bonds among men, themselves vexed by differences of race and rank.

Growing out of current views that texts and histories are never completely unified or stable is the claim that their meanings and values are not permanently fixed by the intentions of their author or the contexts of their first appearance. Critical texts, like plays, alter their shapes in response to historical change and to the ideologies and desires of their different audiences: students, readers, playgoers, scholars. I have been pleased to discover, in writing this preface a decade after the completion of the manuscript, how supple *Broken Nuptials in Shakespeare's Plays* still is. I hope that the book continues to open itself up to questions I did not originally ask, to those its future readers will discover, and to the matters of difference that today engage us both inside and outside the academy and the theater.

NOTES

1 In an earlier essay, "Constructing the Subject," I analyze how new critical practices at first continued to exclude women. In a recent autobiographical essay, "Loss and Recovery," I place *Broken Nuptials* in relation to my own intellectual and family history. This preface is not an overview of recent developments in Shakespeare studies but a delineation of where these intersect with my book. For useful reviews of broader developments, see Cohen, "Political Criticism of Shakespeare," and D. Wayne, "Power, Politics, and the Shakespearean Text." For a feminist critique of these developments, see Boose, "The Family in Shakespeare Studies."

2 For discussions of differences among women, see Anzaldúa, *Borderlands/La Frontera;* Sedgwick, "Introduction"; Spelman, *Inessential Woman.*

3 Gary Taylor (*Reinventing Shakespeare*) and Michael Bristol (*America's Shakespeare*) among many others look at how Shakespeare is culturally appropriated and reproduced. Radical textual editors stress the collaborative nature of Shakespeare's theater and deny

the validity of composite editions, insisting instead on the equal integrity of differing copy-texts. Where there was once one *King Lear*, there are now at least three to attend to. See *The Division of the Kingdoms*, ed. Taylor and Warren, and *The Oxford Shakespeare* and its *Textual Companion*, both ed. Wells and Taylor.

4 The Renaissance has been opened up in part by new editions of women writers such as Mary Wroth and Elizabeth Cary; by work on women's writing (see Jones, *Currency of Eros*, and Beilin, *Redeeming Eve*); and by examinations of women writers' intersections with Shakespeare (see Erickson, *Rewriting Shakespeare*, and *Women's Re-Visions of Shakespeare*, ed. Novy).

5 In "Shakespeare's Women: Historical Facts and Dramatic Representations" I compare the roles of women in Shakespeare's family with those of female characters in the plays. My "Constructing Female Sexuality" examines further how sexuality is regulated in the drama and the period. See also Rose, *Expense of Spirit*. Useful editions are *Half Humankind*, ed. Henderson and McManus; *Daughters, Wives, and Widows*, ed. Klein; and Tilney's *Flower of Friendship*, ed. V. Wayne.

6 For discussions of the Women Controversy and misogyny see Kelly, *Women, History, Theory*; Woodbridge, *Women and the English Renaissance*; Jones, "Counterattacks"; C. Jordan, *Renaissance Feminism*; Ferguson, "Room Not Their Own."

7 See Freedman, *Staging the Gaze*; Montrose, "The Elizabethan Subject"; P. Smith, *Discerning the Subject*.

8 Adelman, *Suffocating Mothers*, attributes women characters' loss of subjectivity to the force of male fantasy. Disjunctive representations are attributed to cultural contradictions by Belsey, "Disrupting Sexual Difference" and *Subject of Tragedy*, and by Rose, "Where Are the Mothers?"

9 See Orgel, "Nobody's Perfect"; B. Smith, *Homosexual Desire*; Dollimore, *Sexual Dissidence*; Traub, "Desire and the Differences It Makes" and "The (In)significance of 'Lesbian' Desire"; Sedgwick, "Introduction."

10 See Greenblatt, "Fiction and Friction," in *Shakespearean Negotiations*; Traub, "Desire and the Differences It Makes"; see also many of the essays in *Erotic Politics*, ed. Zimmerman.

11 See especially essays in *Shakespeare Reproduced*, ed. Howard and O'Connor, and in *The Matter of Difference*, ed. V. Wayne.

12 On race in the period, see W. Jordan, *White Over Black*; Lewis, *Race and Slavery*; Barthelemy, *Black Face, Maligned Race*; and Boose, " 'Getting of a Lawful Race.' " For recent discussions of *Othello*, see

Bartels, "Making More of the Moor"; Newman, " 'And Wash the Ethiope White,' " in *Fashioning Femininity;* and Loomba's excellent book *Gender, Race, Renaissance Drama.* For performance history, see Neill, "Unproper Beds."

SELECTED BIBLIOGRAPHY

This bibliography includes works cited in the Preface as well as works, especially books, that deal with Shakespeare and with the themes of *Broken Nuptials*, and that represent important developments in Renaissance studies in the last ten years.

Adelman, Janet. *Suffocating Mothers: Fantasies of Maternal Origin in Shakespeare's Plays: Hamlet to the Tempest.* New York: Routledge, 1992.

Anzaldúa, Gloria. *Borderlands/La Frontera: The New Mestiza.* San Francisco: spinsters/aunt lute Press, 1987.

Bartels, Emily. "Making More of the Moor: Aaron, Othello, and Renaissance Refashionings of Race." *Shakespeare Quarterly* 41 (1990): 433–54.

Barthelemy, Anthony. *Black Face, Maligned Race: The Representation of Blacks in English Drama from Shakespeare to Southerne.* Baton Rouge: Louisiana State University Press, 1987.

Beilin, Elaine V. *Redeeming Eve: Women Writers of the English Renaissance.* Princeton: Princeton University Press, 1987.

Belsey, Catherine. "Disrupting Sexual Difference: Meaning and Gender in the Comedies." In *Alternative Shakespeares,* ed. Drakakis, pp. 166–90.

———. *The Subject of Tragedy: Identity and Difference in Renaissance Drama.* London: Methuen, 1985.

Boose, Lynda. "The Family in Shakespeare Studies; or—Studies in the Family of Shakespeareans; or—the Politics of Politics." *Renaissance Quarterly* 40 (1987): 707–61.

———. "The 'Getting of a Lawful Race': Racial Discourse in Early Modern England and the Unrepresentable Black Woman." Forthcoming in *Women, Race, and Writing in the Early Modern Period,* ed. Hendricks and Parker.

Bristol, Michael. *America's Shakespeare/Shakespeare's America.* London: Routledge, 1990.

Cary, Elizabeth. *The Tragedy of Mariam.* Ed. Margaret W. Ferguson and Barry Weller. Berkeley: University of California Press, 1993.

Cohen, Walter. "Political Criticism of Shakespeare." In *Shakespeare Reproduced*, ed. Howard and O'Connor, pp. 18–46.

Dollimore, Jonathan. *Sexual Dissidence: Augustine to Wilde, Freud to Foucault*. Oxford: Clarendon Press, 1991.

Dollimore, Jonathan, and Alan Sinfield, eds. *Political Shakespeare: New Essays in Cultural Materialism*. Ithaca: Cornell University Press, 1985.

Drakakis, John, ed. *Alternative Shakespeares*. London: Methuen, 1985.

Erickson, Peter. *Rewriting Shakespeare, Rewriting Ourselves*. Berkeley: University of California Press, 1991.

Ferguson, Margaret W. "A Room Not Their Own: Renaissance Women as Readers and Writers." In *The Comparative Perspective on Literature*, ed. Clayton Koelb and Susan Noakes, pp. 93–116. Ithaca: Cornell University Press, 1988.

Ferguson, Margaret W., Maureen Quilligan, and Nancy J. Vickers, eds. *Rewriting the Renaissance: The Discourses of Sexual Difference in Early Modern Europe*. Chicago: University of Chicago Press, 1986.

Freedman, Barbara. *Staging the Gaze: Postmodernism, Psychoanalysis, and Shakespearean Comedy*. Ithaca: Cornell University Press, 1991.

Greenblatt, Stephen. *Shakespearean Negotiations: The Circulation of Social Energy in Renaissance England*. Berkeley: University of California Press, 1988.

Henderson, Katherine Usher, and Barbara F. McManus, eds. *Half Humankind: Contexts and Texts of the Controversy about Women in England, 1540–1640*. Urbana: University of Illinois Press, 1985.

Hendricks, Margo, and Patricia Parker, eds. *Women, Race, and Writing in the Early Modern Period*. London: Routledge, forthcoming.

Howard, Jean E., and Marion F. O'Connor, eds. *Shakespeare Reproduced: The Text in History and Ideology*. New York: Methuen, 1987.

Jones, Ann Rosalind. "Counterattacks on 'the Bayter of Women': Three Pamphleteers of the Early Seventeenth Century." In *The Renaissance Englishwoman in Print*, ed. Anne M. Haselkorn and Betty S. Travitsky, pp. 45–62. Amherst: University of Massachusetts Press, 1990.

———. *The Currency of Eros: Women's Love Lyric in Europe, 1540–1620*. Bloomington: Indiana University Press, 1990.

Jordan, Constance. *Renaissance Feminism: Literary Texts and Political Models*. Ithaca: Cornell University Press, 1990.

Jordan, Winthrop. *White Over Black: American Attitudes toward the Negro, 1550–1812*. Chapel Hill: University of North Carolina Press, 1968.

Kelly, Joan. *Women, History, and Theory: The Essays of Joan Kelly*. Chicago: University of Chicago Press, 1984.

Klein, Joan Larsen, ed. *Daughters, Wives, and Widows: Writings by Men about Women and Marriage in England, 1500–1640.* Urbana: University of Illinois Press, 1992.

Lewis, Bernard. *Race and Slavery in the Middle East: An Historical Enquiry.* Oxford: Oxford University Press, 1990.

Loomba, Ania. *Gender, Race, Renaissance Drama.* Manchester: Manchester University Press, 1989.

Montrose, Louis Adrian. "The Elizabethan Subject and the Spenserian Text." In *Literary Theory/Renaissance Texts,* ed. Patricia Parker and David Quint, pp. 303–40. Baltimore: Johns Hopkins University Press, 1986.

Mullaney, Steven. *The Place of the Stage: License, Play, and Power in Renaissance England.* Chicago: University of Chicago Press, 1988.

Neely, Carol Thomas. "Constructing Female Sexuality in the Renaissance: Stratford, Windsor, London, Vienna." In *Feminism and Psychoanalysis,* ed. Richard Feldstein and Judith Roof, pp. 209–29. Ithaca: Cornell University Press, 1989. Revised and reprinted in *Sexuality and Politics in Renaissance Drama,* ed. Carole Levin and Karen Robertson, pp. 1–26. Lewiston, N.Y.: Edwin Mellen Press, 1991.

———. "Constructing the Subject: Feminist Practice and the New Renaissance Discourses." *English Literary Renaissance* 18 (1988): 5–18.

———. "Loss and Recovery: Homes Away from Home." In *Changing Subjects: The Making of Feminist Literary Criticism,* ed. Gayle Greene and Coppélia Kahn, pp. 180–94. London: Routledge, 1993.

———. "Shakespeare's Women: Historical Facts and Dramatic Representations." In *Shakespeare's Personality,* ed. Norman N. Holland, Sidney Homan, and Bernard J. Paris, pp. 116–34. Berkeley: University of California Press, 1989.

Neill, Michael. "Unproper Beds: Race, Adultery, and the Hideous in *Othello.*" *Shakespeare Quarterly* 40 (1989): 383–412.

Newman, Karen. " 'And Wash the Ethiope White': Femininity and the Monstrous in *Othello.*" In *Fashioning Femininity and English Renaissance Drama,* pp. 71–93. Chicago: University of Chicago Press, 1991.

Novy, Marianne, ed. *Women's Re-Visions of Shakespeare: On Responses of Dickinson, Woolf, Rich, H.D., George Eliot, and Others.* Urbana: University of Illinois Press, 1990.

Orgel, Stephen. "Nobody's Perfect: Or Why Did the English Stage Take Boys for Women?" *South Atlantic Quarterly* 88 (1989): 7–29.

Parker, Patricia, and Geoffrey Hartman, eds. *Shakespeare and the Question of Theory.* New York: Methuen, 1985.

Rackin, Phyllis. *Stages of History: Shakespeare's English Chronicles.* Ithaca: Cornell University Press, 1990.

Rich, Adrienne. "Compulsory Heterosexuality and Lesbian Existence." *Signs* 5.4 (1980): 631–60.

Rose, Mary Beth. *The Expense of Spirit: Love and Sexuality in English Renaissance Drama.* Ithaca: Cornell University Press, 1988.

———. "Where Are the Mothers in Shakespeare? Options for Gender Representation in the English Renaissance." *Shakespeare Quarterly* 42 (1991): 291–314.

———, ed. *Women in the Middle Ages and the Renaissance: Literary and Historical Perspectives.* Syracuse: Syracuse University Press, 1986.

Rutter, Carol, comp. *Clamorous Voices: Shakespeare's Women Today.* New York: Routledge, 1989.

Sedgwick, Eve Kosofsky. "Introduction: Axiomatic." *Epistemology of the Closet.* Berkeley: University of California Press, 1990.

Smith, Bruce R. *Homosexual Desire in Shakespeare's England: A Cultural Poetics.* Chicago: University of Chicago Press, 1991.

Smith, Paul. *Discerning the Subject.* Minneapolis: University of Minnesota Press, 1988.

Spelman, Elizabeth V. *Inessential Woman: Problems of Exclusion in Feminist Thought.* Boston: Beacon Press, 1988.

Stallybrass, Peter. "Patriarchal Territories: The Body Enclosed." In *Rewriting the Renaissance,* ed. Ferguson, Quilligan, and Vickers, pp. 123–42.

Taylor, Gary. *Reinventing Shakespeare: A Cultural History from the Restoration to the Present.* Oxford: Oxford University Press, 1991.

Taylor, Gary, and Michael Warren, eds. *The Division of the Kingdoms: Shakespeare's Two Versions of King Lear.* Oxford: Oxford University Press, 1983.

Tilney, Edmund. *The Flower of Friendship.* Ed. Valerie Wayne. Ithaca: Cornell University Press, 1992.

Traub, Valerie. "Desire and the Differences It Makes." In *The Matter of Difference,* ed. V. Wayne, pp. 81–114.

———. "The (In)significance of 'Lesbian' Desire in Early Modern England." In *Erotic Politics,* ed. Zimmerman, pp. 150–69.

Wayne, Don. "Power, Politics, and the Shakespearean Text: Recent Criticism in England and the United States." In *Shakespeare Reproduced,* ed. Howard and O'Connor, pp. 47–67.

Wayne, Valerie, ed. *The Matter of Difference: Materialist Feminist Criticism of Shakespeare.* Ithaca: Cornell University Press, 1991.

Wells, Stanley, and Gary Taylor, eds. *William Shakespeare: The Complete Works*. Oxford: Oxford University Press, 1986.

———. *William Shakespeare: A Textual Companion*. Oxford: Oxford University Press, 1987.

Woodbridge, Linda. *Women and the English Renaissance: Literature and the Nature of Womankind, 1540–1620*. Urbana: University of Illinois Press, 1984.

Wroth, Mary. *The Poems of Lady Mary Wroth*. Ed. Josephine A. Roberts. Baton Rouge: Louisiana State University Press, 1983.

Zimmerman, Susan, ed. *Erotic Politics: Desire on the Renaissance Stage*. New York: Routledge, 1992.

Acknowledgments

I began thinking about the essay on *Othello* that was to become the germ of this book in September 1973 while jobless and expecting a third child. In the eleven years since, she and the book have taken on lives of their own which seem wonderfully independent of my designs on them. Throughout these years I have incurred more debts than I can reckon, including some long-standing ones I am happy finally to acknowledge. I learned much from many teachers, but especially from David Mallery and Edward J. Gordon (1914–75) at Germantown Friends School, Kenneth Connelly and Charles J. Hill at Smith College, and Maynard Mack, Louis L. Martz, and William K. Wimsatt (1907–75) at Yale University; their rigorous and passionate commitment to literature and life taught me what criticism should be and prepared me—quite inadvertently—to become a feminist critic. I have been greatly aided in this process by the work of feminist scholars in many disciplines, by the challenges and encouragement of students at the University of Illinois and Illinois State University, and by my long and fruitful collaboration with Gayle Greene and Carolyn Swift in coediting an anthology of feminist Shakespeare criticism. The book has benefited too from my participation in MLA special sessions on "Marriage and the Family in Shakespeare" and

"Feminist Criticism of Shakespeare," in Shakespeare Association of America seminars, and on numerous other panels; I owe thanks to the organizers of these sessions, to their participants, and to their responsive and demanding audiences.

Many different kinds of assistance were crucial to the completion of this book. I am grateful for permission to reprint revised versions of previously published sections of it. An early and condensed version of Chapter 1 appears in *Shakespeare's Rough Magic: Renaissance Essays in Honor of C. L. Barber*, ed. Coppélia Kahn and Peter Erickson (Newark: University of Delaware Press, 1985). Two pages on Ophelia at the end of chapter 2 appeared first in an essay, "Feminist Modes of Shakespearean Criticism: Compensatory, Justificatory, Transformational," *Women's Studies* 9 (1981): 3-15, which will be reprinted in an expanded version in *For Alma Mater: Essays in Feminist Scholarship*, ed. Paula Treichler, Cheris Kramerae, and Beth Stafford (Urbana: University of Illinois Press, 1985). A somewhat different version of chapter 3, "Women and Men in *Othello*," first appeared in *Shakespeare Studies* 10 (1977): 133-58, and was reprinted in *The Woman's Part: Feminist Criticism of Shakespeare*, ed. Carolyn Ruth Swift Lenz, Gayle Greene, and Carol Thomas Neely (Urbana: University of Illinois Press, 1980). An earlier version of the discussion of *The Winter's Tale* in Chapter 5 was originally published in *Philological Quarterly* 57 (Spring 1978): 181-94. Agnes Tobias, my incomparable typist for over fifteen years, fit this manuscript into her overcrowded schedule, generously putting my deadlines ahead of her own. Illinois State University provided funds to assist in the typing, time released from teaching, and summer research grants; the support of my outstanding chairperson, Charles Harris, has been invaluable. Ellen Graham has overseen the book through the Yale University Press with efficiency and grace, and Barbara Folsom has copyedited it with inspired meticulousness.

I cannot possibly name all the friends and colleagues who have aided the progress of this book. Among the wider community of Shakespearean scholars to whom I am indebted I owe special thanks to Madelon Gohlke Sprengnether, Marianne Novy, and Coppélia Kahn, whose work has influenced this book from its inception, whose conversations and criticisms have strengthened it, and whose friendship has sustained me. Janet Adelman's lucid criticism has likewise long been a model for me, and I am fortunate to have had the benefit of her engaged, astute, detailed reader's report; the book has been much improved by my efforts to live up to her challenging commentary. In Champaign and Normal, many friends and colleagues have talked Shakespeare and criticism with me, asked penetrating questions at Renaissance seminars and department colloquia, read drafts and raised cogent objections to them; I am especially grateful to Elin Diamond, Margaret Dickie, David Kay, Joan Klein, Michael Shapiro, Charles Shattuck, and William Woodson. During all of the time that I have been working on this book, Jan Hinely has magnanimously shared with me her room of her own, her rich insights into Renaissance literature, and her stylistic perspicacity; any clumsiness that remains is in despite of her efforts. Dick Wheeler has improved every draft of every chapter, tenaciously uncovering incoherence where I had concealed it from myself and generously discovering coherence where I had despaired of it; again and again his probing questions and his deep knowledge of Shakespeare's plays allowed me to see what I had meant or what Shakespeare had meant.

Finally, I am indebted to my family for their sustained encouragement. My parents, Eleanor and Allen Thomas, have long been supporters of all my enterprises, and Wright, Sophia, Mark, and Juliet Neely have endured with me the vicissitudes of this particular project from its inception to its conclusion. Wright's demanding readings of early drafts strengthened my ideas and my arguments; his painstakingly accurate proofreading of the final version eradicated countless errors; and his years of child care made the writing possible. Sophia, Mark, and Juliet have furthered the progress of this book even while sometimes apparently impeding it; their engagement with their lives has been in fruitful tension with my engagement with literature, and their growth has encouraged my own.

BROKEN NUPTIALS IN
SHAKESPEARE'S PLAYS

Introduction:
Wooing, Wedding, and Repenting

ARRIAGE in Shakespeare's plays is a crucial dramatic action and a focus for tensions and reconciliations between the sexes. Movements toward marriage constitute the subject of the comedies; disrupted marriages are prominent in many of the tragedies; the establishment or reestablishment of marriage in one or two generations is the symbol of harmony in the late romances. The plays' marriages are counterpointed by what I call broken nuptials, extending Leo Salingar's use of the term.[1] These are parodic or irregular wedding ceremonies, premature or postponed consummations, estrangements, mock deaths, and real deaths—anything that disrupts the process of wooing, betrothal, wedding, marriage. These broken nuptials express the anxieties, desires, and conflicts of the couples who enter into marital unions as well as the external pressures placed on these unions by parents, rulers, the community. My study will examine how marriage, achieved or broken, influences the themes and structure of the plays and serves as the focus for the social and emotional relations of the sexes.

My emphasis on marriage is the result of my desire to explore women's roles in Shakespeare's plays. This exploration led me, as it has led feminist scholars in many disciplines, to examine the contexts in which women are defined, a project precisely articulated by the late Michelle Rosaldo in her reflections on the nature of feminist anthropology:

> It now appears to me that woman's place in human social life is not in any direct sense a product of the things she does (or even less a function of what, biologically, she is) but of the meaning her activities acquire through concrete social interactions. And the significances women assign to the activities of their lives are things that we can only grasp through an analysis of the relationships women forge, the social contexts they (along with men) create—and within which they are defined.[2]

Marriage is the social context that centrally defines the female characters in Shakespeare's plays; with few exceptions their conflicts, crises, and character development occur in connection with wooing, wedding, and marriage. Their roles and status are determined by their place in the paradigm of marriage —maiden/wife/widow—which likewise governed the lives of Renaissance women.[3] The introduction to a Jacobean women's legal handbook starkly notes the inevitability and restrictiveness of this paradigm for women: "all of them are understood either married or to be married and their desires [are] subject to their husband. I know no remedy though some women can shift it well enough."[4] Even exceptional historical women like Queen Elizabeth or extraordinary characters like Cleopatra do not escape definition in terms of the paradigm: Elizabeth made strategic use of the conventional roles she eschewed, manipulating her marriageability to gain political advantage and presenting herself as wife to England and as mother to her people,[5] while Cleopatra creates for herself a symbolic marriage to Antony at the end of Shakespeare's play. Examining women characters in the context of marriage facilitates a balanced evaluation of the power and limits of their roles.

There is a long tradition of criticism that scrutinizes the roles of women in Shakespeare; recently such criticism has proliferated and become increasingly self-conscious about its methodology and its goals. This criticism, in both its current and earlier versions, has assessed the place of the women characters in somewhat contradictory ways. One strand concerns itself with analyzing the strength, influence, and complexity of the women in the plays, compensating for their past neglect, misreading, and stereotyping. Nineteenth-century forerunners of this approach, like the historians who studied exemplary women, isolated and extolled prominent female characters, admiring their strength, wit, intelligence, power—and also their charm and beauty.[6] Recent critics, more self-conscious about their goals and more sophisticated in their methods, document the ways in which Shakespeare's women have been misread and stereotyped by critics, editors, and producers.[7] They read Kate's role of shrew and even her speech of subordination positively, make Cleopatra the hero of her play, emphasize Desdemona's sexual assertiveness.[8] They analyze the implications of female conversations and friendships, of female doubling, of women's commentary.[9]

Another strand of criticism stresses instead the constrictions placed on the female characters by the patriarchal structures within the plays and by the male-authored text in which they exist. Such critics show that Shakespeare's female characters inevitably are defined and define themselves in relation to men. They demonstrate that even strong, central women like Lady Macbeth and Cleopatra are socially and sexually contained by the structures of patriarchy, that the assertive comic heroines are restricted by the marriages which conclude their stories.[10] They analyze how these marriages achieve social and political harmony for the patriarchy as well as providing emotional union for the couple.[11] They reveal how the tragic heroes' fantasies of women cripple men and destroy female characters, illuminating the way in which the men's development of their own identity depends on and exploits women.[12]

Some very recent studies, drawing on and benefiting from both strands of criticism, analyze the relationship between the commanding heroines and the confining culture, between the idealization and degradation of women, and trace changes in

gender relations through different genres. Linda Bamber explores how women conceived of as the other, as the representatives of external reality, assume different functions in
comedy, history, tragedy, and romance.[13] Peter Erickson examines how men and women take on each other's qualities
and roles, and how women are granted power or deprived of
it in different plays.[14] Marianne Novy weighs the varying interactions between mutuality and patriarchy, between reason and emotion, and their effects on women's roles.[15]

My book grows out of and has been nourished by all this
work, extending earlier explorations by focusing on the relations of the sexes in marriage. I examine the plays primarily as
dramatic structures without reference to their determinants in
Shakespeare's psyche. I explore the social relations of the sexes
within the plays but do not draw extensively on social history
(an analogous body of texts, as I show later in the Introduction)
to interpret these relations. My concern is with the ways in
which the plays are influenced by other literary texts: by the
conventions of drama, by the effects of their disparate sources,
by generic expectations. I focus particularly on the ways in
which gender relations are shaped by and shape the different
genres in which Shakespeare wrote: the comedies of the 1590s,
the problem comedies and tragedies (1600–08), and the romances that end his career. As Shakespeare responds to the
demands of a variety of genres, recasting them in response to
the overall development of his own art, the role of women, the
nature of relations between the sexes, and the place of marriage alter. In exploring these transformations, each of the
book's five chapters offers a sustained interpretation of a single
play, which places it in the context of contemporaneous plays
to provide a broad reading of a key phase of Shakespeare's
development.

The five plays I reinterpret—*Much Ado About Nothing, All's
Well That Ends Well, Othello, Antony and Cleopatra,* and *The Winter's Tale*—share a number of concerns and motifs. All have
marriage as a central issue and each contains more than one
courtship or marriage. Taken together, these plays encompass
the whole process of wooing, wedding, and repenting. *Much*

Ado begins with the beginning of courtship. The wedding ceremony and delayed consummation occur in acts 2 and 4 of *All's
Well*. The opening of *Othello* is coterminous with Othello's and
Desdemona's elopement. Antony and Cleopatra employ the rituals of courtship long after their affair is established and do not
complete their union until after the rupture of Antony's actual
marriages. In *The Winter's Tale* the long-standing marriage of
Hermione and Leontes is disrupted early in the play and is restored only after the betrothal of their daughter, Perdita.

All of these plays embody the conflicts attendant on marriage by the incorporation of broken nuptials; these range from
Claudio's denunciation of Hero during their wedding ceremony in *Much Ado* to Polixenes's interruption of Perdita's and
Florizel's betrothal in *The Winter's Tale*. The mending of these
ruptured nuptials is achieved primarily through the women's
apparent or actual deaths. The strategic mock deaths of Hero,
Cleopatra, and Hermione, accomplished with the assistance of
other women, Helen's pretended death on a pilgrimage, and
the real death of Desdemona engender—however problemati-
cally—their lovers' repentance and the rejuvenation of the
unions. Although bonds between males are in conflict with
courtship and marriage, prominent female characters, female
friendships, and female doubles further heterosexual relations.
Love relationships and marriages are also impeded by social
and political tensions: patriarchal rivalry and friendship in
Much Ado, class distinctions in *All's Well*, racial divisions in
Othello, imperial war between Rome and Egypt in *Antony and
Cleopatra*, estrangement between court and country, fathers
and sons in *The Winter's Tale*.

I explore the pressures that make the transition from wooing to wedding so difficult and examine its effects on relations
between the sexes, and especially on the status of the female
characters. One way to start thinking about this transition as it
is experienced by the women and men in the plays is to examine certain of the ideologies that shape it—to look at the
functions, interactions, and implications of the conventions of
courtly love, which is associated with courtship, and of cuckoldry, which is associated with marriage. These conventions

coexist in all the plays examined here.[16] The men idealize their beloveds, and the women deny, mock, and qualify their lovers' protestations of commonplaces of what I will call Petrarchan love, the attenuated, formulaic Renaissance version of medieval courtly love relegated here to the period of courtship. Through this mockery the women enhance, but ultimately threaten, their status. By debunking Petrarchanism, they expose the emptiness of male idealization and the unrealiability of male vows of undying love. They are able to seize control of courtship, to insist on the reality of female sexuality and shrewishness, and to affirm for themselves and other women a complex identity beyond the Petrarchan stereoypes. Apparently freer in courtship than most upper-class Renaissance daughters were, these heroines typically defy their fathers, choose their own marriage partners, and woo them aggressively. In the bedtricks of *All's Well* and *Measure for Measure*, women even coerce their husbands to consummate their marriages. But by attaining verbal superiority, and taking themselves off the pedestal, by asserting their desires and acting on them, Shakespeare's maids are moving toward and necessitating their subordination as wives—their domestication by silence, by removal of disguise, and by giving themselves, their possessions, and their sexuality to the husbands.

Deidealization, as it prepares the way for marital sexual union, activates the misogyny that coexists with idealization. Having dismantled the conventions of Petrarchan love, Shakespeare's maids, when they become wives or are about to, ignite the comic—or tragic—conventions of cuckoldry. Cuckoldry derives from misogyny and is the inverse of both medieval and Renaissance courtly love; it subordinates women in a variety of ways. Both conventions express anxiety about or hostility toward marital sexuality. Courtly love does so, in its medieval form, by encouraging adulterous love and, in its Renaissance form, by idealizing unattainable women and denying their sexuality. Cuckoldry does so by emphasizing women's dangerous sexuality and promiscuity and the precariousness of their possession by their husbands. On the other hand, courtly love implies some mutuality, either in a physically adulterous or sublimated relationship or in a mutually chaste courtship, whereas cuckoldry assumes asymmetry: the motif concerns itself only with female infidelity; women cannot be cuckolded. In this way, cuckoldry subordinates as well as denigrates women. The woman is the focus of courtly love conventions, however attenuated her presentation or self-absorbed her lover; the central image of courtly love is the woman's eyes, symbol of her ennobling influence over her lover. In contrast, the focus of cuckoldry is entirely on cuckold and cuckolder; in fact, there is not even a term comparable to *adulteress* to designate the woman's role in the cuckoldry triangle; nor is there a special term for her if she is the victim of infidelity. Cuckoldry's central emblem is, of course, the cuckold's horns, symbol of the sexual potency that has been appropriated by his rival.[17] The convention acknowledges the power of women's sexuality but represses this knowledge. Instead, male sexuality is emphasized, and wives are treated as property that serves to validate husbands' manhood, honor, and status.

The effect of the motif in Shakespeare's plays is complicated by the fact that usually the men are only imaginary cuckolds; the women are almost invariably chaste and faithful. Though they are vilified in misogynist commonplaces, they are eventually vindicated, and the plays prove them superior to the men in their fidelity, love, strength, endurance, while the men are made to look foolish or murderous and to experience guilt, punishment, repentance, forgiveness. So women's power is enhanced and confirmed by the men's slander, but only at the price of confinement in the most restrictive of stereotypes—only if they remain chaste, loving, obedient, and long-suffering, only if they are willing to die for love (or to pretend to die for love), to return after marriage to something resembling the chaste immobility of the Petrarchan beloved. In the plays as in the period, women's sexuality is a source of potential power and considerable anxiety.

Marriage especially may be the locus of sexual anxiety in the plays because it was the focus of multiple pressures in the culture in which Shakespeare lived and worked. Traditionally, the state, the church, the family, the local community, and the marriageable couple had powerful and conflicting designs on the institution of marriage. In Shakespeare's England these conflicts were particularly acute because of the political tensions which accompanied the establishment of an independent Protestant state, the religious changes which attended the Reformation and the creation of the Anglican church, the influential programs of the humanist reformers, and the extensive theoretical controversy about the nature of women, possibly generated by unsettling changes in their social roles. Attitudes toward the place of women, the nature of sexuality, and the function of marriage were contradictory and in flux in the Elizabethan period as they are in the plays, so that reading the social representations of women is as complicated a business as reading the literary ones. But those representations in the prescriptive literature provide a useful backdrop and an illuminating analogue to the literary representations that are the focus of this book.

Just as literary critics have arrived at various assessments of the role of female characters in the plays, so historians propound conflicting views on the status of women in the period. Traditionally, historians have assumed that ferment over women, sexuality, and marriage generated improvements in the status of women as well as that of men. They cite as evidence the presence of exemplary women who achieved political power or exhibited impressive intellectual accomplishments (Mary Tudor, Queen Elizabeth I, Margaret Roper, Lady Jane Grey, the Howard sisters, the Countess of Pembroke),[18] the humanists' advocacy of education for women, and Protestantism's new ideology of companionate marriage.[19] But most contemporary scholars of women, marriage, and the family argue that the status of women relative to that of men and to that of women in earlier periods diminished and emphasize their new restrictions. They discover that the remarkable accomplishments of exemplary women were anomalous, manifested asymmetries, and generated anxieties;[20] they argue that education for women was less available, less serious, more problematic than that offered men;[21] they show that women's economic freedom and potential declined;[22] they argue that companionate marriage in a patriarchal society demanded the increased subordination of women.[23] The evidence and arguments supporting the two assessments, taken together, reveal the paradoxical mixture of gains and losses that was the lot of Renaissance women.

In the period as in the plays, the ideology of marriage brings into sharp focus the contradictory attitudes toward women and the complicated blend of power and subordination which characterized their status. The Reformation had begun to transform the old ideology without altering the prescribed form of marriage, its traditional functions, or the attitudes that accompanied them. To the two conventional functions of the institution—the accomplishment of legitimate procreation and the avoidance of fornication—the state-and-church sponsored homilie on marriage joined a new one, the loving amity of the couple. Marriage "is instituted of GOD, to the intent that man and woman should live lawfully in a perpetuall friendship, to bring foorth fruite, and to avoid fornication."[24] Advocacy of companionate marriage—the loving sexual partnership of husband and wife—went hand in hand with other changes in attitude that had potentially positive implications for women. Love, once denounced as a dangerous disrupter of marriage, was now decreed essential to it. Celibacy having been demoted by the Reformation, marital sexuality was no longer viewed as a necessary evil but as a positive good—and not only by Protestants. Erasmus, for example, in his *Epistle in laude and praise of matrimonie*, extravagantly extolled copulation as a law of God and nature (even trees and rocks do it).[25] He implied that sexuality provides not just progeny (the main argument of the epistle) but intrinsic fair pleasure: "I here nat hym whiche wyll saye unto me that that foule ichynge and pryckes of carnall lust have come nat of nature, but of syn. . . . And as touchyng the fowlnes surely we make that by our imaginacion to be fowle, which of the selfe nature is fayre and holy" (sig. B8). He points out that men who fail to till their fields are punished and asks "what punyshment is he worthy whyche refuseth to tylle that ground which tylled beareth men? And in tyllage of the erthe is requyred a longe and paynefull labour, here the short tyllage is also entysed with a pleasure as it wer a reward prepared therefore" (sig. C6ᵛ). Since a harmonious sexual companionship requires the consent and compatibility of the couple, enforced marriage and the custom of wardship were increasingly condemned; and since sexual satisfaction was to be found in marriage by husband as well as wife, adultery was condemned for both and the double standard denounced,[26] as it is in Shakespeare's plays; directly by Emilia in *Othello* and indirectly by the paucity of either wayward wives or philandering husbands throughout the canon.

There are, however, a number of external and internal impediments to the success of companionate marriage. The new demand for the couple's mutual affection and sexual satisfaction was inevitably in conflict with the desire of parents to control their childrens' marriages for family advancement or consolidation, a conflict that is central to many of the plays. Although children were theoretically able to negotiate their own marriages, parents, especially upper-class parents, continued to regulate spousals in order to achieve or maintain status, cement alliances, gain economic advantage, and ensure continuity of family and property. Indeed, parental pressures may have been especially strong in the period (as they certainly are in the plays) due to economic and demographic factors that tended to increase competition for suitable matches. Since aristocratic fortunes were in decline, heirs from the peerage needed to marry lower-born brides from the expanding mercantile class, whose large dowries would restore depleted family reserves. At the same time, because the population (and hence the number of marriageable daughters) was increasing and the number of male heirs in the peerage was not, the competition to marry these daughters into the aristocracy was fierce. This competition is reflected in the doubling of the average size of dowries in the period from 1570–1590 (with still greater increases later) and in the increase in the ratio of dowry to jointure, the husband's provision for the wife after his death.[27] Hence fathers continued to betroth their children before they reached the age of consent (twelve) and to control their children's marriage prospects even after their deaths, through wills more restrictive and less imaginative than that of Portia's father in *The Merchant of Venice*. Although legal marriage required only the consent of the couple, economic arrangements could not be accomplished without a ceremony and parental contracts;[28] therefore parental consent was often essential. Children who were wards (like Bertram and Helen) were under still more severe restraints, as their marriages could be auctioned off to the highest bidder and they had no appeal to parental affection.

Even when the couple's choice met the requirements of their parents and their society, they themselves (like Claudio and Hero) might find negotiating an amicable relationship difficult. These difficulties were exacerbated by the contradictory attitudes of the period toward women, sexuality, and male-female relations. In spite of the mutuality and companionship urged, in fact the woman had unequal status at every point in the process of wooing and wedding. She gave up more, she had to endure more, and she bore greater responsibility for the success—or failure—of the marriage. The very assumption of her emotional and sexual equality in the context of a male-dominated social order seems to have had the consequence of creating restrictions on her.

The prescriptive literature, while urging men to marry and providing them with detailed instructions on the choice of wives, rarely provides assistance for women beyond a vague admonition to choose a spouse wisely. This lack of helpful advice implies that women had no choice other than marriage, that their marriages were controlled by their parents even more than men's, and that men took the initiative in courtship—as they probably usually did in the period, if not always in Shakespeare's plays. Women, moreover, like Iago's "deserving woman" are warned to be wary of their wooers: "See suitors following, and not look behind" (*Oth*, II.i.157). Both the conservative Catholic Vives, in *Instruction of a Christian Woman*, written at the beginning of the fifteenth century, and the progressive anonymous compiler of *The Lawes Resolution of Womens Rights*, written at the beginning of the seventeenth century,

sternly warn women to guard against the inevitable deceits of
their wooers:

> Give none ear unto the lover, no more than thou
> wouldst do unto an enchanter or sorcerer. For he
> cometh pleasantly and flattering, first praising the
> maid, showing her how he is taken with the love of
> her beauty, and that he must be dead for her love, for
> these lovers know well enough the vainglorious
> minds of many, which have a great delight in their
> own praises, wherewith they be caught like as the
> birder beguileth the birds,[29]—

and against the violence which furthers these deceits:

> But to what purpose is it for women to make vowes,
> when men have so many millions of wayes to make
> them break them? And when sweet words, faire
> promises, tempting, flattering, swearing, lying will
> not serve to beguile the poore soule: then with rough
> handling, violence, and plaine strength of armes,
> they are, or have beene heretofore, rather made pris-
> oners to lusts theeves, than wives and companions to
> faithfull honest lovers: So drunken are men with their
> owne lusts, and the poysen of Ovids false precept,
> *Vim licet appellant, vis est ea grata puellis*: That if the
> rampier of Lawes were not betwixt women and their
> harmes, I verily thinke none of them, being above
> twelve yeares of age, and under an hundred, being ei-
> ther faire or rich, should be able to escape ravishing.
> [p. 377]

Having survived the perils of courtship, the woman, at marriage, became in the apt term, a *femme couverte,* losing all her
possessions along with her legal and economic rights: *That
which the Wife hath is her Husbands.* "For thus it is, If before
Marriage the Woman were possessed of Horses, Neate,
Sheepe, Corne, Wool, Money, Plate, and Jewels, all manner of
moveable substance is presently by conjunction the Husbands,
to sell, keepe or bequeath if he die."[30]

Once married, the wife suffered more severely than the husband the consequences of the injunction to procreate; she endured the dangers of repeated pregnancies and childbirths (a poignant theme in the romances) and the difficulties of nursing and weaning (she is advised to nurse her children herself) and of child raising. Even the homilie on marriage acknowledges women's heavier burden: "Trueth it is, that they must specially feele the griefe and paines of their Matrimonie, in that they relinquish the liberty of their owne rule, in the paine of their travailing, in the bringing up of their children. In which offices they be in great perils, and be grieved with great afflictions, which they might be without if they lived out of Matrimonie" (p. 243). A similar but more radical acknowledgment occurs in *Lawes Resolutions* when, at the beginning of its chapter on laws pertaining to widows, they are counseled to rejoice rather than grieve at their husband's death: "Why mourne you so, you that be widowes? Consider how long you have beene in subjection under the predominance of parents, of your husbands, now you be free in libertie, *'frée proprii juris,'* at your owne Law, . . . the vow of a widow, or of a woman divorced no man had power to disallow of, for her estate was free from controlment" (p. 232). As the passage suggests, the death of her husband was the wife's only escape from the afflictions of marriage. Although judicial separation, *divortium a mensa et thoro* (which did not legally dissolve the marriage or allow remarriage), was available to the wife in the case of the husband's adultery, brutality, or desertion, and although remarriage in the case of a husband's adultery was tolerated, most wives could not practically avail themselves of this option, since they had no money, property, or legal power.[31]

Even those parts of the ideology of marriage that might have been expected to alter and enhance women's status engendered demands for their subordination. The assumptions that sexuality was superior to celibacy and that sexual satisfaction was to be achieved in marriage by both men and women placed the wife's sexuality in a new light; she was no longer merely a necessary vessel for procreation but an active sexual partner. But sexuality, and in particular female sexuality, con-

tinued to be associated with sin and Eve's fall, and lasciviousness, inconstancy, and frailty were attributed especially to
women.[32] The enhancement of women's sexual role made female incontinence more threatening. Hence chastity became
the primary duty required of women throughout life in the
forms of virginity, marital fidelity, widows' abstinence. Not
only did the wife have to remain faithful but, unlike the husband, she had to prove her faithfulness by exhibiting the pe-
culiarly Renaissance virtue of shamefastness and by avoiding
all appearances of immodesty or wantonness. Elaborate restrictions on dress and behavior grew out of this emphasis on
chastity and shamefastness. The liberal Tilney's advice to
wives on how to protect their reputations is identical with if
less elaborate than the counsel the conservative Vives gave
to maids: stay at home. Going abroad was dangerous, Vives argues, because

> if a slander once take hold in a maid's name by folks'
> opinion, it is in a manner everlasting, nor cannot be
> washed away without great tokens and shows of
> chastity and wisdom. If thou talk little in company
> folks think thou canst but little good; if thou speak
> much they reckon thee light. If thou speak uncun-
> ningly, they count thee dull witted; if thou speak cun-
> ningly thou shalt be counted but a shrew. If thou an-
> swer not quickly thou shalt be called proud or ill
> brought up; if thou answer [readily] they shall say
> thou wilt be soon overcome. If thou sit with demure
> countenance, thou art called a dissembler. If thou
> make much moving, they will call thee foolish. If thou
> look on any side, then will they say, thy mind is
> there. If thou laugh when any man laugheth, though
> thou do it not of purpose, straight they will say thou
> hast a fantasy unto the man and his sayings, and that
> it were no great mastery to win thee. Whereto should
> I tell, how much occasion of vice and naughtiness is
> abroad.[33]

The woman's militant chastity was essential to counteract both
her own "frailty" and men's deceit and aggression. While

Shakespeare's women do not always stay at home, they do protect their chastity assiduously.

As the emphasis on sexual partnership in marriage resulted in more stringent demands for female chastity, likewise the call for a loving partnership between men and women resulted in or was accompanied by a contradictory insistence on rigid hierarchy. The husband's and the wife's contributions to marital amity were distinct and asymmetrical. The husband's duty was to govern his wife lovingly, firmly—untyrannically but absolutely. Tolerating the frailties of the "weaker vessel," he was to ignore small faults and correct large ones, not brutally but subtly, a strategy recommended as being effective as well as humane: "And therefore considering all her frailties she is to be rather spared. By this meanes thou shalt not onely nourish concord: but shalt have her heart in thy power and will. For honest natures will sooner be reteined to do their duties, rather by gentle wordes than by stripes."[34] Tilney's dialogue argues that the wife's sexuality could be similarly controlled: "In this long and troublesome journey of matrimonie, the wise man maye not be contented onely with his Spouses virginitie, but by little and little must gently procure that he maye also steale away her private will and appetite, so that of two bodies there may be made one onelye hart, which she will sonne doe, if love raigne in hir" (sig. B6). Many Shakespearean husbands, among them Petruchio, Benedick, Othello, and Leontes, manifest the desire to control their wife's will and appetite.

The wife's love, in contrast to the husband's, was to be expressed through the obedience promised by her (but not by her husband) in the Anglican marriage ceremony and enjoined on her by all the prescriptive literature and by the homilie on marriage: "But as for their husbands, them must they obey, and cease from commanding, and performe subjection. For this surely doth nourish concord very much when the wife is ready at hand at her husbands commandement, when she will apply her selfe to his will, when shee endehoureth her selfe to seek his contentation, and to doe him pleasure, when shee will eschewe all things that might offend him" (p. 242). If husbands should have faults, wives are to admonish them gently and tactfully, preferably in bed.[35] Women are urged to love and "endeavor to please" even vile, vicious, or vice-ridden husbands: "howe much more the husbande bee evill, and out of order, so much more is the woman's prayse, if shee love him" (Tilney, sig. D5). Hero, Helena, Desdemona, and Hermione all deserve such praise. Writings on marriage assume that conflict is inevitable but offer men and women complementary strategies of control and obedience for alleviating it.

The relative status of men and women when relations of the sexes were at their most friendly and civilized, the competing forces that interacted in companionate marriage, and the surface equality that masked and upheld male authority are not only expounded in Edmund Tilney's *The Flower of Friendshippe*, they are also embodied in its frame and its dramatic interplay. This pleasing work by a future master of the revels is a combination of instructive marriage treatise and witty dialogue with roots in Castiglione's *Courtier*, Pedro de Luján's *Coloquios Matrimoniales*, and Erasmus's marriage colloquies.[36] Superficially, the dialogue represents dramatically the equality for men and women in marriage which it advocates. The pastime is first undertaken in preference to various sports rejected because the women in the company cannot participate. The husband's duties, delineated by Don Pedro, guest and game leader, and the wife's, expounded by Madame Julia, the hostess, are parallel and reciprocal. Husband and wife are urged to love and care for each other, to tolerate the spouse's weaknesses, to avoid various faults including adultery, to be discreet, perform their duties, raise the children. The dramatic interplay concerns sexual politics and is carefully balanced. Isabella, Julia's "feminist" daughter attacks women's subordination and defends their rights, like her prototype, Lord Julian, in *The Courtier* and like her successors in Shakespeare, Adriana and Emilia. Opposing her, Gualter mounts commonplace attacks on women's shrewishness and desire for mastery. His name, the same as that of Griselda's husband, marks him as a conventionally witty misogynist with many counterparts in dialogues, colloquies, the women controversy, and the drama, including Berowne, Benedick, and Iago.[37]

But in spite of its attention to balance and equality, the dialogue responds to the anxieties Gualter voices about female domination and unruliness by implicitly and explicitly affirming male authority. The frame arrangements, which apparently promote shared authority, are in fact controlled by Pedro, who proposes the pastime and, even as he delegates to Julia the garland of sovereignty for the first day, determines the topic. Her immediate return of the garland, ceding him the right to speak first, is inevitable; her token authority gives her no actual control over either topic or speaker. On the second day, Julia passes the garland to her friend and contemporary Aloisa, and when it is predictably returned to her, she willingly but obediently accepts the role of speaker: "For disobedience is a fault in all persons, but the greatest vice in a woman" (sig. D3). The duties enjoined are also not quite parallel. While both husband and wife are forbidden to commit adultery, only the wife is counseled to maintain a perfectly chaste reputation. Considerably more forbearance is urged for the wife than for the husband. An extreme case of wifely forbearance is represented in Pedro's example, which is welcomed by Julia as an apt conclusion to *her* lecture on the wife's duties. He tells of a wife who cures her husband's adultery by enhancing it for him: she brings a fine bed and hangings to make the bare surroundings in which he carries on his affair with a poor woman more pleasant, and in this way wins him back to her love (and more attractive bedchamber). "He should . . . have had a bed of nettles, or thornes, had it bene to mee" (sig. E6), retorts Aloisa, unmoved by the exemplary tale.

The tensions underlying equality and the mode of their resolution are clearest in the contrasting treatments of Gualter and Isabella. Gualter's misogynistic generalizations about the evils of women are not taken entirely seriously or adopted by Pedro, but they are never denied. Gualter's interpolations reiterate that, even at their best, women pose problems for husbands—that, for example, rich, fair, noble, and virtuous women all make bad wives because these advantages can turn a husband into a "slave" or a "bondman" (sigs. B5^v, B5), and that, at their worst, "they be shrewes all, and if you give the simplest of them leave to treade upon your foote, tomorrowe she will tread upon thy head" (sig. C7ᵛ). Although the women persistently (but playfully) demand that Gualter be banished or silenced for his digressive and intrusive "prattle," Pedro tolerates him, significantly arguing that "he increaseth our sporte, and we cannot well want him" (sig. B7). Isabella, with equal persistence, inserts her own witty interpolations on behalf of women, disagreeing with Pedro's claim that marital equality is achieved by joining an older man to a younger woman, arguing that wives cannot be expected to love adulterous husbands, and asking sarcastically whether the wives should accommodate themselves to husbands who are mad or drunk. Julia and Aloisa similarly remark women's oppression and mock at excesses of male authority. But in contrast to the tolerance afforded Gualter's witty misogyny, Isabella's earnest arguments for equality between women and men in marriage are vigorously refuted.

No one supports Isabella in her direct challenge to the key doctrines of the wife's obedience. Isabella argues that this obedience should be reciprocated: "but as meete is it, that the husbande obey the wife, as the wife the husband, or at the least that there be no superioritye betweene them, as the auncient philosophers have defended. For women have soules as wel as men, they have wit as wel as men, and more apte for procreation of children, than men. What reason is it then, that they should be bound, whom nature hath made free" (sig. D8). She extends her case with an example from the Achaians in which gender roles are reversed, with the women ruling and the men doing the housework. Her argument is authoritatively attacked by the whole company. Gualter expresses the dangers in such role reversal when he responds to her utopian example by asking mockingly of such a wife's treatment of her husband, "and might she beat him too?" Julia for the first time in the dialogue asserts her maternal authority over Isabella, condescendingly urging her not to believe everything she hears and dismissing another sort of potential "equality"—that of separate spheres with men ruling outdoors and women in the home. This, she claims, is a barbarian and dangerous custom because it gives women a sphere, if only a limited one, for potential disobedience. She is immediately seconded by "father Erasmus" who has spoken only once before in the dialogue and whose succinct, unqualified assertion—the last word on the topic—is lent weight by his age, his reputation, and his appeal to religion: "both divine, & humaine lawes, in our religion giveth the man absolute authoritie, over the woman in all places" (E1). Julia then provides a rational, secular, psychological justification for Erasmus's declaration, arguing that men are naturally suited for sovereignty and women only rarely so.[38] Through this exchange the tensions that emerge from female demands for equality in marriage are decisively resolved.

But this resolution is temporary and fictional. The continuing dialectic between women's small gains in power and status and the restrictions urged in response to them characterizes the period and makes conclusive assessments of the woman's part difficult. These assessments, historians now emphasize, will differ according to which women are examined—women of what century, what country, what class, what marital status; according to which sources are used—diaries, letters, court depositions, demographic data, prescriptive or ideological texts, literature or drama; and according to what criteria are employed, which features isolated for analysis. Gualter's attacks on women may be extracted from Tilney's dialogue to emphasize the period's pervasive misogyny or Isabella's spirited and sensible arguments may be cited as evidence of its enlightened awareness of women's authority and inequality. When the complex, witty interplay of the prescriptive dialogue as a whole is taken into account, its relationship to actual marriages in the period becomes even harder to explicate. Do its form and symmetry and the presence of women as active eloquent participants reflect or condone new liberties gained by women? Does its final unequivocal support for male authority reflect or advocate increased restrictions for women? Or is it merely a playful fiction unrelated to women's lives?

Precisely the same questions can be asked about Shakespeare's plays, whose strong female characters are often silenced at the conclusions; they can be answered only with difficulty. Unless there were real women whose power and activities seemed threatening, it is hard to account for the numerous works like Tilney's devoted to the regulation of female behavior. But neither the fact of ideological ferment about women and marriage nor the presence of some exceptionally powerful women is proof of significant changes in the lives of most women, in the Renaissance or today. Most historians of women, marriage, and the family in the period would answer Joan Kelly's provocative question, "Did women have a Renaissance?" as she did—with an unqualified no.[39] But as these historians marshal evidence for the negative, they nonetheless make heretofore invisible women visible, devote sustained and subtle attention to them, and reweave their lives into the texture of history, redefining it. It is, ironically, as if today's historians were creating for those long dead women the Renaissance they never enjoyed.[40]

The contradictory assessments of women's place made possible by the complex evidence the period provides are neatly summed up in Juliet Dusinberre's *Shakespeare and the Nature of Women* (1976) and Lisa Jardine's *Still Harping on Daughters: Women and Drama in the Age of Shakespeare* (1983),[41] books which extend these assessments to encompass fictional women. Both books examine attitudes toward women in the drama by examining attitudes toward women in the period; both look at the effects of Protestantism and puritanism, virginity and chastity, humanist education, cross-dressing in drama and social life, the roles of exemplary historical women, and the influence of powerful female stereotypes. Employing similar material with similar aims, they construct precisely contradictory theses encompassing the period, the drama, and Shakespeare.[42] Dusinberre argues that the "feminism" (p. 1) of the period is reflected in drama which is "feminist in sympathy" and that Shakespeare questioned received stereotypes about women, "saw men and women as equal" (p. 308), and created strong, complex female characters who reflect the period's elevation of women's status. Jardine reads the drama as a reaction to, not a reflection of, social realities, a misogynist response to "the patriarchy's unexpressed worry about the great social changes which characterize the period" (p. 6). Strong, passionate women like Kate in *Taming of the Shrew*, the Duchess of Malfi, or Moll Cutpurse in Middleton's *Roaring Girl* (chap. 3 passim; chap. 4 passim; pp. 159–61) are not exemplary or liberating but are satiric creations or cautionary warnings. Such women are invariably contained or chastised by the drama; like Isabella in Tilney's dialogue, they are set up to be suppressed. Shakespeare's plays reflect this misogyny; his treatment of strong women reflects patriarchal anxieties, and his admirable heroines fit the "saving stereotypes" which the period created of patient, chaste, long-suffering, self-martyring women (pp. 184–93). Although these two books are in sharp contradiction to each other, each reflects, I think, one side of the complex truth about the representations of women both in the period and in the drama. Although Shakespeare certainly did not speak as a woman or in defense of women, he did represent them fully, absorbing and recreating in another dimension all of the contradictions that surround women's status. His created male and female characters articulate tensions in relations between men and women as clearly, and sometimes perhaps more clearly, than does the historical record, with its persistent tendency to erase female voices.

My study examines the complex ways in which women's roles are represented in Shakespeare's plays. The status of the female characters varies according to their place in the maiden/wife/widow paradigm. It varies, too, from genre to genre, from play to play, and from moment to moment in individual plays. In the comedies (and—with more strain—in the problem comedies) the women are maidens who "can shift it well enough." Their assertions of verbal, social, and sexual power enable them to evade or manipulate financial pressures, fathers' commands, the intricacies of marriage contracts, and the stereotyping of themselves by romantic or misogynist lovers. They do so by using the resources of disguise, wit, greenworld escapes, parodic or postponed nuptials, salutory mock deaths, generative bedtricks. But at the conclusions of the comedies, the maidens' approaching subordination as wives is manifested dramatically not only in Kate's speech advocating obedience, but in the women's sudden silence, their removal of disguise, their return from the green world, their forgiveness of husbands "molded out of faults" (*MM*, V.i.441). Yet Portia maintains her power even *after* her extravagant giving away of herself; she manifests it through her ability in the final scene to use her sexuality positively, to keep control of cuckoldry jokes (usually the male prerogative on the eve of consummation), and to engineer the commitment she desires from Bassanio and Antonio.

In the tragedies, maidens become wives and must often "relinquish the liberty of their owne rule." Their released sexuality is now execrated, their disobedience is experienced by the men as threatening, their subordination is demanded. Many of the women characters in the tragedies, however passionately loving or brutally strong-willed, move at the end of the plays toward isolation, passivity, madness, or suicide. Almost all die as a result of their love of men—Juliet, Portia, Ophelia and Gertrude, Desdemona and Emilia, Goneril, Regan, and Cordelia, Lady Macbeth and Lady Macduff. But Cleopatra's suicide is not obedient, not a punishment, not enacted just for love. In the romances, these tragic paradigms are averted by the splitting of female characters into mothers and daughters. The wife/mothers—good or bad—die or appear to die and can be idealized or scapegoated. The daughters, though they do not stay at home, remain impeccably pure maidens; their loving chastity regenerates (literally or symbolically) the virtues of their mothers and reconciles their fathers (who have mitigated their tyranny) with their suitors (who have tempered their desires). But Paulina is anomalous; neither a daughter nor a mother (we know she has three daughters, but she is never put in any dramatic relation to them), when "free in libertie," she makes use of her widow's role to sustain the long friendships with Hermione and Leontes which enable her to serve as catalyst to their reunion.

The rich characterization, dramatic development, and symbolic implications of the women's roles in the plays are, of course, far more difficult to interpret than this summary can begin to suggest. In this study I will explore the intricately interwoven contexts that define the meaning of women's actions in Shakespeare's plays: the relationships they forge with men and with each other; the dramatic and psychological significance of the institution of marriage and of the motif of broken nuptials; the structures of particular plays and their interactions with their sources; the nature of genres; and the development of the canon. It is not only that these contexts define women's actions. Making women newly visible in them transforms the meaning of marriage and broken nuptials, the texture of the plays, the shape of the genres, and the configurations of Shakespearean development.

CHAPTER ONE

Broken Nuptials in Shakespeare's Comedies:
Much Ado About Nothing

ARRIAGE, no one doubts, is the subject and object of Shakespeare's comedies, which ordinarily conclude with weddings celebrated, recelebrated, or consummated. But throughout these plays broken nuptials counterpoint the festive ceremonies, revealing male and female antagonisms and anxieties that impede the movement toward marriage.

Leo Salingar finds broken nuptials the distinctive feature of a number of Shakespeare's plays that have Italian *novelle* as sources.[1] I extend the implications of the expression, using it to refer to all of the parodic, unusual, or interrupted ceremonies and premature, postponed, or irregular consummations that occur in nearly every comedy from *Love's Labor's Lost*'s deferred weddings to *Measure for Measure*'s premature consummations. The centrality of the motif is reinforced by the fact that Shakespeare added broken nuptials when they are absent from his sources and altered and enlarged those he found there, imbuing them with more complex and wide-ranging functions and significance than they originally had.

Love's Labor's Lost and *A Midsummer Night's Dream* lack sources for the plays as a whole, and there are no clear-cut antecedents for the deferred weddings of the one or the Titania-Bottom union of the other.[2] In *The Taming of A Shrew*, the source/analogue to Shakespeare's play, there is no farcical wedding ceremony, although Ferando, the Petruchio figure, is "basely attired" (scene vii, 1.27) and drags Kate home before the wedding feast (Bullough, 1:84, 87–88). *Merchant of Venice*'s postponed consummation is absent from its primary source, the first tale of the fourth day of Ser Giovanni Fiorentino's *Il Pecorone*, in which the lover, in order to win the lady, "bestow[s] on her the bliss of holy matrimony" and then enjoys her for several months more after the marriage before the bond expires and he must leave for Venice (Bullough, 1:470). The ring precipitates only a minor incident when it is given to Portia's analogue, who returns it quickly to her husband without any emphasis on its symbolic value or reconfirmation of the wedding vows. The mock wedding ceremony in *As You Like It*'s source, Thomas Lodge's *Rosalynde*, is a one-sentence joke initiated by Aliena and Rosalynde: "and so with a smile and a blush, they made up this jesting match, that after proovde to a marriage in earnest" (Bullough, 2:214). Touchstone and Audrey and their aborted ceremony by Oliver Martext are missing altogether from Lodge's romance.

Where broken nuptials are present in the source, their significance is emphasized and complicated by Shakespeare in his plays. The interrupted ceremony of *Much Ado About Nothing*, the precipitous marriage of Olivia and Sebastian in *Twelfth Night*, and the bedtrick consummations of *All's Well That Ends Well* and *Measure for Measure* derive from important plot incidents in the sources: Bandello's novella 22, "Timbreo and Fenicia"; the anonymous *Gl'Ingannati*; the ninth story of the third day of Boccaccio's *Decameron*; the fifth of the Eighth Decade of Cinthio's *Hecatommithi*, "The story of Epitia"; and George Whetstone's *Promos and Cassandra*. Claudio's violent disruption of the wedding ceremony itself is missing in Bandello, where Timbreo merely sends a friend to Fenicia's house before the wedding to announce the breaking-off of the match (Bullough, 2:118). In *Gl'Ingannati*, the wedding between the Olivia and Sebastian figures is undertaken with comical haste because Isabella, locked in a room with Fabrizio, has received conclusive proof that he is not a woman in disguise: "before he gave her the ring, my young mistress had given him something too!" (Bullough, 2:336). Although in the sources of *All's Well* and *Measure for Measure* broken marriages and premature consummations are as central as they are in the plays, Bertram's and Helen's single dark consummation is an event blithely repeated numerous times in Boccaccio's tale, while in none of the sources of *Measure* is there a surrogate for the Isabella analogue or a bedtrick. Shakespeare appears to have been drawn to sources that contain broken nuptials; he multiplies instances of the motif, heightens its importance, and complicates its significance.[3]

The existence of the motif has implications for study of the comedies' connections, continuity, and development. The pervasiveness and patterning of the motif may provide a way of looking at them as useful as those provided by C. L. Barber's implicit distinction between festive and other comedies, Sherman Hawkins's division between green-world comedies of extrusion and closed-heart comedies of intrusion, and Salingar's categories of farcical, woodland, and problem comedies.[4] Exploration of the motif will show that the most important impediments to comic fulfillment lie within the couples themselves and not, as Northrop Frye has influentially argued, within the blocking figures, repressive laws, and humor characters of an anticomic society in need of transformation.[5] *Senex* figures in Shakespearean comedy are marginal, weak, or altogether absent, as in *Love's Labor's Lost* and *Twelfth Night.* The fathers in *Two Gentlemen of Verona* and *As You Like It* are peripheral to the matchmaking. Attempts by Leonato in *Much Ado* and the King in *All's Well* to arrange marriages go awry. Even Portia's father's will, which Frye takes as an example of a repressive law, actually preserves her from unwelcome suitors and selects the desired one. The fathers who deny their daughters' wishes and try to control their matches—Egeus in *Midsummer Night's Dream*, Baptista in *Taming*, and Page in *Merry Wives*—are easily thwarted and ultimately compliant. Shylock, the plays' most clear-cut and ruthless senex figure, is powerless to prevent Jessica's elopement and is only an indirect impediment to the marriage of Portia and Bassanio.

Humor characters are more numerous and more important than *senex* figures. They rarely hinder matches but sometimes reflect in exaggerated form the rigidities, anxieties, and defenses of the lovers themselves. Armado is even more absorbed in his own wit than the lords are in theirs; Malvolio's "love" for Olivia is more fantastical than Orsino's. But often the humor or subplot characters not only parody their betters' affectations but abandon them sooner. Armado gets Jaquenetta pregnant while the lords are still writing sonnets. Bottom acquiesces in his enchantment by Titania more easily than the lovers do in theirs. Gratiano expresses the sexual aspect of marriage more vigorously than Bassanio does, and Parolles's letter to Diana forthrightly exposes both Bertram's intentions and his own. The couples in the plays must overcome their own anxieties, not the blocking mechanisms of a restrictive society. But their inner anxieties of course reflect society's formulaic and constricting attitudes toward male and female roles, sexuality, and the structure and function of marriage.

The broken nuptials express these anxieties and are one means of achieving the release of emotion moving toward clarification which C. L. Barber has explored in the festive comedies. I shall argue, extending Barber's insights, that release of emotion is necessary in all of the comedies, as is some transformation of released emotion, although not precisely the sort that Barber finds characteristic of the late romances.[6] Within the continuity of the comedies which the motif manifests, overall development is likewise apparent. In earlier comedies, irregular nuptials identify and release conflicts, engendering their resolution. In later comedies in which conflicts are severe and anxieties deeply rooted, nuptials are more severely disrupted and resolutions increasingly strained.[7]

In Shakespearean comedy, if wooing is to lead to a wedding ceremony and consummation of the marriage, separation from family and friends must occur, misogyny must be exorcised, romantic idealizing affection must be experienced and qualified, and sexual desire must be acknowledged and controlled. Only then can romance and desire be reconciled in a formal social ceremony. Resistance to marriage is variously manifested and mitigated and is different for men and women. Women often bear a double burden. Once released from their own fears, usually through the actions of other women, they must dispel men's resistance and transform men's emotions. Various impediments to the comic project are revealed and re-moved by the irregular nuptials in three early comedies: Kate's opposition to romantic affection in *The Taming of the Shrew*, which is transformed by Petruchio; the men's vacillation be-tween misogyny and romanticism in *Love's Labor's Lost*, which is mocked and countered by the ladies; and the capricious, ag-gressive action of desire in *Midsummer Night's Dream*, which is experienced and manipulated by both men and women and transforms them. I will examine the significance of the broken nuptials in these three plays and trace the development of each one's version of the motif through later comedies. Then I will focus on the central instance of broken nuptials in *Much Ado About Nothing*, showing how this thematically pivotal comedy extends earlier uses of the motif and anticipates its darker con-figurations in the problem comedies and contemporaneous tragedies.

Taming of the Shrew is unusual among the comedies both because it addresses so explicitly the conflicts about and be-tween the social/economic, the romantic, and the sexual as-pects of marriage and because of the anomalous attitudes of Kate and Petruchio; she resists marriage more vigorously than any of the other women, while Petruchio is more pragmatic about it than most of the men. The play explores the arbitrari-ness, variety, and fluidity of roles and their constructive as well as constricting potential in a range of family and social relationships—husband/wife, father/daughter, father/son, mas-ter/servant, teacher/pupil. Through its array of role changes, *Taming* demonstrates that stable identity can persist beneath radical transformations of role, that unconventional roles can be assumed to achieve conventional goals, and that role play-ing can create some flexibility within social hierarchies without threatening their essential stability.[8] Petruchio's farcical disruptions of his and Kate's nuptials—the mocked ceremony, interrupted feast, and postponed consummation—while arrogant and misogynist, reveal and temper the sources of Kate's resistance to affection and marriage. This method of his taming is double-edged; he presents Kate with exaggerated images of disruptive shrewishness and contrasting images of roles that are socially more desirable—those of idealized beloved, sexual partner, cooperative wife. These potentials are all present in their first exchange when he insults, praises, and seduces her as "plain Kate, / And bonny Kate, and sometimes Kate the curst. / But Kate, the prettiest Kate in Christendom, / Kate of Kate Hall, my super-dainty Kate" (II.i.185–88).[9] His wild antics at the wedding extend his strategy. Mirroring and exaggerating Kate's uncooperative behavior, they suggest the advantages of conventional cooperation and decorum but at the same time imply that formal ceremonies do not necessarily reflect individual commitment. His cuffing of the priest reveals a disdain for conventional hierarchies, while his loud oath to marry and his louder kiss affirm his enthusiasm for Kate as a wife and sexual partner. His subsequent removal of her from the wedding feast likewise has both positive and negative implications. It parodies the authoritarian possessiveness which constitutes a genuine threat to wives. At the same time, it dramatically enacts the separation from her family that will enable Kate to discard the restrictive aspects of the role of shrew through which she has defined her place in that family. By carrying her off, Petruchio celebrates the sexual bond generated through their bawdy exchanges and puts a comically romantic construction on it, picturing her as a threatened damsel with a devoted protector: "Fear not, sweet wench; they shall not touch thee, Kate, / I'll buckler thee against a million" (III.ii. 237–38). Petruchio is as unconventional a husband as he is a wooer. Unlike many other Shakespearean husbands—Romeo leaves his nuptials to join his friends, Bassanio leaves Portia to go to his friend's trial, Claudio plans an immediate return to the battlefield, and Bertram, Othello, Antony, Macbeth, and Coriolanus all go to war—Petruchio stays home and devotes all his time, energy, and attention to Kate.[10] But he refuses her food, sleep and the consummation of the marriage until he has bullied her into a more affectionate commitment.

In response to his disorienting performances, Kate gradually shifts roles without abandoning her identity, as we see in their verbal games on the road to Padua, in their public kiss, and in her concluding affirmation of marriage, the prelude to their completed nuptials. On the road, Kate pleases Petruchio while at the same time playfully asserting herself and confirming their mutual dominance over the rest of the world. Agreeing to agree with Petruchio and call the sun what he wishes, Kate mocks his madness, elaborates upon instead of resisting his declarations, and insists on her own untransformable identity by naming herself "Katherine" instead of "Kate," Petruchio's name for her:

> Then God be blessed, it is the blessèd sun.
> But sun it is not when you say it is not,
> And the moon changes even as your mind.
> What you will have it named, even that it is
> And so it shall be so for Katherine.   [IV.v.18–22]

Katherine's ability to combine assertion and accommodation and her newfound pleasure in giving and receiving affection are confirmed in her final speech, a celebration of reciprocity.[11] In it she deftly draws on a number of male/female stereotypes to reconcile patriarchal marriage with romantic love and mutual desire. She defines marriage not just as a hierarchical social institution in which an obedient wife dutifully serves her lord but, conversely, as a playful Petrarchan romance in which an ardent lover courageously serves a beautiful woman:

> Thy husband is thy lord, thy life, thy keeper,
> Thy head, thy sovereign—one that cares for thee,
> And for thy maintenance commits his body
> To painful labor both by sea and land,
> To watch the night in storms, the day in cold,
> Whilst thou li'st warm at home, secure and safe;
> And craves no other tribute at thy hands
> But love, fair looks, and true obedience.
> [V.ii.148–55]

Underlying both fictions is a reciprocal sexual bond in which the woman is a clear, life-giving fountain, responsive to her husband's "honest will" (V.ii.160):

A woman moved is like a fountain troubled,
Muddy, ill-seeming, thick, bereft of beauty,
And while it is so, none so dry or thirsty
Will deign to sip or touch one drop of it.   [144–47]

As Petruchio transforms Kate's shrewishness into spirited devotion, she redefines his bullying as service, "painful labor by sea and land," which will leave her in peace. Following this joyous reassertion of her marriage vows and the recelebrated wedding feast, the couple can go off to bed for the belated consummation of their marriage.[12]

Female resistance to wooing and wedding is rare in the comedies and is not elsewhere dispelled by men. But other women—Beatrice, Phebe, Olivia, Diana, and Isabella—do "usurp" themselves, as Viola puts it to Olivia (I.v.185); their withdrawal from men has something in common with Kate's. It is characterized by unsparingly accurate attacks on male pride and romanticism and by the self-pride and suppression of desire most thoroughly manifested in Isabella. Olivia and Isabella, like Kate, must loosen paralyzing bonds to family. All of these women are released—at least partially—by vehement attacks on their pride and beauty and by the preliminary movement into temporary, partial, or counterfeit relationships— Kate's farcical marriage, Beatrice's witty "wars" with Benedick, Phebe's and Olivia's adolescent attachments to the disguised women who attack them, Diana's pretended acquiescence in Bertram's seduction of her, and Isabella's pretended participation in the bedtrick. All but Kate are urged toward their release by other women. The attacks on Beatrice by Hero, Ursula, and Margaret, on Phebe by Rosalind, and on Olivia by Viola, and the bedtrick substitutions of Helen for Diana and Mariana for Isabella, engender in each of the women partial identification with the situation of the woman she is paired with.

These attacks serve a double purpose. The mockers break down the defenses of the objects of their scorn, enabling them to know themselves better. In the process they express their own anxieties and reveal their own pride, because the women they mock reflect aspects of themselves. Hero's participation in the gulling of Beatrice vents her own sharp wit; the praise of male worthiness and the mockery of female disdain may help her to exorcise her own scarcely expressed fears of being "over-mastered" in marriage (*Ado*, II.i.58). Rosalind more obviously shares with Phebe the tendencies she mocks in her. She, too, discounts her lover's rhetoric and refuses satisfaction to him (although Orlando, to be sure, seems in no hurry to demand it). Her wooing games, like Phebe's scorn, postpone the moment of submission. Viola grieves for a lost brother as Olivia does, and her disguise is a "reserving" of herself more protective than Olivia's veil (I.v.187). Her service to Orsino is a project apparently as futile and self-abnegating as Olivia's mourning. The mockery perhaps helps Hero, Rosalind, and Viola, like the women they have released from pride, to give themselves unhesitatingly to the men they love when the moment comes to do this. In the problem comedies the relationships are more reciprocal, their effects more inconclusive. The intimacy and sympathy of Helen and Diana, Isabella and Mariana, leads to the cooperation in the bedtricks that permits Helen and Mariana to achieve the sexual union they desire (and for which they willingly sacrifice pride). It is not clear that their passionate example alters the vigorously defended chastity of Diana and Isabella—necessary given the aggressiveness of male lust in these plays. The two make no response to the offers of marriage presented to them at the end of the plays; their release is deferred—or perhaps permanently averted.

Male resistance to marriage is more pervasive and persistent than women's; it typically takes other forms and is dispelled in somewhat different ways. Men's conflicting bonds are not usually to family but to male peers. Instead of withdrawing, they defend themselves against women and protect their self-esteem by aggressive misogyny or witty idealization. The men are released in the early comedies by women's mockery, designed to reveal the men's absurdity and the limitations of the women they worship. In *Love's Labor's Lost*, the comedy in which women's control and men's folly go unchecked, the women mock the men's wooing and postpone the weddings until after the play has ended. In the original academe scheme, the men banish women in order to cement their fellowship and to overcome "devouring Time" and the "disgrace of death" by warring against "the huge army of the world's desires" (I.i.3–4,10). Their facile shift from misogyny to romanticism is incomplete and reveals the similar functions of the two poses. The formulaic wooing, like the ascetic retreat it replaces continues to protect the men from women and sex and time and strengthens their bonds with each other. In the play, love, like scholarship, is a protective game played by strictly conventional rules. The academe prohibitions degrade women and the love sonnets idealize them, but both serve to suppress desire for the individual women who are banned or wooed. The unacknowledged connections between misogyny, idealization, and desire are implicit in the series of speeches that document the men's shift from asceticism to romance. Berowne's idealistic justification of submission to love—"It is religion to be thus forsworn / For charity itself fulfills the law, / And who can sever law from charity?" (IV.iii.360–62)—leads immediately to a call for sexual assault: "Advance your standards, and upon them, lords! / Pell-mell, down with them! But be first advised, / In conflict that you get the sun of them" (364–66). The bawdy challenge generates the cynical acknowledgment that female infidelity can render male victory barren—"Allons! allons! Sowed cockle reaped no corn, / And justice always whirls in equal measure. / Light wenches may prove plagues to men forsworn; / If so, our copper buys no better treasure" (380–83)—and a more cautious plan to advance, masked as Muscovites.

At the end of the play the men brutally mock the Worthies' pageant and the revelation of Armado's impregnation of Jaquenetta as "one show worse than the king's and his company" (V.ii.512) without recognizing their own reflections in the longing for unattainable ideals embodied in the pageant or in the harkening after the flesh acted on by Armado. Their untimely marriage proposals deny once again the reality of death. The women, responding to their own desires and to the threat posed by the men's arrogant misogyny and romantic folly, abort the expected festive conclusion—"These ladies' courtesy / Might well have made our sport a comedy" (V.ii. 873–74)—and refuse the offers. They impose on the men separate, year-long penances that are to be a fruitful transformation of the "little academe" to which they were originally pledged. The king will be sent to a "forlorn and naked hermitage, / Remote from all the pleasures of the world" (V.ii. 793–94) where he will have no games to play and no audience to play to. Berowne, confined to a hospital, will have to confront the mortality he had evaded and to employ his wit in the service of others or discard it. Oaths once sworn to each other will now be sworn to their beloveds. The penances, however, do not deny time; they encourage the use of it to achieve not immortal fame but mortal satisfaction. Through them, romance, wit, and male friendship, having had their season, may give way in time to the fulfillment, the prosaic familiarity, and the heterosexual "binding" and "breaking" (*AYL*, V.iv.58) imaged in the seasonal songs.[13] Awaiting the men's growth, the women undergo a complementary withdrawal to mourn the king's death; in later comedies and in the tragedies, female withdrawal becomes increasingly defensive and involves greater risks. Because the outcome of penance and withdrawal is "too long for a play," (V.ii.876) Jack does not have Jill, and the nuptials are not mended in *Love's Labor's Lost*.

In *The Merchant of Venice* and *As You Like It* the threats of male friendship and idealizing romance are again confronted and released in parodic ceremonies imposed by the women on the men they love. At the end of *Merchant*, Bassanio must reassert his wedding vows and again receive Portia's ring before the mid-play marriage can be consummated; and Orlando must rehearse his vows with Rosalind/Ganymede/Rosalind in preparation for the actual wedding that concludes *As You Like It*. Portia and Rosalind use the pseudoceremony to mock the conventionally extravagant commitments of the men; both assert the possibility of female infidelity to emphasize the sexual dimension of women and marriage not fully acknowledged by their beloveds. Bassanio's bond with Antonio—for which he leaves Portia and gives away her ring in a kind of mock be-trothal—has constituted a genuine threat to his marriage. In the last scene he is brought to recognize this and to recommit himself more fully to Portia. Antonio must also pledge himself to the marriage, in effect giving Bassanio away with the return to him of Portia's ring, which has come to represent Portia's chastity and sexuality, Bassanio's lapsed and reaffirmed fidel-ity, and the sexual consummation of the marriage that will fol-low their re-wedding. Bassanio's recommitment reciprocates Portia's earlier submission of herself to him: "This house, these servants, and this same myself / Are yours—my lord's. I give them with this ring" (III.ii.170–71). Orlando's romantic pledge to die for love is likewise transformed by means of a mock cere-mony into a more realistic commitment to marry, knowing that the sky will change and the wife may wander and that he can "no longer live by thinking" (V.ii.50). His alteration precipi-tates Rosalind's removal of her disguise and reciprocal submis-sion: "To you I give myself, for I am yours" (V.iv.117). Portia and Rosalind, in disguise and in control, can playfully employ misogynistic fantasies of female promiscuity to qualify ro-mance because their sexual infidelity is perceived as a joke, not as a genuine threat to the securely patriarchal structures of the plays.[14]

But in *Midsummer Night's Dream* desire, symbolized by the operations of the fairy juice, is urgent, promiscuous, and threatening to women as well as to men. Its effects mock the protestations of constancy by Lysander and Demetrius and exaggerate the patriarchal possessiveness of Theseus and Obe-ron: "every man should take his own. . . . The man shall have his mare again, and all shall be well" (III.ii.459, 463–64). All is made well in part because the erratic or aggressive desires of the controlling men are "linger[ed]" (I.i.4) by the chaste con-stancy of Hermia and Helena and the poised detachment of Hippolyta, or tempered by the inconstancy of Titania with Bot-tom. Oberon, engineering this union, imagines it as an ugly, bestial coupling with "lion, bear, or wolf, or bull" (II.i.180), an apt punishment for Titania's multiple desires and intimacies. But from Titania's perspective (and ours) it is a comically fulfilling alternate nuptial—and was staged as such by Peter Brook, complete with streamers, the wedding march, a plumed bower of bliss, and a waving phallus.[15] The union is a respite for Titania from the conflicts of her hierarchical marriage. She and Bottom experience not animal lust but a blissful, sensual, symbiotic union, characterized, like that of mother and child, by mutual affection and a shared sense of effortless omnipotence. Their eroticism, the opposite of Oberon's bestial fantasies or Theseus's phallic wooing, is tenderly gynocentric: "So doth the woodbine the sweet honeysuckle / Gently entwist; the female ivy so / Enrings the barky fingers of the elm" (IV.i.43–45). Although Titania disavows her "enamored" visions (IV.i.77–78), and Oberon misconstrues them, the couple's "amity" (IV.i.88) depends on that prior union: freed by it to relinquish her other love object, the Indian boy, to Oberon, Titania's submission generates in him the tenderness she craves.

While Theseus and Hippolyta await their nuptials, marital harmony is reestablished by Titania and Oberon, and the chaotic desires of the young lovers are sorted out. During the last-act interval between the weddings and their consummations, the violent potentials in love, sex, and marriage are comically incorporated in the rejected and enacted entertainments. "The battle with the centaurs" interrupted the wedding of Theseus's friend Pirithous when the drunken centaurs attacked the Lapiths to capture the bride; during "the riot of the tipsy Bacchanals," the Bacchantes tore Orpheus to pieces, enraged by his devotion to Eurydice and his scorn of other women. The Pyramus and Thisbe play dramatizes a lovers' union aborted by parental obstructions, a devouring lion, and the lovers' deaths. The play within the play's joining of parodic romance with bawdy innuendo brings into the festive conclusion the two dimensions of love—conventional romanticism and uncontrollable desire—which, converging, threatened but did not harm the couples in the forest and which facilitated the union of Titania and Bottom.[16]

Later, in *Twelfth Night*, another dream-nuptial is similarly commanded by the woman and acquiesced in amazedly by the

man. Sebastian, like Bottom, is the bemused recipient of female bounty. But the romantic and sexual attraction of Olivia
and Sebastian is legitimized in a chapel by the priest, who describes the exquisitely formal and decorously conventional
wedding: "Confirmed by mutual joinder of your hands, /
Attested by the holy close of lips, / Strength'ned by inter-
changement of your rings; / And all the ceremony of this
compact / Seal'd in my function, by my testimony" (V.i.
156–60). While perfectly completed, this is, perhaps, the most
irregular nuptial of all, for Sebastian both "is and is not" (V.i.
216) the object of Olivia's desires. (More farcically and less happily, in *The Merry Wives of Windsor*, the sexual mismatches of
Caius and Slender, whose brides turn out to be "lubberly"
boys (V.v.186), cancel their nuptials and reflect the ludicrous
impotence of their desires and of Falstaff's). In *Twelfth Night*
the union is wondrous, not troublesome; the fortunate appearance of twin Sebastian "unties" all the "knots" (II.ii.41) of the
play, releasing Olivia from proud disdain into satisfied desire,
allowing Orsino's free-floating fancies to anchor on Viola, his
"fancy's queen" (V.i.389), and transforming Viola's romantic
and self-sacrificing pledge to die for Orsino—"And I, most jocund, apt, and willingly, / To do you rest a thousand deaths
would die" (V.i.131–32)—into a fulfilling sexual commitment.
But the simultaneously regular and irregular nuptial points to
the sheerly contingent connection of sexual desire with romantic affection and with wedding ceremonies and anticipates the
more radical substitutions that are necessary to untie the tan-
gles of the problem comedies.

In these comedies, as idealization becomes more difficult
to maintain and desire less easy to control, both pose greater
threats. Misogyny and romanticism interpenetrate when, in
Angelo (as in *Much Ado*'s Claudio), idealization of women becomes a brittle, easily shattered defense against sexual desire
and anxiety, and when, as in Troilus and Bertram, romantic
rhetoric is employed as a weapon of aggressive seduction, as
foreshadowed in Proteus's arrested rape in *Two Gentlemen of
Verona*. The desire induced in the earlier comedies to generate
release—through the fairy juice, the witty mockery of the her-

oines, the bawdy of fools, clowns, and subplot characters—
now degenerates into degraded lust. This lust, untransformed,
cannot be displaced from the central couple and absorbed into
the ritualistic conclusions, as Touchstone's is after Jaques interrupts his earlier attempt to contrive a quasi-legitimate union
with Audrey. The comically irregular ceremonies and postponed consummations of the earlier comedies give way in *All's
Well* and *Measure for Measure* to "cozen'd" and premature consummations that "Defile the pitchy night" (*AWW*, IV.iv.
23–24), consummations that feel like prostitution in *All's Well*
and like rape in *Measure for Measure*. The submission of Helen
and Mariana in the bedtricks is painfully humiliating, and in
the last scenes of the plays Diana and Isabella must take this
humiliation on themselves. The men are not merely mocked
into acknowledgment of the risks of marriage and the limitations of the beloved; they are forced into marriages they dread
with women they dislike.

Much Ado About Nothing contains the most clear-cut example of broken nuptials—Claudio's interruption of his wedding
ceremony to accuse Hero of infidelity. Poised at the center of
the comedies, the play looks both backward and forward.[17] Its
tensions and its poise are achieved by the interactions of its
two plots, its two couples. None of the other comedies includes two such sharply contrasted, subtly interrelated, and
equally important couples. While, despite some uneasiness
about the issue, critics are generally in agreement that the
Claudio/Hero story is the main plot and the Beatrice/Benedick
story the subplot, they also concur that the subplot couple is
rhetorically richer, dramatically more interesting, and psychologically more complex than the mainplot couple.[18] Discrep-
ancies in the sources, the tone, and the nature of the two plots
have generated charges of disunity that have been countered
by claims that the two are unified by one or another theme:
giddiness, moral complacency, the deceptiveness of appearances.[19] Varied, hesitant, or inadequate attempts to categorize
the play, focusing usually on one plot or the other, also suggest that the relationship between the two plots has not been
fully understood and confirm and illuminate *Much Ado*'s affinities with both festive and problem comedies.

C. L. Barber implies at a number of points in *Shakespeare's Festive Comedy* that *Much Ado* is like a festive comedy with a holiday world in which Beatrice and Benedick experience festive release; but the absence of an extended discussion suggests that it does not fit easily into his category.[20] Sherman Hawkins, likewise emphasizing Beatrice and Benedick, includes the play with *Comedy of Errors*, *Taming of the Shrew*, and *Twelfth Night* as a closed-heart comedy based on "sexual antagonism" (p. 67) in which men and women must overcome internal obstacles to love; but his description fails to account for the Hero/Claudio plot.[21] Northrop Frye, when attending to Beatrice and Benedick, likewise identifies the play as a humor comedy (like *Love's Labor's Lost* and *Taming*) in which the witty couple and Claudio must discard the humors that are impediments to love. But elsewhere Frye, focusing on Hero's death and rebirth, groups the play with *All's Well* as an extension of the ritualistic "green-world" comedies—*Two Gentlemen of Verona*, *Midsummer Night's Dream*, *As You Like It*, *Merry Wives of Windsor*.[22] Other critics who emphasize the Hero/Claudio plot have also noted *Much Ado*'s connections with later plays. R. G. Hunter, in *Shakespeare and the Comedy of Forgiveness*, by stressing Claudio's error, contrition, and our forgiveness of him, is led to place the play at the beginning of a line stretching through *All's Well* to *Cymbeline* and *The Tempest*; but this forgiveness is only peripheral in *Much Ado*.[23] Leo Salingar, as we have seen, places *Much Ado* in his category of problem comedies along with *Merchant of Venice*, *All's Well* and *Measure for Measure*; although *Much Ado* manifestly includes broken nuptials, the distinguishing mark of the category, the other characteristic features—the complex of the judge and the nun, the trial scene, and the conflict between justice and mercy—are attenuated or altogether absent, and the Beatrice/Benedick story does not fit the pattern.[24] A. P. Rossiter, focusing on the themes and tone of the play rather than its plots, explores most fully and persuasively *Much Ado* as an immediate precursor of the group that he designates "problem plays" or "tragi-comedies"—*Henry IV, Part II*, *Troilus and Cressida*, *All's Well*, *Hamlet*, *Measure for Measure*, and *Othello*. He finds *Much Ado* balanced neatly on a tonal frontier between comedy and tragicomedy just before the "point at which a sense of humour *fails*" and is replaced by "cynicism" — "where the attitudes I called 'hardness' (self-defensive) and 'farce' (offensive, debunking) combine to 'place' love, honour, truth, only to devalue them."[25]

As these various explorations suggest, *Much Ado About Nothing* combines elements from almost all of the other comedies in a unique mixture. It is linked with both the romantic comedies and the problem comedies by virtue of the interactions of its two couples, its two plots. In the Claudio/Hero plot, the anxieties and risks underlying the conventions of romantic love are expressed and contained by the broken nuptials, Hero's vilification and mock death, and Claudio's penitence and acceptance of a substitute bride, motifs that are developed further in *All's Well, Measure for Measure,* and the late romances. In the Beatrice/Benedick plot, the mutual mockery, double gulling, and Benedick's acceptance of Beatrice's command to "Kill Claudio" function, as do the mockery, trickery, parody, and tamings of the festive comedies, to break down resistance and to release desire and affection. The Beatrice/Benedick plot protects the Hero/Claudio plot by ventilating and displacing it and by transforming its romance elements. In turn, the impasse of the Hero/Claudio plot generates movement in the Beatrice/Benedick plot and, by permitting the witty couple the expression of romantic affection, initiates the transformation of their "merry wars" into a witty truce.[26] Together the two plots release and control elements that will generate greater uneasiness and distrust in the problem comedies. Together they maintain an equilibrium between male control and female initiative, between male reform and female submission, which is characteristic of the romantic comedies but is disrupted in the problem comedies. In this play, wit clarifies the vulnerability of romantic idealization while romance alters the static, self-defensive gestures of wit.

The two plots are played out against a backdrop of patriarchal authority , which is protected by the extensive bawdy, especially the cuckoldry jokes, and contained by the ineffectuality of the men's exercise of power, especially when exaggerated in the Dogberry subplot. The play's lighthearted, witty bawdy expresses and mutes sexual anxieties; it turns them into a communal joke and provides comic release and relief in specific ways. It manifests sexuality as the central component of marriage and emphasizes male power and female weakness. Its clever, inventive innuendo emphasizes the anatomical "fit" between the sexes: "Give us the swords; we have bucklers of our own" (V.ii.19).

The bawdy persistently views sex as a male assault on women. Men "board" (II.i.138) women, "put in the pikes" (V.ii.20), and women cheerfully resign themselves to being "made heavier . . . by the weight of a man," and "stuff'd" (III.iv.26, 62–63). The women counterattack by mocking the virility that threatens them: the "blunt foils" (V.ii.14), "short horns" (II.i.22), and "fine little" wit (V.i.161) of the men. They do not, however, see their own sexuality as a weapon. They joke about female "lightness" (III.iv.36, 43, 45) to warn each other against it, not to threaten men; even the term itself identifies women with weakness rather than strength.

But women's proverbial "lightness" is also a source of power. Women fear submission to men's aggressive sexual power. Men, likewise perceiving sexuality as power over women, fear its loss through female betrayal. They defend themselves against betrayal in three ways: they deny its possibility through idealization, anticipate it through misogyny, or transform it, through the motif of cuckoldry, into an emblem of male virility. As Coppélia Kahn shows, cuckoldry is associated with virility through the horn, which symbolizes both.[27] The reiterated motif "In time the savage bull doth bear the yoke" (I.i.254) emphasizes the bull's potency as well as his submission to dull domestic life and inevitable cuckoldry. Similarly, to be "horn-mad" (I.i.262) is to be both furious with jealousy and sexually voracious; both halves of the pun imply aggressiveness. The defensive function of these jokes is especially apparent in the extended one that precedes the couples' pledge to marry. In it the scorn due the cuckold is ingeniously swallowed up in the acclaim awarded the cuckolder for his "noble feat" by which he attains power over both the woman and the husband:

> *Claudio.*   Tush, fear not, man! We'll tip thy horns
> with gold,
>   And all Europa shall rejoice at thee,
>   As once Europa did at lusty Jove
>   When he would play the noble beast in love.
>
> [V.iv.44–47]

All rejoice with the woman. The cuckold is crowned, the cuckolder is noble, and even the illegitimate calf will be proud of, if intimidated by, his father's virility—and may even inherit it.[28]

> *Benedick.*   Bull Jove, sir, had an amiable low.
>   And some such strange bull leaped your father's
>   cow
>   And got a calf in that same noble feat
>   Much like to you, for you have just his bleat.
>
> [V.iv.48–51]

Here Benedick implies that Claudio, like his putative father, may become a cuckolder, and Claudio subsequently jokes that Benedick, too, may be a "double-dealer" (V.iv.114). Cuckoldry has thus been deftly dissociated from female power and infidelity and identified instead with masculine virility and solidarity, which are emphatically reasserted on the eve of the weddings.

Marriage and cuckoldry, both potentially threatening to male bonds and power, have become assurances of them. But male authority in the play remains lame and diffused. Leonato is a weak father; Claudio, a passive protaganist; Don John, a conventional villain. Don Pedro is potentially the most powerful man in the play by virtue of his age, rank, and multiple connections with the others. But this potential remains subdued. He phases himself out of the plots he initiates, is moved from the center of the action to the periphery, and is curtailed as a rival suitor. His illusory competition with Claudio for Hero is abruptly dropped, and what could become a courtship of Beatrice—"Will you have me, lady," (II.i.314)—when politely dismissed by her as a joke, is immediately abandoned in favor of the project of uniting her with Benedick. The men's rivalry evaporates, and their violence is defused. First Leonato's and Antonio's attempts to avenge Hero are comically presented, and then Benedick's challenge is laughed off.

Male power in the play also remains benign because it is blunted by its ineffectuality and rendered comic by Dogberry's parody of it. Most of the men's schemes—Pedro's to woo Hero, the Friar's to reform Claudio, Don John's and Leonato's to get revenge, Benedick's to kill Claudio, the Watch's first to "offend no man" (III.iii.80) and later to bring wrongdoers to justice—are botched, backfire, or fall apart. But though none of the schemes works as it is supposed to, they all achieve their goals. Dogberry's bungling attempts to arrest Borachio and Conrade on some charge or other mirror and parody the inept strategy and good luck of the other men. Whereas at the end of the church scene Beatrice and Benedick transcend melodrama and create witty romance, in the following scene (IV.i) Dogberry transforms melodrama downward into farce, parodying the perversions inside the church. The arraignment precedes any examination of the evidence, malefactors and benefactors are confused with each other, and judges as well as accused have charges brought against them. When, at the end of the scene, Dogberry defends himself, he becomes a comic spokesman for his betters. He endearingly articulates the men's testy response to insults real or imagined, their reliance on conventions—of dress, rank, wit, institutions—to protect and confirm their self-importance, and the potential for assininity that goes along with their desires for swaggering and safety:

> I am a wise fellow; and which is more, an officer; and which is more, a householder; and which is more, as pretty a piece of flesh as any is in Messina, and one that knows the law, go to! And a rich fellow enough, go to! And a fellow that hath had losses; and one that hath two gowns and everything handsome about him.
>
> [IV.ii.80–86]

The play's presentation of male power is further symbolized by the sheerly linguistic invention, "the Prince's officer Coxcomb" (IV.ii.72), whose denomination suggests deference and pride, elegant arrogance and assinine folly, but also embodies comfortable security. Such security is threatened by those outsiders who wish to usurp legitimate authority and who are perhaps symbolized by Coxcomb's antithesis, the "thief Deformed": "'a has been a vile thief this seven year; 'a goes up and down like a gentleman" (III.iii.125–27). Yet in spite of the men's rivalry, ineffectuality, and silliness, all of the play's plot-generating deceits and revelations are controlled by them, and it is they who fit women with husbands. Their authority and solidarity are confirmed in the play's conclusion, which reconciles male power and alliances with marriage.[29]

But first conflicts disrupt both the male bonds and the two couples. The Claudio/Hero alliance is thinly sketched as a conventional one in which the functions of romantic idealization are made clear. Claudio protects himself from Hero's sexuality by viewing her as a remote, idealized love object who is not to be touched or even talked to: "she is the sweetest lady that ever I looked on" (I.i.183).[30] Patriarchal marriage customs conveniently coalesce with romantic rhetoric, enabling him to maintain Hero as an object of social exchange and possession: "Lady, as you are mine, I am yours," he cautiously vows (II.i.296).[31] He lets Don Pedro do his wooing for him. He scarcely acknowledges Hero's sexual attractiveness, and his only reference to his own desires seems oddly passive and gynocentric in a play crammed with aggressively phallic innuendo: "But now I am returned and that war-thoughts / Have left their places vacant, in their rooms / Came thronging soft and delicate desires, / All prompting me how fair young Hero is" (I.i.294–97).[32] Claudio thus alleviates his anxieties about marriage by viewing it both as a romantic ideal and as a conventional social arrangement that will occupy the time between battles. Once married, he intends to go off to Aragon immediately with Don Pedro, their companionship uninterrupted (III.ii.3).

Hero's willingness to be the passive object of her father's negotiations, Don Pedro's decorous wooing, and Claudio's low-keyed proposal provide her with a parallel defense against sexuality. She is as unforthcoming as Claudio at their first ex-

change, and perhaps she welcomes his silence, for she asks
Don Pedro as he begins his wooing to "say nothing" (II.i.83).
Her own uneasiness about sex is suggested in her unhappiness
on her wedding day, and the one bawdy innuendo that she
contributes to the banter, "There thou prick'st her with a this-
tle" (III.iv.74) is as tentative as Claudius's allusion. Hero is the
perfect object of his "delicate" desires: modest, chaste, virtuous, silent.

The witty verbal skirmishes comprising Beatrice's and
Benedick's "merry wars" explicitly express the anxieties about
loss of power through sexuality, love, and marriage that lie beneath Claudio's and Hero's silent romanticism. Their verbal
wars fill up the silence of the Hero/Claudio plot and reveal the
fundamental asymmetry of the battle of the sexes. Benedick ex-
pressly equates loving with humiliation and loss of potency; he
imagines it as a castrating torture: "Prove that ever I lose more
blood with love than I will get again with drinking, pick out
mine eyes with a ballad maker's pen and hang me up at
the door of a brothel house for the sign of blind Cupid"
(I.i.243–47). He likewise fears being separated from his friends
by marriage and loss of status with them if he must "sigh away
Sundays" or, feminized, "turn spit" like Hercules (I.i.196;
II.i.244). He defends himself against a fall into love and marriage and against fears of female betrayal by distrust of women
—"I will do myself the right to trust none" (I.i.237). Distrust,
coupled with the claim that all women dote on him, allows him
to profess virility without putting it to the proof. Mocking
Claudio's romantic idealization, he is similarly protected by
misogyny; the parallel function of the two poses is evident in
Benedick's admission that, could he find an ideal woman, he
would abandon the pose: "But till all graces be in one woman,
one woman shall not come in my grace" (II.iii.27–29). As he
continues his description of the ideal woman, it is clear that
she, like Claudio's Hero, meets the conventional prescriptions
for a suitably accomplished and submissive wife: "Rich she
shall be, that's certain; wise, or I'll none; virtuous, or I'll never
cheapen her; fair, or I'll never look on her; mild, or come not
near me; noble, or not I for an angel; of good discourse, an ex-

cellent musician" (II.iii.29–33). Benedick's misogyny puts him in a position of unchallengeable power; his wit is consistently belligerent, protective, and self-aggrandizing. But his bawdy incorporates, as romantic rhetoric does not, the aggressiveness and urgency of desire even while defending against it.

Instead of defensively asserting power and certainty, Beatrice's sallies often directly reveal weakness and ambivalence; her wit, in contrast to Benedick's, is consistently self-deprecating. Her mockery of marriage and men poignantly reveals her desire for both. The fear of and desire for women's roles that generate her merry mask are suggested in her description of her birth and her mother's response to it—"No, sure, my lord, my mother cried; but then there was a star danced, and under that was I born" (II.i.322–23)—and in Leonato's similarly paradoxical description of her—"She hath often dreamt of unhappiness and waked herself with laughing" (II.i.333). Her repartee, like that of the others, embodies anxiety about being unmarried, as it does about being married: "So, by being too curst, God will send you no horns" (II.i.23). She does not mock Hero's marriage plans as Benedick does Claudio's but only urges her to marry a man who pleases her. Hero's engagement does not engender smug self-satisfaction in her but a sense of isolation: "Thus goes everyone to the world but I, and I am sunburnt. I may sit in a corner and cry 'Heigh-ho for a husband!'" (II.i.306–08). Even her allusion to living "as merry as the day is long" in heaven "where the bachelors sit" shows her desire to continue to share equally in easy male camaraderie rather than a desire to remain single (II.i.45–47).[33]

Beatrice's ambivalence about marriage is rooted in her fear of the social and sexual power it grants to men. Her bawdy jests manifest both her desire for Benedick and her fear of the potential control over her which her desire gives him. In the first scene it is she who quickly shifts the play's focus from Claudio's deeds of war to Benedick's deeds of love. She refers to him as "Signior Mountanto," suggestively initiates dialogue by asking, "Is it possible Disdain should die while she hath such food to feed it as Signior Benedick?" (I.i.29, 117), and from behind the safety of her mask admits to Benedick (of him)—"I would he had boarded me" (II.i.137). But her jesting about the unsuitability of husbands with beards and those without them both mocks Benedick's beard and reveals her ambivalent attitude toward virility: "He that hath a beard is more than a youth, and he that hath no beard is less than a man; and he that is more than a youth is not for me, and he that is less than a man, I am not for him" (II.i.34–37). Because she is apprehensive about the social and sexual submission demanded of women in marriage and wary of men's volatile mixture of earthly frailty with arrogant authority, Beatrice does not want a husband:

> Till God make men of some other metal than earth.
> Would it not grieve a woman to be overmastered with
> a piece of valiant dust? To make an account of her life
> to a clod of wayward marl? No, uncle, I'll none.
> Adam's sons are my brethren, and truly I hold it a sin
> to match in my kindred.   [II.i.56–61]

Neither hating nor idealizing men, she does not wish to exchange kinship with them for submission to them. Given the play's dominant metaphor of sex as a male assault, the subordination demanded of Renaissance women in marriage, and the valiant cloddishness of many of the men in the comedies, Beatrice's fear of being "overmastered" seems judicious. But her anxieties, like Benedick's, grow out of pride and fear of risk as well as out of justified wariness.

Beatrice and Benedick, both mockers of love, cannot dispel these anxieties or admit to love without intervention. The asymmetrical gullings perpetrated by their friends (the "only love-gods" in this play, II.i.372) resemble the ceremonies mocking men and the attacks on female recalcitrance already examined. These garrulous deceits follow upon and displace Hero and Claudio's silent engagement and confront anxieties there left unspoken. As male and female anxieties are different, the two deceits are contrasting. The men gently mock Benedick's witty misogyny while nurturing his ego. Their gentle ribbing of Benedick's "contemptible spirit" is tempered with

much praise of his virtues; he is proper, wise, witty, and valiant "As Hector" (II.iii.180–87). They alleviate his fears about
Beatrice's aggressiveness by a lengthy, exaggerated tale of her
desperate passion for him: "Then down upon her knees she
falls, weeps, sobs, bears her heart, tears her hair, prays,
curses—'O sweet Benedick! God give me patience!'" (II.iii.
148–50). The story dovetails perfectly with his fantasy that all
women dote on him (and presumably it gratifies the other men
to picture the disdainful Beatrice in this helpless state). The
men also reassure Benedick that Beatrice is sweet and "out of
all suspicion, she is virtuous" (160–61). The gulling permits
Benedick to love with his friends' approval while remaining
complacently self-satisfied. Even these protective assurances
of his power win from him only a grudgingly impersonal acknowledgment of his feelings: "Love me? Why, it must be requited" (II.iii.219). This he must justify by relying, like Claudio, on friends' confirmations of the lady's virtue and
marriageability, and by viewing marriage not personally but
conventionally as a social institution designed to control desire
and ensure procreation: "the world must be peopled" (236).

The women's gulling of Beatrice is utterly different in
strategy and effect. They make only one unembroidered mention of Benedick's love for her, and even that is interrogative—
"But are you sure / That Benedick loves Beatrice so entirely?"
(III.i.36–37). They praise *his* virtues, not Beatrice's. Instead of
treating sex with detachment, as the men do with their joke
about "'Benedick' and 'Beatrice' between the sheet" (II.iii.139),
the women include an explicit, enthusiastic reference to it:
"Doth not the gentleman / Deserve as full as fortunate a
bed / As ever Beatrice shall couch upon?" (III.i.44–46).
Throughout most of the staged scene, they attack at length and
with gusto Beatrice's proud wit, deflating rather than bol-
stering her self-esteem. The men emphasize Beatrice's love
whereas the women emphasize her inability to love as a means
of exorcising it: "She cannot love, / Nor take no shape
nor project of affection, / She is so self-endeared" (54–56).
Beatrice, accepting unabashedly the accuracy of these
charges—"Contempt, farewell! And maiden pride, adieu!"

(109)—is released into an undefensive and personal declaration of love and of passionate submission to Benedick: "Benedick, love on; I will requite thee, / Taming my wild heart to thy loving hand. / If thou dost love, my kindness shall incite thee / To bind our loves up in a holy band" (111–14). She views marriage not as a social inevitability but as a ritual expressing affectionate commitment. Benedick's "love" will be requited with "kindness," not merely with the production of "kind." And, unlike Benedick, she trusts her own sense of his worth more than her friends' praise: "For others say thou dost deserve, and I / Believe it better than reportingly" (115–16).

The effect of the gullings is to engender parallels between the two women and the two men and to emphasize differences between the men and women, manifesting in this way the connections between the two plots. Hero asserts herself for the first time during the gulling of Beatrice. She zestfully takes the lead in the mockery, parodying Beatrice's contemptuous wit and scorning her scorn; her vehemence perhaps reveals some resentment of Beatrice's domination and shows her own similar capacity for aggressiveness, realism, and wit. In their next scene together on her wedding day, Hero for the first time expresses her own apprehensiveness about marriage by being heavy of heart and refusing to join in the sexual banter of the other women. Like Hero, Beatrice is now "sick" with love, and her wit is out of tune.[34] Claudio welcomes Benedick's lovesickness even more gleefully than Hero does Beatrice's. During the gulling, his comic descriptions of the doting Beatrice and the valiant Benedick are caricatures of his own romantic ideals, while his description of Beatrice dying for Benedick (II.iii.173–77) hints at the violence, anxiety, and desire for female submission that lie beneath the romantic veneer. Benedick in love is, like Claudio, "sadder"; his wit is curtailed ("governed by stops"), and he has shaved off his beard, marking his new vulnerability (III.ii.15, 56). Claudio, with the other men, takes advantage of him, reiterating his tale of Beatrice's "dying."

The anxieties about sexuality and submission that are the source of the men's lovesickness then erupt violently in Don John's slander. It is ironically appropriate that, though Hero has never talked to Claudio at all and he had "never tempted her with word too large" (IV.i.52), he should immediately accept Don John's report that she "talk[ed] with a man out at a window" (IV.i.308) as proof of her infidelity. Though he does not "see her chamber window ent'red" (III.ii.108), this imagined act transforms defensive idealization to vicious degradation, as will occur later with Angelo, Troilus, Hamlet, Othello, Posthumus, and Leontes. His former cautious, silent worship inverted, Claudio denounces Hero at their wedding with extravagantly lascivious, but still conventional, rhetoric:

> Out on thee, seeming! I will write against it.
> You seem to me as Dian in her orb,
> As chaste as is the bud ere it be blown;
> But you are more intemperate in your blood
> Than Venus, or those pamp'red animals
> That rage in savage sensuality.   [IV.i.55–60]

He perverts the ceremony that had seemed to protect him and seeks from friends confirmation of her corruption, as he had formerly needed proof of her virtues.

When unanchored idealization turns to degradation here, nuptials are shattered more violently and irretrievably than in the other comedies. The possibility of future reconciliation is kept alive, however, by the Friar's scheme for Hero's mock death, by Dogberry and crew's knowledge of the truth about Don John's deceit, and by Beatrice's command to Benedick. The slander of Hero tempers Beatrice's commitment to love. But Claudio's failure of romantic faith in Hero parallels and helps to rectify Benedick's lack of romantic commitment to Beatrice. Both men, along with Hero, must risk a comic death and effect a comic transformation to affirm their love. Although only Dogberry's revelation influences the plot, the three "deaths" function together to engender the play's comic reconciliations and festive release.

Hero's mock death, transforming the strategies of self-concealment through masking, disguise, or withdrawal practiced by women in romantic comedies, anticipates the development of the motif in later plays. The women in *Love's Labor's Lost* mask themselves, and they go into seclusion at the end;

Kate plays shrew and Titania evades Oberon; Julia, Rosalind, Portia, and Viola are disguised. The literal masks of Beatrice and Hero at the ball mirror their defensive facades of wit and silence. But, unlike these festive disguises, women's mock deaths do not merely parody or postpone nuptials voluntarily; they are designed by the woman and/or her confidantes to mend nuptials shattered by the men. It is now not idealization of women which must be qualified but their slander and degradation which must be reformed. The mock death is both an involuntary, passive escape from degradation and a voluntary constructive means to alter it.[35]

Hero's play death incorporates many of the elements found in later versions of the motif; the Friar, who engineers the death with Leonato's approval, outlines its constructive purpose and potential effects. The death—real or imagined—of the slandered woman satisfies the lover's desire for revenge while alleviating his fear of infidelity: "Yet she must die, else she'll betray more men" (*Oth*, V.ii.6). Then relief and guilt working together will change "slander to remorse" (IV.i.210). Freed from the pain of desiring her and the fear of losing her, the lover can reidealize the woman, a process that is described in detail by the friar, walked through in this play, and dramatized more completely in *All's Well That Ends Well*, *Hamlet*, *Othello*, *Antony and Cleopatra*, *Cymbeline*, and *The Winter's Tale*.

> For it so falls out
> That what we have we prize not to the worth
> Whiles we enjoy it; but being lacked and lost,
> Why then we rack the value, then we find
> The virtue that possession would not show us
> Whiles it was ours. So will it fare with Claudio.
> When he shall hear she died upon his words,
> Th' idea of her life shall sweetly creep
> Into his study of imagination
> And every lovely organ of her life
> Shall come appareled in more precious habit,
> More moving, delicate, and full of life,
> Into the eye and prospect of his soul
> Than when she lived indeed.   [IV.i.216–29]

Through the death—pretended or actual—of the corrupted beloved, the lover can repossess her, purified. In this way, the Friar hopes, the "travail" of restoring the image of the woman will culminate in a "greater birth" (IV.i.212), her death in life.

But for women the strategy is bold, painful, and risky. Whereas in earlier comedies, female disguise, control, and wit brought men to their senses, in later ones, more disturbingly, female submission generates male affection. Hero must put herself in the hands of the friar, practice patience, and accept, if the trick fails, chaste seclusion in a religious retreat[36]—the fate Hermia is threatened with in *Midsummer Night's Dream*, Helen pretends to in *All's Well That Ends Well*, and Isabella desires in *Measure for Measure*. Women pretend to die of unrequited love as Beatrice is said to be doing; they "die" sexually, validating male virility as Helen and Mariana do in bedtricks whose deceit makes them a form of mock death; and they die, or pretend to, as retribution for their imagined betrayals; Juliet undergoes a double confrontation with death—her deathlike swoon induced by the Friar's potion and her interment with dead bodies in the Capulet monument—before she actually dies; Hermione must remain in seclusion sixteen years. In the tragedies women actually die. But the woman's pretended or real death, even when combined with the vigorous defense of her virtues by her friends—Beatrice, the Countess, Emilia, Paulina[37]—does not by itself ensure penitence. Ophelia's and Desdemona's deaths do engender in Hamlet and Othello the penitent reidealization the friar describes. But Juliet's and Cleopatra's mock deaths kill Romeo and Antony. Claudio's and Bertram's penitence is perfunctory and coerced. Claudio seems utterly unaffected by the death until Borachio testifies to Hero's innocence (as Emilia will testify to Desdemona's and the oracle to Hermione's); then reidealization is instantaneous: "Sweet Hero, now the image doth appear / In the rare semblance that I loved it first" (V.i.250–51). Only Antony and Posthumus forgive the woman without proof of her innocence. Only in *Antony and Cleopatra* and *Cymbeline* does the mock death by itself lead to the guilt, penitence, and forgiveness predicted by the Friar. And only at last in *The Winter's Tale* does the death lead to penitence, transformation, and full reconciliation. Although the motif appears in all genres, playing dead can perhaps be seen as a female version of the tragic hero's literal and symbolic journeys.[38] Its effect is not to transform the woman as the tragic hero is transformed, but to achieve the transformation of her image in the eyes of the hero and to alter and complicate the audience's view of her.[39] The motif satisfies the male characters' fantasies of control and the audience's need to sympathize with the slandered women.

But in *Much Ado* the festive conclusion is not only made possible by Hero's mock death, Claudio's enforced penance, and Dogberry's apprehension of the "benefactors" who expose the deceit. Equally important is Benedick's willingness to comply with Beatrice's command to "Kill Claudio" (IV.i.288). Benedick's acquiescence signals his transformation and reconciles him with Beatrice. Although the gullings bring Beatrice and Benedick to acknowledge their affections to themselves, they have not risked doing so to each other. The broken nuptials provide the impetus for this commitment. The seriousness of the occasion tempers their wit and strips away their defenses. Weeping for Hero, Beatrice expresses indirectly her vulnerability to Benedick, just as Benedick's assertion of trust in Hero expresses indirectly his love for Beatrice and leads to his direct, ungrudging expression of it: "I do love nothing in the world so well as you" (IV.i.267). This reciprocates Beatrice's earlier vow to "tame her wild heart" for him. But the broken nuptials have encouraged Beatrice to be wary still; her vow is witty, and she asks for more than vows from Benedick, taking seriously his romantic promise, "Come, bid me do anything for thee." "Kill Claudio," she replies (IV.i.287–88).

Extravagant and coercive as her demand may be, Benedick's willingness to comply is a necessary antidote to the play's pervasive misogyny and a necessary rehabilitation of romance from Claudio's corruption of it.[40] Benedick's challenge to Claudio, by affirming his faith in both Hero's and Beatrice's fidelity, repudiates his former mistrust of women and breaks his bonds with the male friends who shared this attitude. Because romantic vows and postures have proved empty or unre-

liable—"But manhood is melted into cursies, valor into com-
pliment, and men are only turned into tongue, and trim ones
too" (IV.i.317–20)—they must now be validated through
deeds. The deed Beatrice calls for is of a special sort. Male aggression is to be used not in war but for love, not against
women but on their behalf. Beatrice calls on Benedick to become a hero of romance in order to qualify his wit and verify
his commitment to her. Similar transformations are demanded
by the women of other men in the comedies: the lords in *Love's
Labor's Lost* must test their wit and prove their vows during a
year of penance; Bassanio must relegate friendship to surety
for his marriage; Orsino and Orlando are led to abandon silly
poses for serious marriage vows. But while the grave estrangement of Claudio and Hero is displaced by Beatrice's and Benedick's movement into romantic love, the wits' love for each
other is also protected by their commitment to the cause of
Hero. Beatrice can weep for her friend as she does not weep for
Benedick, and Benedick is "engaged" simultaneously to Beatrice and on behalf of Hero.

   The scene of the challenge itself also deftly intertwines
two tones—the romantic and the comic—and the two plots.
Although it shows the bankruptcy of Claudio's wit, it also absorbs Benedick's challenge back into a witty comic context before actual violence can disrupt this context irrevocably. Benedick, having abandoned his wit, proposes to substitute a
sword for it: "It [wit] is in my scabbard. Shall I draw it?"
(V.i.126). Seriously challenging Claudio, he refuses to join in
his friend's effort to use wit to transform swords back into
jests, a duel to a feast, his adversary to a dinner: "he hath bid
me to a calf's head and a capon; the which if I do not carve
most curiously, say my knife's naught. Shall I not find a wood-
cock too?" (V.i.154–57).[41] In fact, swordplay *is* absorbed back
into wordplay when the slandering of Hero is revealed, Claudio guiltily does penance, and the challenge is dropped. Benedick's delivery of it releases him and Beatrice into the affectionate banter through which, "too wise to woo peaceably"
(V.ii.71), they reanimate the conventions of romantic rhetoric
as they did those of romantic valor: "I will live in thy heart, die

in thy lap, and be buried in thy eyes; and, moreover, I will go with thee to thy uncle's" (V.ii.99–101). The dynamics of the Beatrice/Benedick plot invert and counteract the dynamics of the Claudio/Hero plot. Whereas Hero must "die" in response to Claudio's misogynistic fantasies of her corruption in order to restore his romantic attachment, Benedick must agree to kill Claudio in compliance with Beatrice's demand in order to establish the replacement of witty misogyny by romantic affection.

At the conclusion, Claudio's and Hero's pat reaffirmation of their wedding vows ignores rather than transforming the conflicts which erupted through the broken nuptials. First Claudio performs a ritualistic but impersonal penance: "Pardon, goddess of the night, / Those that slew thy virgin knight; / For the which, with songs of woe, / Round about her tomb they go" (V.iii.12–15). Then he asserts his faith in women by agreeing to accept a substitute bride. But his willingness to "seize upon" any bride seems to suggest that the possessiveness and conventionality which fuel romance are not exorcised. When she unmasks, Claudio declares, "Another Hero," and it is Don Pedro who must assert the continuity between the two Heros, one "defiled" and destroyed, the other pure, a "maid": "The former Hero! Hero that is dead!" (V.iv.62–65). But there is no sense of rebirth. Claudio and Hero give no sign of establishing a new relationship or of incorporating desire. They move mechanically back into their former roles: "And when I lived I was your other wife / And when you loved you were my other husband" (V.iv.61).[42] In the problem comedies, Bertram's and Angelo's repentance and acceptance of substitute brides is even less spontaneous; in them the crucial presence of two women at the endings— the one the chaste object of lust (Diana, Isabella), the other the substitute bride and enforced marriage partner (Helen, Mariana)—emphasizes the continuing division between idealization and degradation, between romance and desire, which is glossed over here.[43]

In *Much Ado*, however, Beatrice and Benedick, displacing the Claudio/Hero plot one final time, create the festive conclu-

sion. Disruptive elements continue to be expressed and exorcised in their bantering movement into marriage. Their refusal
to love "more than reason" or other than "for pity" or "in
friendly recompense" (V.iv.74–93) acknowledges wittily the
fear each still has of submission and the desire each has that
the other be subordinate. They are finally brought to their nuptials only by a wonderfully comic "miracle," (91) but one not
dependent on removal of disguise, recognition of other kinds,
or the descent of a god. The discovery of their "halting" sonnets signals their mutual release into the extravagance of romance and is followed by the kiss which, manifesting their
mutual desire, serves as a truce in their merry wars. This kiss
"stop[s]" Beatrice's mouth as she had earlier urged Hero to
"stop" Claudio's at their engagement (V.iv.97; II.i.299). But
while affirming mutuality in one way, the kiss ends it in another, for it silences Beatrice for the rest of the play. Similarly,
other strong, articulate women are subdued at the ends of their
comedies—Julia, Kate, Titania, Rosalind, Viola.[44] This kiss,
then, may be seen as marking the beginning of the inequality
that Beatrice feared in marriage and that is also implicit in the
framing of the wedding festivities with male jokes about cuckoldry, in the reestablishment of male authority by means of
these jokes, and in Benedick's control of the nuptials.

This inequality is confirmed as Benedick presides over the
play's conclusion, using his wit to affirm the compatability of
manhood, friendship, and marriage. Through the cuckoldry
motif, Benedick has transformed a potentially humiliating submission in marriage into a proof of power. He likewise transforms the women's "light heels" into a sign of joy, not infidelity (V.iv.119). His final unifying gesture invites Don Pedro to
join him and Claudio in marriage to alleviate his sadness, attain authority, and reestablish ties with his war companions:
"get thee a wife, get thee a wife! There is no staff more rever-
end than one tipped with horn" (V.iv.122–25). Beatrice's and
Benedick's sparring is transformed by the broken nuptials into
romantic attachment, and Hero's mock death and the revelation of her innocence transform Claudio's degradation of her
into a ritualistic penance. Throughout the comedies broken

nuptials, even when initiated by men, give women the power to resist, control, or alter the movement of courtship. But with the celebration of completed nuptials at the end of the comedies, male control is reestablished, and women take their subordinate places in the dance.

While rejoicing in the festive conclusion of *Much Ado* we should perhaps remember Beatrice's acute satire on wooing and wedding—and their aftermath:

> wooing, wedding, and repenting is as a Scotch jig, a measure, and a cinquepace. The first suit is hot and hasty like a Scotch jig (and full as fantastical); the wedding, mannerly modest, as a measure, full of state and ancientry; and then comes Repentance and with his bad legs falls into the cinquepace faster and faster till he sink into his grave.   [II.i.69–75]

Beatrice's description, which sees marriage as a precarious beginning, not a happy ending, is anticipated by the many irregular nuptials of earlier comedies and is embodied in the troubling open endings of *All's Well That Ends Well* and *Measure for Measure*. In these plays the balance between wit and romance, between male authority and female power is lost. The culmination "fantastical" romance and "hot and hasty" desire in a "mannerly modest" ceremony does not preclude the repenting which follows in the problem comedies and tragedies. In the romantic comedies "the catastrophe is a nuptial," as Armado proclaims with relish in his love letter to Jaquenetta (*LLL*, IV.i.78), but later nuptials prove to be catastrophic in a sense other than the one Armado consciously intends. His own reversal of customary nuptials by getting Jaquenetta pregnant before the ceremony foreshadows a source of difficulty. And in *Much Ado About Nothing* there is one final nuptial irregularity: the dancing begins even before the weddings are celebrated.

CHAPTER TWO

Power and Virginity in the Problem Comedies:
All's Well That Ends Well

S we have seen, in Shakespeare's romantic comedies broken nuptials, often in the form of parodic ceremonies or postponed consummations, release and exorcise male and female anxieties about marriage; they break down resistance, transform misogyny, qualify romantic idealization, and acknowledge sexuality. In doing so, they make possible the union of love, desire, and social necessity celebrated in the festive conclusions. In these comedies the virginity of the heroines is taken for granted, and the consummation of the marriages is never enacted but merely anticipated at the ending. All of these elements are altered in a group of plays written at the beginning of the seventeenth century and often called problem plays—*Hamlet, Troilus and Cressida, All's Well That Ends Well, Othello, Measure for Measure.*

The term "problem-plays" was first used by Frederick Boas in 1896 to refer to *Hamlet, All's Well That Ends Well, Troilus and Cressida,* and *Measure for Measure.*[1] A. P. Rossiter, much later and with good reason, includes *Othello* in this group; he is, I believe, the only critic to do so.[2] The term, which has been used to designate various groups of plays, has been defined in quite different ways and is often employed with apologies and disclaimers.[3] But the fact that it remains current after almost a hundred years suggests that its very amorphousness contributes to its utility. Boas's brief paragraph of explanation neatly introduces all the different kinds of problems—social, moral, psychological, structural, affective—which later critics have explored in the plays. He finds that these works include the social problems of societies "whose civilization is ripe unto rottenness" as well as moral problems, "intricate cases of conscience [which] demand a solution by unprecedented methods." These thematic concerns generate aesthetic problems: the characters are neither likeable nor tragic, and as "the issues raised preclude a completely satisfactory outcome," the plays' endings are inconclusive. Responses to them are, therefore, mixed: "at the close our feeling is neither one of simple joy nor pain." The source of the problems is to be found, Boas suggests, in some unidentifiable crisis of Shakespeare's life; the dramatic consequence is generic blends, plays that cannot "be strictly called comedies or tragedies" (p. 345). Most later discussions of the plays are similarly affective and circular. Registering puzzled, mixed, or negative responses, they assume a biographical catalyst without actually specifying one and seek the justifications of both author's crisis and critic's feelings in the plays' problematic content and structure. E. K. Chambers and J. Dover Wilson, for example, assimilate the moral problems *in* the plays to aesthetic ones *with* the plays and find them failures, unpleasantly negative reflections of Shakespeare's cynicism.[4] In contrast to mainstream critics, W. W. Lawrence, who focuses only on the three non-tragedies and terms them, as I do, problem comedies, discounts biographical influence and critical perturbation. He looks at the plays in the light of their folktale sources and finds that then their moral and aesthetic problems evaporate.[5] But in spite of Lawrence's optimistic readings and C. J. Sisson's denunciation of "The mythical sorrows of Shakespeare," the problems of the plays and the implicit problems of the playwright have not disappeared.[6]

Although Lawrence's analysis is much cited, few have

found his solutions as compelling as the plays' problems. Recent critics continue to imply some basis for the plays in Shakespeare's life without specifying a particular event or attitude which generated them. They tend to downplay the social and moral problems of the plays and stress psychological problems, assimilating these to aesthetic flaws. E. M. W. Tillyard's discussion reflects continuing bifurcation in the meaning of the term as he compares problem plays to problem children, each problematic in different ways, and finds that *All's Well* and *Measure for Measure* are disturbed and incoherent whereas *Hamlet* and *Troilus and Cressida* contain interesting problems.[7] The two most extended, precise, and useful attempts to define the term and the plays, those of A. P. Rossiter in *Angel with Horns* and Richard P. Wheeler in *Shakespeare's Development and the Problem Comedies*, likewise reflect the two poles of definition—that the plays anatomize problems and that they have them. Rossiter for the most part eschews psychological/historical explanation and aesthetic evaluation. He attributes the special quality of these plays to their genre (tragicomedy), to their subject ("tragi-comic man," 116), to their attitude toward this subject ("scepticism of man's worth, importance, and value," 116), and to their mixed tone, in which ideals are deflated, unhappiness is treated comically, and funny subjects are treated as serious. The plays are seen as an "inquisition into human nature and humanism," (152), a deliberate skeptical probing.[8] In contrast, Wheeler, examining only the core problem comedies, *All's Well* and *Measure for Measure*, especially in relation to the earlier festive comedies and the late romances, links their psychological and aesthetic problems; he argues that their comic designs are not adequate to permit the mastery of the profound conflicts they embody.[9]

Whether the problems of the plays are defined as deliberate or involuntary, as moral or aesthetic, as matters of content or of form, they are invariably connected with sexuality and its vexed relation to social authority, with controversial actions by and mixed responses to the women characters, and with the weakness or nastiness of the young men: Boas, for example, comments that they are all "painful studies of the weakness, levity, and unbridled passion of young men" (345). Since these very issues are the focus of my study, it is the problems *in* the plays, especially in *All's Well That Ends Well*, rather than those *of* the plays that I will explore in this chapter. Although I think that comic form is under pressure in the problem comedies, as are the marriages which constitute their conventional endings, I do not think that the plays' form is inadequate to their complex content. Comic structure is expanded and altered but not thereby weakened. The women, too, play different roles from those in the romantic comedies. But although they are subject to more negative and intransigent attitudes than in the earlier comedies, their characterizations transcend the corrupted and stereotyped views of them held by the male characters, and they function to temper the skepticism and cynicism which some critics have found in these plays. The plays seem to me neither completely cynical inquisitions nor failed comedies. But because they differ from the festive comedies by rendering the elements of sex, love, and marriage deliberately problematic and in conflict with each other, the generic term *problem play* seems to be entirely appropriate, as does the more specific term, *problem comedies* referring to *All's Well That Ends Well*, *Measure for Measure*, and *Troilus and Cressida*.

The romantic comedies are protected in ways that the problem plays are not. Their conventions serve to contain sexuality and to mitigate its threatening aspects. The heroines' disguises allow them to acknowledge female promiscuity while detaching themselves from it; they also make the direct expression of male desire impossible. However, the green-world setting often permits the release of desire in a playful context and links it positively with the rhythms of nature, with growth, fertility, and procreation. The bawdy also enables sexuality to be expressed in a witty, conventional way, acknowledging the universality of desire while separating it from individuals. Desire is protected further in these plays by being linked inevitably with love and marriage. Degraded or non-marital sexuality is rare, marginal, benign. The only prostitute is the Courtesan in *Comedy of Errors*, the only coercive sexuality is the bizarre and soon thwarted rape at the conclusion of *Two*

Gentlemen of Verona. Seduction attempts by Touchstone and the Falstaff of *Merry Wives* are comic failures, and the promiscuity of Titania with Bottom is a funny, charming liaison.

In the problem plays, however, there are no male disguises for the heroines, no green worlds, no fairies, no parody couples to express desire and protect the main couples; even the bawdy is changed in tone. Sexuality is now frequently dissociated from marriage and procreation. It finds expression in seduction (*Troilus and Cressida* and *All's Well*), aggressive lust (*Measure for Measure*), prostitution (*Measure for Measure, Othello*), promiscuity (*Troilus and Cressida*), and, perhaps, adultery (*Hamlet*). Instead of being connected with imagery of growth and fertility, sexuality is associated with corruption, loss, disease, death.[10] It also plays a larger part in the language, imagery, characterization, and plot of these plays than it did in the comedies. Meanwhile, romantic love, which is less pervasive than it was in the comedies, no longer controls desire and, suitably qualified, engenders the mutuality that brings about happy marriages. In the problem plays, romantic love is easily manipulated and easily shattered. Troilus and Bertram use its rhetoric to seduce Cressida and Diana. Hamlet and Othello manifest its corruptibility. Women withdraw from idealizing love. Helen and Mariana come to pursue romantic desires in practical ways; Ophelia, in madness, hallucinates seduction and betrayal and Diana anticipates them; Cressida seems to eschew ideals altogether and Isabella, sexuality.

Stripped of the adornments of romantic love and no longer a guarantee of controlled or satisfied desire, marriage is put under even more pressure as its social and institutional complications are emphasized. In the romantic comedies the external social impediments to marriage were conventional and conventionally flimsy: male disguise, easily removed; the father's will, easily complied with; the father's veto, easily canceled. But in the problem plays, marriages are beset with tangled social, economic, and legal problems: the coercive power of wardship, the radical incompatibility of race and social class, the absence of dowries, the intricate legalities of contracts and precontracts, the sin of incestuous second marriage. There are, of course, other kinds of social and moral problems in the plays besides marriage—the deflation of heroism and honor in *Troilus and Cressida*, for example, or Hamlet's inability to act to avenge his father's murder. But even in these two plays the dissociation of sexuality from marriage and the disruption of marriage underlie other sorts of corruption.

As sexuality becomes more central and more debased in the problem plays and as marriage becomes legally and socially more difficult, the protection of virginity, an underlying assumption in the festive comedies, becomes a matter for debate. On the one hand, virginity is seen as a value and a virtue; on the other, as a commodity to be exchanged. Ophelia and Diana are lectured on the necessity of the vigilant defense of theirs. Isabella values hers over her brother's life. Hamlet urges abstinence upon Gertrude even in marriage. But Parolles argues that Helen should lose her virginity expeditiously, and she and Cressida do so. Mariana, likewise, loses her virginity under deceitful circumstances to achieve the marriage she desires. But the loss of virginity, while enabling the women in these plays to achieve their goals, also endangers them: they lose the kinds of power they could take for granted in the romantic comedies.

The inevitable virginity of the heroines of the festive comedies generated desire, tempered it, and constrained it within the context of marriage and procreation. In the problem plays loss of virginity constricts or compromises women's power in three ways. First, at the crudest level, virginity is power, seductive power, as Angelo learns, and bargaining power, as Cressida knows. Her well-known expression of this—"Men prize the thing ungained more than it is; . . . Achievement is command; ungained beseech" (I.ii.296–300)—is validated in all the problem plays. Her value falls precipitously after she is won, as does that of Diana and Isabella. After apparent seductions they are vilified as whores—as are Gertrude and Desdemona even within marriage. Second, when women lose their virginity, they lose their position as idealized beloveds and hence their ability to inspire male adoration and mitigate male anxieties, to keep men "amiable" (the virtue of the handkerchief in *Othello*). In the problem plays, even when participating in loving and faithful marriages, the women trigger male fears of female sexuality and wantonness, of male impotence and degradation. Invariably they are "bewhored" by the men in the plays. Third, women's loss of virginity is the emblem of their social transformation from beloved to wife and of the changed status this entails. "Ay, so you serve us / Till we serve you" (IV.ii.17–18), Diana's wry retort to Bertram's protestations of eternal service, has implications beyond sexual ones for courted beloveds who become wives. The consequent loss of independence, initiative, and control is apparent in the submission of Desdemona to her husband, and in the partial, potential, or pretended submissions of Helen and Diana, Mariana and Isabella.

Like the romantic comedies, *All's Well That Ends Well* and *Measure for Measure* specifically dramatize broken nuptials that culminate in achieved marriages. In these problem comedies, romantic love, sexual union, and social accommodation are again examined, but arranged in a different balance, put under more pressure, and brought more profoundly into conflict with one another than in the romantic comedies. In the earlier plays, love provides the crucial link between the personal imperatives of desire and the social imperatives of marriage and procreation. But in the problem comedies love is peripheral and unrequited, sexuality is corrupted and divorced from love and marriage, and the social pressures enforcing marriage are enormous. Hence the reconciliation between the couple's desires and society's demands is more difficult to achieve than in the earlier comedies. In *All's Well That Ends Well*, I shall argue, a precarious reconciliation is achieved with full acknowledgment of its cost. The marriages that conclude *Measure for Measure*, however, are enforced, joyless, and without promise. *All's Well* transforms the motifs of the comedies, while *Measure for Measure* anticipates the themes, attitudes, and conflicts of the tragedies.

All's Well dramatizes fully all of the strains in courtship and marriage that were potential or muted in the festive comedies: the older generation's attempt to control marital choice, the men's corrupted views of women and sexuality, the women's consequent powerlessness and conflicting need to pursue their desires aggressively. In this play the older generation is prominent and authoritative. More fully drawn than in the romantic comedies, it is more emphatically in decline and hence dependent on the marriages of youth for its own rejuvenation. But parent figures in the problem comedies endanger nuptials more by insisting on them than fathers and rulers in earlier comedies did by impeding them. Because the apparently dying king and Bertram's mother are implicated in the broken nuptials, they must participate directly in their restoration. This intervention by the elders is necessary partly because the young couple is unable to negotiate marriage themselves as the couples of the romantic comedies could. Helen's[11] anxieties are more deeply rooted and less easily dispelled than was the proud resistance to love of earlier heroines. Her sense of personal unworthiness and social inadequacy are reinforced by Bertram's rejection. In him, the witty misogyny of the heroes of comedy deteriorates into revulsion against women, and erotic desire turns into irresistible lust seeking satisfaction outside of marriage. Bertram's attitudes are reinforced by the military environment to which he flees (one never central in the romantic comedies) and by his relations with Parolles, a bond more corrupt and corrupting than earlier male friendships.

In order to counter Bertram's misogyny and lust and his flight from social responsibilities, Helen must combine the roles of chaste beloved (through her idealizing rhetoric, her pilgrim's disguise, and her mock death), of sexual partner (through the bedtrick), and of wife (through her legal betrothal, marriage ceremony, and pregnancy). She must cooperate with other women, change places and identities with Diana, and undergo the losses and gains which are the consequence of her mock death and of the bedtrick. Bertram must, however perfunctorily, undergo sexual initiation, the exposure of Parolles, the loss of his wife, and submission to the authority of his elders. The marriage that is ratified at the end of the play is presented not as a joyous lovers' union but as a compromised bargain, not as a happy ending but as a precarious beginning.

Although *All's Well* ends as vexed comedy, it begins as attenuated tragedy. The themes of its first scene are those of *Hamlet*: the death of fathers, the power and impotence of kings, and the future of a young son, an "unseasoned courtier" (I.i.72). Like Hamlet, Bertram is urged to heed platitudinous advice, assume the virtues of his dead father, and submit to the authority of his king, ensuring in this way the stability of family and state. Bertram, like Hamlet and other tragic heroes, is the focus of a variety of demands; unlike these others, however, he does not make demands of his own. Bertram remains throughout most of the play "evermore in subjection" (I.i.5) to his elders. Unlike both the heroes of the comedies, who are usually parentless,[12] and those of tragedy, who often struggle with fathers or father figures, Bertram either submits or flees.

Although *All's Well* opens by sketching dilemmas that might be enlarged to full tragic dimensions, this enlargement emphatically does not happen. Early in the first scene the play denies expectations[13] by its abrupt shift of attention from Bertram to Helen, who, as a poor female orphan, is not likely to be the repository of familial or social expectations. Her first soliloquy transfers the focus of the play from education to love, from social demands to personal desires, from the dead and dying to the living: "I think not on my father" (I.i.82). Throughout the rest of the first act Helen establishes herself as the protagonist, the play's subject as marriage, and its genre as comedy.

The first scene, moreover, reveals sharp differences from the romantic comedies as well as from *Hamlet* and the tragedies. Helen's soliloquy is characteristic of the tragic heroes; exactly like Hamlet's first soliloquy, it reveals that it is not only her father's death that is upsetting her. In it, surprisingly, she, like the heroes of the romantic comedies, is a Petrarchan lover, idealizing Bertram as a "bright particular star" (89), providing a conventional blazon of his beloved parts, and humbly lamenting her inadequacy and the unattainability of her beloved. But she is more self-conscious about the excessiveness of her posture than an Orsino or an Orlando—"My idolatrous fancy / Must sanctify his relics" (100–01)—and her lament is grounded in the real difference in social status between her and her beloved. Her hopelessness is therefore realistic as well as conventional; precisely this blend of romantic conventionality and shrewd realism characterizes Helen throughout the play.

One means of overcoming the distance between Helen and Bertram is obliquely implied by Parolles in his dialogue with Helen on virginity. Demystifying chastity, the virtue honored by romantic love, he defines it as a valuable commodity that can be spent for personal and social gain: "Within ten year it will make itself ten which is a goodly increase and the principal itself not much the worse" (I.i.149–51). Under Parolles's tutelage Helen rapidly comes to recognize her own desires and potential and moves from vowing to die to protect her virginity to wishing to "lose it to her own liking" (152)—from worshiping distant stars to finding "remedies" within herself. Her two soliloquies are not, however, simply opposites; both contain Helen's characteristic ambiguousness. The first soliloquy testifies, however humbly, to "Th' ambition in my love" (93), while the second voices its assertions only tentatively in a couplet sonnet composed of obscure images and nervous questions: "Who ever strove / To show her merit that did miss her love?" (I.i.227–28). In both soliloquies, as throughout the rest of the play, Helen is paradoxically proud and humble, self-assertive and self-effacing, passionate and chaste, vigorous and passive. Her particular blend of idealized virtue and urgent desire differentiates her from the comedy heroines and accounts for the critics' sharply contrasted responses to her.[14] Her actions are, however, the result not only of her complex character but of the complex situation in which she finds herself. Unlike most of the heroines of the romantic comedies, she is not the pursued but the pursuer; the shape her pursuit takes is in part forced on her by her constricted social role, by the interventions of the elders, and by the fragmented and paradoxical attitudes toward women held by the men in the play.

Helen's dialogue with Parolles on virginity reveals some aspects of this attitude and provides the impetus for Helen to conceive her strategy of pursuit. It also introduces the play's emphasis on the sexual component of marriage, sets the subject and tone of its extensive bawdy, and manifests its central thematic paradox—loss in gain and gain in loss. The dialogue's subject is the loss of virginity—intercourse; its metaphors are martial and commercial, and its tone is realistic, crude, somewhat funny; this tone is neither as good-natured as the bawdy in the romantic comedies nor as bitter as that in *Troilus and Cressida* and *Measure for Measure*. Sexual encounters are imaged as mutual aggression with mixed victory and defeat on both sides.

> *Parolles.*   Man, setting down before you, will undermine you and blow you up.
> *Helen.*   Bless our poor virginity from underminers and blowers-up! Is there no military policy how virgins might blow up men?
> *Parolles.*   Virginity being blown down, man will quickly be blown up; marry, in blowing him down again, with the breach yourselves made you lose your city.
>
> [I.i.121–29]

The dialogue's reiterated image of tumescence and detumescence encapsulates a central pattern of the play. An alternation of fullness and emptiness characterizes the plot with its gaining, losing, and regaining (the general theme of Boccaccio's Third Day, present in the source tale[15] but expanded here), the development of the characters with their alternating potence and impotence, confidence and collapse, and the verse with its alternating compression and slackness.

The scenes in which Helen proposes her cure to the King and chooses Bertram manifest her blend of virtuous modesty and sexual energy, of self-confidence and self-deprecation. The sexual innuendo that imbues both scenes is not, I think, intended to undermine the audience's sympathy with Helen or to impugn her motives, but to reveal the mixed nature of both her motives and her power, the result of the mixed nature of the love that drives her and of the goal she seeks.[16] The combination of Helen's high-minded virtue and seductive sexuality is apparent in comments made about her by others, in her own language, and in the structuring of the two scenes. When Lafew announces Helen to the King, he praises her "wisdom and constancy" (II.i.87) and later refers to the cure as a "miracle" (II.iii.1). However, his innuendo as he describes her as one "whose simple touch / Is powerful to araise King Pippen, nay, / To give great Charlemain a pen in's hand, / And write to her a love-line" (II.i.78–81), his allusion to Pandarus as he leaves her alone with the King, and his lecherous jests in the choosing scene about the frigidity of the young courtiers, all call attention to her rejuvenating sexual appeal rather than to her intellectual or spiritual powers. As the scene with the King progresses, Helen, although restrained and moderate at first, gains warmth and passion.[17] Significantly, the King is moved to consider her services not when she appeals to the power of her father's art or to the possibility of divine aid, but when she asserts her confidence in her own art to effect his cure: "But know I think, and think I know most sure / My art is not past power, nor you past cure" (II.i.160–61). He is persuaded to attempt her remedy only after she has associated her cure of his "parts" with the renewing forces of nature as well as of faith—"The greatest grace lending grace, / Ere twice the horses of the sun shall bring / Their fiery torcher his diurnal ring" (II.i.163–65)—and has promised to risk for him her chaste reputation, or even her life. She will venture: "Tax of impudence, / A strumpet's boldness, a divulgèd shame, / Traduced by odious ballads; my maiden's name / Seared otherwise; ne worse of worst, extended / With vilest torture, let my life be ended" (II.i.173–77). In the first of the play's many agreements, the King and Helen agree to risk death together, to serve each other's "will" with their "performance" in couplets that are both hieratic and sexually suggestive:

> Sweet practicer, thy physic I will try
> That ministers thine own death if I die.
>
> [II.i.188–89]

> Here is my hand; the premises observed.
> Thy will by my performance shall be served.
>
> [204–05]

The choosing scene manifests still more explicitly the erotic energy that has rejuvenated the King. The scene is framed by Lafew's innuendos and his description of the King as "Lustig" and "able to lead her a coranto" (II.iii.42, 44). Helen commences her choice by an explicit leave-taking of "Dian's alter" and each of her rejections of the lords is more sexually explicit than the one before, as she refers to her "suit" (77), to "great Love" (86), to "your bed" (92), and "mak [ing] yourself a son out of my blood" (98). This series emphasizes the modesty and submissiveness of Helen's final offer of herself to Bertram. Her extraordinary seductiveness mitigates our sympathy with him in his violent rejection of her and focuses attention on the sexual as well as the social basis for it.

Bertram is not yet even at the beginning of the journey toward sexual maturity that Helen is already embarked on. Hence, he is an utterly recalcitrant beloved, aptly characterized by Parolles's definition of narcissistic virginity: "Peevish, proud, idle, made of self-love which is the most inhibited sin in the canon" (I.i.144–48). Self-love leads to Bertram's rejection of Helen and of all three components of marriage: love, sex, and social union. His first response to her choice—"I shall beseech your Highness / In such a business, give me leave to use / The help of mine own eyes" (II.iii.107–09)—shows the absence of romantic "fancy"; its necessary subjectivity is often symbolized by eyes in the earlier comedies. The bawdy innuendos of his second exchange with the King manifest Bertram's revulsion from Helen's sexuality, his sense of his own sexual inadequacy, and his understandable refusal to be a surrogate for the King, repaying *his* debts and acting on *his* desires.

> *King.* Thou know'st she has raised me from my sickly bed.
> *Bertram.* But follows it, my lord, to bring me down
> Must answer for your raising.   [II.iii.112–14]

Bertram's anxieties are emphasized by Lafew's commentary, which associates the imagined rejections of the other lords with the unnatural frigidity of "eunuchs," "boys of ice," and asses. Finally, articulating and disguising his sexual recoil, Bertram expresses contempt for her social class: "A poor physician's daughter my wife! Disdain / Rather corrupt me ever!" (II.iii.116–17). The King futilely fixes on the third component of the refusal, the only one he has control over, and agreeing to "create" social eminence in Helen, enforces the marriage.

The nature of Bertram's capitulation only confirms the sexual roots of his aversion. He submits to the social disgrace of the wedding ceremony but evades love and sexual consummation. Although he weds Helen, he emphatically refuses to "bed" her—or even kiss her. Parolles encourages and articulates his distaste for sexual union, warning: "He wears his honor in a box unseen, / That hugs his kicky-wicky here at home / Spending his manly marrow in her arms" (II.iii.282–84). His perversity in the matter is highlighted, too, by Shakespeare's alteration of Boccaccio's story, in which the count, Beltramo, seems to find Giletta, the heroine, attractive but rejects her for social reasons.[18] And there is in the source none of the emphasis on the seductiveness of Helen, which Shakespeare includes in both the cure and the choosing scenes. The impossible condition under which he would reestablish his marriage—"show me a child begotten of thy body that I am father to, then call me husband" (III.ii.59–61,—both expresses his sexual loathing and suggests that if Bertram could desire Helen and prove himself with her, the marriage would be acceptable. But before this can happen, Bertram must escape the suffocating authority of his mother and the King. He must prove his manhood as a warrior before risking it as a lover—as do Claudio, Benedick, and Othello. He must be sexually initiated not in a marriage sanctioned by his elders but in an illegitimate liaison in which he appears to act as the seducer.

Bertram must begin his education anew in the "nursery" (I.ii.16) of the Italian wars. But it is Helen who brings it to completion through her flight, her mock death, her doubling with Diana, and the bedtrick. She puts to use literally now the erotic power that metaphorically played a part in the King's recovery, but at the same time she mutes the expression of it. She wins

Bertram by both submitting to his commands and actively fulfilling her desires. Her ambigous self-effacement permits Bertram's growth:

> Nothing in France until he has no wife!
> Thou shalt have none, Rousillion, none in France;
> Then hast thou all again.   [III.ii.100–02]

This is a prophecy of her flight from France, but (by virtue of
the parenthetical, "none in France") also of the play's end.

The witty overtones of Helen's mock death connect it, by
means of the familiar Renaissance pun, with her sexual death
in the bedtrick and embody the double role she must play to
win Bertram. Both the bedtrick and the "death" combine aggressiveness and humility in a constructive deceit that is characteristic of Shakespearean mock deaths. Helen's pilgrimage
and her mock death acquire double meaning in her sonnet letter to the Countess, through the confusion about the destina-
tion of her journey, and by the precise placing of the bedtrick
in the structure of the play. Having soliloquized that she
would rather die herself than be the cause of Betram's death
(III.ii.99–129), her letter to the Countess declares that she will
relinquish Bertram and make a pilgrimage to the shrine of
Saint Jaques; however, its sonnet form and its Petrarchan rhetoric imply that she will pursue him and hint at the means she
will use. Helen presents herself in the conventional image of a
lover as pilgrim—humble ("Ambitious love hath so in me of-
fended"), penitent ("barefoot plod I the cold ground upon"), in
search of forgiveness and death. She does not, however, plan
to renounce love: "Bless him at home in peace, whilst I from
far / His name with zealous fervor sanctify" (III.iv.4–17). The
sonnet, in fact, seems as much metaphorical as expository,
rendering futile debates about whether Florence is really on
the way to Spain, just which Saint Jaques's shrine is meant,
what Helen's real intentions are. Perhaps these matters are as
unclear to her as to the audience; she only knows that she
wants to die for Bertram. The Countess's response ignores ge-
ography. Discounting the literal meaning of the sonnet, she
hopes it may promise the couple's reconciliation.

The "death" Helen seeks may likewise be metaphorical. The sonnet's couplet, viewed in the context of the play as a whole and of the sonnet tradition, may hint that the death will be sexual, not literal: "He is too good and fair for death and me, / Whom I myself embrace to set him free." The fuzziness of its pronouns (*whom* and *him*), usually straightened out in glosses, suggests deliberate confusion about whether Helen will embrace death or Bertram. In fact she will do both, and the letter wittily hints that Helen's passion will be fulfilled, not renounced. The suggestiveness is comparable to the clever overtones the tale of Giletta gains when read in the context of the other stories of the *Decameron*'s Third Day, in which religious stratagems are repeatedly used to further sexual gains, in which bedtricks are less high-minded than Giletta's, and in which religious and courtly language is ripe with sexual innuendos.[19] The ambiguity of Helen's "death" is further emphasized by its timing. The announcement of her "death" by the Lords occurs (without preparation or explanation) at precisely the moment of her assignation with Bertram.[20] This death, then, is a clever "unmetaphoring," to use Rosalie Colie's apt term, of the conventional pun on *die*.[21] Helen is a passionate pilgrim who dies for love. Her double "death" is not merely a nasty trick but a rich metaphor expressing her loss of virginity and identity and her gain of a new identity for Bertram and for herself.

The bedtrick's success requires the presence of Diana, Helen's "Motive / And helper to a husband" (IV.iv.20–21). The chaste virgin and the whore embody men's polarized fantasies of women. But the play, through the women's names, their role reversals, the substitution, and their identification with each other, controverts the fragmented views of the men and affirms the reconciliation or potential reconciliation of sexual partner and loving wife in both.

Helen's name carries implications of wantonness; Diana's implies militant virginity. These associations are emphasized in the play. The clown's song links Helen with her famous predecessor, mocking both: "Was this fair face the cause, quoth she, / Why the Grecians sackèd Troy? / Fond done, done fond, / Was this King Priam's joy?" (I.iii.71–74). Shakespeare's audience may have connected her especially with the silly and sensual Helen of Shakespeare's *Troilus and Cressida*, probably written and produced at about the time of *All's Well*.[22] More generally, Helen of Troy was, for the Renaissance, the exemplum of a bad wife. But this Helen, belying her name, begins the play as a virgin resigned to unrequited and unconsummated love. In contrast, Diana, namesake of the goddess of chastity, seems, when we first see her, ripe for seduction by the "handsome," "gallant," and "brave" gentleman Bertram (III.v.51, 78–79), as the caustic warnings against him by Mariana and her mother suggest. But soon the two switch places to move into roles more consonant with their names. Helen's persuasion of the king and her choice of Bertram are both presented as metaphorical seductions. When Bertram flees her, she must, in effect, prostitute herself in the bedtrick, engaging in an anonymous sexual encounter and receiving his ring as payment. Diana, meanwhile, becomes a militant virgin, defending herself adamantly against Bertram's advances, wittily attacking his protestations of love, and expressing generalized distrust of men, which leads her to vow, "To live and die a maid" (IV.ii.74), Helen's original resolve. In the last scene yet another reversal occurs, as Diana assumes, for Helen, "a strumpet's boldness" (II.i.174) and accepts the slander that Helen had once risked; Helen assumes her desired role as a chaste wife. If Diana were to accept the King's offer of her choice of husband, the identification between the two would be complete.

Not only does the play identify Helen and Diana, but all the women also identify with each other, feeling sympathy and offering help where hostility and rivalry might have been expected. The Countess warmly supports the affection of her poor ward for her son and heir, remembering the passions of her own youth. Diana's attraction to Bertram is qualified by her sympathy for his unknown wife even before she meets Helen, and her private and public attacks on Bertram are on Helen's behalf as well as her own. The Widow, seeing Helen's plight, plants the idea of the bedtrick: "This young maid might do her / A shrewd turn, if she pleased"(III.v.66–67). Helen has only to extend the Widow's suggestion, recognizing that she might shrewdly turn Bertram's unlawful purpose into "lawful meaning" (III.vii.46). Following the bedtrick the bonds of sympathy between the women deepen. The Widow and Diana become pilgrims with Helen, and Helen, in her reflections on the experience and in her remark, "When I was like this maid . . ."(V.iii.309), acknowledges her connection with and dependence on Diana. The three women are "maid, widow and wife" (*MM*.V.i.177) illustrating the marriage paradigm and comprising the socially acceptable roles for women in the period. Though Diana is Helen's rival and Helen makes use of her, there is no envy or hostility between them. Intimacy, mutual aid, and instinctive sympathy are characteristic of most female relationships delineated by Shakespeare. Women's sympathy for and identification with each other cross boundaries of age, class, role, and value, existing between Julia and Sylvia, Beatrice and Hero, Desdemona and Emilia, Cleopatra and her waiting women, Hermione and Paulina. But at the same time, female friendships consistently support and further women's bonds with men. Unlike male friendships, they are not experienced or dramatized as in conflict with heterosexual bonds.

Bertram and Parolles, like Helen and Diana, are parallel and contrasted figures whose friendship serves as a defense against women and sexuality far more explicitly than did the male friendships in the comedies. Parolles's attitude toward sexuality as a degrading commodity influences or perhaps merely reflects and supports Bertram's. He looks to sex for profit—either money or children—and so he instructs Helen in the market value of her virginity, encourages Bertram's decision not to "spend" his "manly marrow" (II.iii.284) by bedding her, gratuitously uses or invents the sexual exploits of his companions to please his imagined captors. As a hypocritical pander in his truncated sonnet letter to Diana, he urges her to be paid in advance for the loss of her virginity:

> When he swears oaths, bid him drop gold, and take it;
> After he scores, he never pays the score.

Half won is match well made; match and well make it;
He ne'er pays after-debts, take it before.

[IV.iii.228–31]

At the same time, he woos her himself in a parody of the bargain Bertram wishes. Self-interest rather than desire motivates his wooing, for, as Parolles knows, Helen and Diana see through him; a relationship with either would end Parolles's easy exploitation of his "sweetheart" (II.iii.271).

The friendship of Bertram and Parolles is as hypocritically self-serving on both sides as their heterosexual relationships. Instead of bailing each other out, as Helen and Diana do, each attempts to sell the other out to save his own skin. Nor is there any hint of identification or sympathy between the two for their parallel predicaments. Although the exposure of Parolles's hollow martial rhetoric is placed to emphasize the parallel with Bertram's similarly hollow amorous rhetoric, and although each is exposed, asks pardon, and embraces shame, they acknowledge no connections with each other. Diana is a conscious, willing scapegoat for Helen; Parolles is an unwitting and unwilling one for Bertram.

As Parolles attempts to protect himself by condemning his comrades and Bertram, so the characters and the play seek to exonerate Bertram by attacking and exposing Parolles. A number of characters blame Bertram's faults on Parolles's influence, although, as many critics note, these faults are in fact not created by Parolles. The contrasts between the two do, however, have the effect of making Bertram look better than he otherwise might have.[23] Parolles's cowardice makes Bertram's lauded courage the more impressive, and Parolles's willingness to embrace shame if it will help him to survive perhaps turns Bertram's arrogance into a kind of virtue. Most importantly, Parolles's "fixed evils" (I.i.105) underline Bertram's malleable immaturity, his potential for growth. The comic setpiece of the exposure of Parolles distracts attention from Bertram's treatment of Diana, and Parolles's attacks on Bertram there and in the last scene engender some sympathy for the Count. His dissociation from Parolles at the end of the play serves as a manifestation of Bertram's reform—which is not much dramatized in other ways.

Bertram's final severance from Parolles and Helen's enduring bond with Diana are both essential to the completion of the marriage that culminates an extended series of separations and affiliations. Comic action characteristically weakens or breaks old bonds to make way for new ones. In the romantic comedies the younger generation easily loosens its ties with the older: benignly, as through Rosalind's disguise; cruelly, as through the elopement of Jessica and Lorenzo; or inevitably, as through the death of the King in *Love's Labor's Lost*. *All's Well* recapitulates these separations. At the beginning of the play, Helen's father has recently died, and she has put aside remembrance of him to dote on Bertram. She symbolically rejects the Countess as a mother (desiring her as a mother-in-law) and, after her marriage, she leaves the Countess and the King to seek Bertram. Bertram, too, forgets the memory of his father's virtue and flees his mother and his King.

But whereas in the romantic comedies heterosexual bonds begin forming early in the plays, Helen and Bertram are isolated from each other throughout most of *All's Well*; they have only three curt exchanges, and none between the fifth scene of act 2 and the third scene of act 3. Apart, they associate themselves with separate male and female communities that function as a prolonged respite between their participation in a family as children (the role each emphatically plays at the start) and their creation of a new family as husband and wife and as parents (the project they embark on at the end). But the communities are joined for different reasons and function differently for the two protagonists. Bertram flees to the brotherhood of military life to evade love, marriage, and responsibility, and he gives up the ring that symbolizes his father's heritage. In contrast, Helen uses the skill inherited from her father to cure the King and later joins the Widow and Diana in an association which encourages her marriage and her own growth. Bertram must be separated from Parolles and military life, whereas Helen's cooperation with the Widow and Diana continues to the end of the play. Diana enacts seduction and betrayal and absorbs shame for Helen in the last scene. Her presence allows Shakespeare to mute in Helen's characterization the polarized traits—aggressive manipulation and degraded submission—required of the protagonists of the tales on which the play draws.

In all the variations on the motifs of the Fulfillment of the Tasks and the Substitute Bride examined by W. W. Lawrence,[24] the huband's flight and the tasks imposed express the husband's fears of female sexuality and marital responsibility along with his contradictory desires for illegitimate satisfaction and the achievement of family continuity through an heir. The central task requires the production of an heir by the wife, and the supplementary tasks all involve obvious symbols of male and female sexuality—the obtaining of rings, swords, or the husband's stallion, the digging of a well, construction of a hall or throne, the filling of a trunk. The entire burden of sexual union is symbolically placed on the woman, who must contrive to fulfill both halves of it. In order to do so, she must be both aggressive and submissive, both "clever" and a "wench." In several of the tales, the wife in fact disguises herself as a man, gains access to her husband, beats him at cards, and offers to provide him with a woman, displaying traditional male qualities of ingenuity, stamina, and courage. But to fulfill the female part of the bargain and to put to rest their husbands' sexual anxieties, the women must be helpless, seduceable, whores. The wives hence take on the roles of lower-class, powerless, or degraded women—a cowherd's daughter, a slave, an imprisoned princess, a poor Florentine maid—women who, like whores, can be used contemptuously to supply sexual satisfaction and abandoned with ease without concern for consequences or heirs. In this connection, it seems significant that Diana's mother is a poor widow; the daughter's lack of paternal or financial protection puts her in an especially vulnerable position in a patriarchal society. In these tales the women must be still more manipulative and ingenious than Helen, whose stratagem presents itself to her accidentally. And while the sexual component of Helen's achievement is emphasized in her cure of the King, the presence of Diana allows it in certain ways to be deemphasized, as she does not directly seduce nor is she seduced by Bertram.

At the same time, however, the bedtrick by which Bertram is won is presented so as to be more troubling and richer than those in the folktale sources, in Boccaccio's tale, or in other analogues. This irregular nuptial both completes and further complicates the marriage of Helen and Bertram. It is the center of the "mingled yarn" of the play, the point where good and ill, loss and gain are most intricately intertwined. The encounter is, in numerous ways, a "death" for both Bertram and Helen, culminating their isolation, humiliation, and loss of identity but also commencing their union. To achieve his desires, Bertram must give up his ring, the emblem of his social rank and family connections. We learn later that Helen, too, has given up the King's ring, emblem perhaps of her dependence on him as a surrogate father. It also symbolizes her honor, which, Diana argues, has a social value for women equal to the male heritage embodied in Bertram's ring: "mine honor's such a ring; / My chastity's the jewel of our house / Bequeathèd down from many ancestors" (IV.ii.45–47). Both embark on the sexual encounter without the sanctioning contexts of family, rank, secure marriage. But the loss of virginity is riskier and more irrevocable than the loss of the ring, and Helen has nothing else to bargain with. The nature of the bedtrick necessitates that Bertram, in accord with his wishes, be bereft of all connections with his beloved other than the sheerly sensual one and that Helen, against her wishes, be a substitute body in the dark who gives up name and speech and employs nakedness as a disguise. She is unaccommodated woman at the place where divine aid, the King's authority, rank, role, and identity have been cast off. The bedtrick both depends on and expresses the radical anonymity of sexual union, its separation from love and marriage. And the union itself, as the bawdy in the play graphically shows, means a physical loss for both—the loss of Bertram's "manly marrow" and Helen's virginity.

But from these losses come gains—or at least the promise of gains. First at the physical level with Helen's pregnancy, which the play has anticipated through Lavatch's and Parolles's witticisms: "The danger is in standing to't; that's the loss of men, though it be the getting of children" (III.ii.41–42) and "Loss of virginity is rational increase, and there was never virgin got till virginity was first lost" (I.i.130–32). Their marriage and the getting of a child reunite sexuality with family. There are more immediate gains as well. Bertram's seduction of the "wondrous cold" Diana (III.vi.116) completes his rebellion against the authority of his mother, the King, and Helen: "he fleshes his will in the spoil of her honor; he hath given her his monumental ring, and thinks himself made in the unchaste composition" (IV.iii.16–18). His cheerful dispatch of "sixteen businesses" (IV.iii.86) in conjunction with the encounter manifests the energizing effects of his sexual initiation and adolescent rebellion. These accomplished, perfunctory reform follows; he is able to claim to have loved his dead wife and mourn for her, to ask forgiveness of his elders and reconcile himself with them, even tô agree to marry a woman of their choosing.

But if the impersonal nature of the encounter satisfies Bertram, its deceitful anonymity disillusions Helen in her extraordinary reflection on the event:

> But, O strange men,
> That can such sweet use make of what they hate,
> When saucy trusting of the cozened thoughts
> Defiles the pitchy night! So lust doth play
> With what it loathes for that which is away.
>   [IV.iv.21–25]

The fact that Helen seems alone among the perpetrators of bedtricks in expressing her humiliation and defilement emphasizes the cost of her stratagem, not its success. But she also acknowledges the sweetness of her pleasure and the growth that will ensue: "the time will bring on summer, / When briars shall have leaves as well as thorns, / And be as sweet as sharp" (IV.iv.31–33). This affirmation by Helen of the ordinary fruition that will accompany her painful initiation qualifies the cynicism of Diana's anticipation of deflowering: "Ay, so you serve us / Till we serve you; but when you have our roses, /

You barely leave our thorns to prick ourselves / And mock us with our bareness"(IV.ii.17–20) and corroborates the Countess's realistic and parodoxical memory of youthful desire: "Even so it was with me when I was young; / If ever we are nature's, these are ours; this thorn / Doth to our rose of youth rightly belong" (I.iii.129–31). All three women use the image of the thorn in the flower to express the mingled pain and pleasure of sexual experience. Only Helen imagines not just the antitithetical rose and thorn but the development of sustaining leaves as the consequence of sexual experience.[25]

The bedtrick is a sexual and psychological death and rebirth for both Bertram and Helen. It is also a symbolic prostitution and the central bargain of *All's Well That Ends Well*. Like the many other agreements in the play, it is both fraudulent and fair, both corrupt and restorative. Helen uses her erotic potency to cure the King, and he in return agrees to satisfy her desires (and sublimate his) by granting her a husband: "If thou proceed / As high as word, my deed shall match thy deed" (II.i.212–13). Bertram eventually complies with the match in order to retain the King's favor: "As thou lov'st her, / Thy love's to me religious; else does err" (II.iii.183–84). Bertram in turn enters into an agreement with Helen: "When thou canst get the ring upon my finger, which never shall come off, and show me a child begotten of thy body that I am father to, then call me husband" (III.ii.58–60). To meet Bertram's conditions, Helen strikes a bargain with the Widow: "Take this purse of gold, / And let me buy your friendly help thus far, / Which I will over-pay and pay again / When I have found it" (III.vii. 14–17), providing Diana with a dowry in return for her help in the consummation of Helen's marriage. In the bedtrick, there are three layers of agreement which, like the other bargains, involve deceit. Bertram falsely promises marriage to Diana in return for her loss of honor; Diana falsely promises the loss of her honor in return for marriage and Bertram's ring. Helen deceives Bertram in order to fulfill his conditions and transform sin into law, creating the paradoxes of the bedtrick which "Is wicked meaning in a lawful deed, / And lawful meaning in a lawful act, / Where both not sin, and yet a sinful fact"

(III.vii.45–47). The deceitfulness of Bertram's deal is mocked by Parolles's warning to Diana: "He ne'er pays after-debts, take it before" (IV.iii.231).

The two rings participate in all these contracts. They become associated with chastity and sexuality, with betrothal and consummation, and with the commercial flavor of the transactions. They embody the sexual, social, and emotional aspects of marriage and symbolize their fragmentation and degradation. The King gives one ring to Helen as reward for her cure. Helen gives it to Diana to give to Bertram in return for his ring; he, in turn, tries to send it to Maudlin as an "amorous token" in preparation for the "main consents" (V.iii.68–69) of their betrothal, which he agrees to in return for his reconciliation with his elders. The recognition of the ring by the King and Lafew precipitates the entrance of first Diana and then Helen, Bertram's two wives. The ring and the series of contracts lead to the reestablishment of Helen's and Bertram's marriage at the play's end; this marriage itself is viewed as a conditional bargain, an agreement in which each party pays something and receives something, and one that has consequences that spread beyond the couple to others who both contribute to the nuptial and benefit from it. The final benefit (and final bargain) of the play is potentially Diana's, as the King offers to repay her contribution to the fulfillment of his bargain with Helen by entering into an identical one with her and providing her with a husband.

The clown, Lavatch, parodies cynically the view of marriage as a corrupt but serviceable agreement, wittily dissecting the conflicts about marriage which the play enacts. In an early conversation with the Countess (which precedes Helen's revelation of her marital project), he declares his intention to marry, joking about his conventional reasons for doing so—to curb lust and produce progeny: "My poor body, madam, requires it. I am driven on by the flesh, and he must needs go that the devil drives." "Service is no heritage, and I think I shall never have the blessing of God till I have issue of my body; for they say barnes are blessings" (I.iii.28–30, 23–26). His satire reveals that these traditional religious justifications for marriage rest on assumptions about the sinfulness of sexuality and the untrustworthiness of all but "one good woman in ten" (I.iii.83) that undermine the very institution they seek to defend. Lavatch's bawdy pun, holy reasons/hole-y raisings, (I.iii.32) wittily reconciles the church's belief in the corruption of the flesh with its upholding of marriage as a sacramental and spiritual union rooted in a fleshly one. He perhaps hints, too, that progressive Puritan attitudes toward marriage are not really that different from conservative Catholic ones: "for young Charbon the puritan and old Poysam the papist, howsome'er their hearts are severed in religion, their heads are both one; they may jowl together like any deer i' th' herd" (I.iii.52–56). Lavatch also reconciles cuckoldry and marriage, making female frailty beneficial. He proves that cuckoldry can save husbands from the sexual, economic, and spiritual deprivations of marriage: "He that ears my land spares my team, and gives me leave to in the crop: if I be his cuckold, he's my drudge. He that comforts my wife is the cherisher of my flesh and blood; he that cherishes my flesh and blood loves my flesh and blood; he that loves my flesh and blood is my friend" (I.iii.45–51). The companionate marriage newly advocated in the period is here ironically achieved by cuckold and cuckolder, who join together in a mutually satisfying enterprise that comically exaggerates the male solidarity generated by the cuckoldry jokes in *Much Ado*. In the clown's pseudologic, cuckoldry and marriage become interdependent; both institutions serve patriarchal society in identical fashion by subordinating women in the service of men's sexual, social, and economic needs.

The characters, however, have difficulty living out these sophistical and paradoxical formulations. Lavatch, who would embrace marriage and cuckoldry together, loses his "stomach" (III.ii.16) for both during his visit to the corrupt court and withdraws into abstinence when he returns home. Bertram, who leaves Helen and pursues an adulterous relationship, in effect cuckolds himself and fulfills the clown's demonstration when he unknowingly sleeps with his wife. But because he consummates his marriage and begets a child, the apparently illicit union can be interpreted as a legitimate one. This highly irregular fulfillment of the conventional functions of marriage dramatizes the strains on the institution that the clown's wit has identified.

The completion of Bertram's marriage to Helen is made possible not only by the bedtrick but by his reform and his reconciliation with his mother and the King. It is rendered acceptable in part by the inadequacy of the alternatives to it— loveless marriage with Lafew's daughter, Maudlin, or socially unacceptable marriage with Diana. The basis of these potential marriages and the circumstances of their disruption reflect continuing conflicts involving marriage and manifest Bertram's still polarized attitudes toward women. The completion of his nuptials with Helen has the potential to reconcile these divisions—in Bertram and in the play.

Before this happens the older generation must reestablish their authority over the younger, attentuated through the flights of Bertram and Helen. Because they need the new generation to make up their losses, they agree to "bury" the past (I.i.1; V.iii.24). The King, the Countess, and Lafew agree not only to "forgive" but to "forget" Bertram's "natural rebellion": "Let him not ask our pardon; / The nature of his great offense is dead, / And deeper than oblivion we do bury / Th' incensing relics of it" (V.iii.9, 6, 22–25). In return Bertram apologizes and asks pardon. He, too, tries to bury the past, reshaping his to accord with his elder's wishes, and to effect the penitent re-idealization characteristic of other Shakespearean husbands with safely dead wives. He declares himself to have loved Maudlin and to have come to love Helen in a speech so vague, compressed, and contorted that it reflects perfectly his abstract and unspontaneous affection.

> At first
> I stuck my choice upon her, ere my heart
> Durst make too bold a herald of my tongue;
> Where, the impression of mine eye infixing,
> Contempt his scornful perspective did lend me,

Which warped the line of every other favor,
Scorned a fair color or expressed it stol'n,
Extended or contracted all proportions
To a most hideous object. Thence it came
That she whom all men praised and whom myself,
Since I have lost, have loved, was in mine eye
The dust that did offend it.   [V.iii.44–55]

This affection is a crabbed parody of the involuntariness and objectlessness of romantic love by virtue of the ugliness of "stuck my choice," the different antecedents for the two pronouns "her" and "she," neither specified, the lack of antecedent for the pronoun "where" and the spurious logic of the adverb "Thence," which points to a connection that has not been explicitly made.[26] Bertram, it appears, fakes love for both Maudlin and Helen so he can confirm his reform, accommodate himself to the marriage the elders desire, and regain the social status he lost by giving up the ring. This is one of the few marriages in Shakespeare that is contracted by parents before the couple even talk to each other, although this was common enough in the period.[27] Claudio's proposed marriage in *Much Ado* to a masked bride—the supposed cousin of the dead Hero—is a similarly arranged and acquiesced-in marriage, as is Octavia's in *Antony and Cleopatra*. The fact that Maudlin never appears onstage at all emphasizes her role as an object of exchange. It is furthermore ironically appropriate that Bertram pledges to marry a woman named Maudlin, the vernacular form of Magdalene and, in the early seventeenth century, a noun meaning a penitent (*OED* 2). Mary Magdalene's traditional roles as reformed harlot and weeping penitent figure forth Bertram's own penitence and reform; they coincide with those of the promiscuous Diana and the saintly Helen that Bertram imagines and foreshadow the surprises still to come in the play.

The socially conventional, parentally arranged nuptial is, however, disrupted by its antithesis—Diana's claims on Bertram as a result of their (supposed) sexual coupling. She asserts (falsely) that Bertram has completed all of the nuptial requirements with her and demands that their union be confirmed by the King:

> If you shall marry,
> You give away this hand, and that is mine;
> You give away heaven's vows, and those are mine;
> You give away myself, which is known mine;
> For I by vow am so embodied yours
> That she which marries you must marry me,
> Either both or none.   [V.iii.169–75]

Bertram denies Diana's claims by vicious denigration of her as a "common gamester" (188) and by his cowardly characterization of their union as prostitution, a commercial transaction instituted by her:

> Her infinite cunning with her modern grace
> Subdued me to her rate. She got the ring,
> And I had that which any inferior might
> At market-price have bought.
>   [V.iii.216–19]

This denigration reveals Bertram's lust for the whore beneath the goddess he praised, manifesting yet again his polarized view of women.

The King and Lafew echo Bertram's attitude as they join him in his attack on Diana: "This woman's an easy glove, my lord; she goes off and on at pleasure"; "I think thee now some common customer" (V.iii.277, 286). Her maddening equivocations delineate the fragmented roles that rigid social expectations and uncontrolled male sexual fantasies impose on women: "Great King, I am no strumpet; by my life / I am either maid or else this old man's wife" (292–93). Diana, through her identification with Helen, both is and is not a maid and a wife and hence must accept the title of whore. A woman, the extended scene suggests, is not acceptable as a wife if she is a whore who serves men's lust, but cannot be accepted as a wife without risking whoredom. This last rupture of nuptials, however, has the power to generate completed ones.

Both Bertram and Helen are now ready to transform their views of each other and marriage. Bertram's nasty clarification of the nature of his encounter with Diana seems cathartic and may prepare him for a fuller and more permanent sexual relationship. His false avowal of love for the dead Helen suggests that he may be able to learn to love a live Helen. His humiliation in the final scene reciprocates hers in the bedtrick. But Helen, at her entrance, testifies to her irreconcilable roles, her fragmented identity: "'Tis but the shadow of a wife you see, / The name and not the thing" (V.iii.307–08). She has the name of wife conferred by the marriage ceremony and the shadowy sexual death in the pitchy dark, but these remain separate. They are potentially mediated, however, by the child that kicks within her, and Bertram, finishing her line, affirms the reconciliation of her hitherto mutually exclusive roles of wife and sexual partner: "Both, both. O, pardon!" (308), acknowledging her as fully his wife before the fulfillment of the tasks is proved.[28] Helen, in turn, alters her view of their sexual encounter, tenderly describing Bertram as "wondrous kind" (310).

Throughout *All's Well That Ends Well* various "endings" have proved illusory as subsequent events have altered their apparent conclusiveness: the marriage of Helen and Bertram is disrupted; the bedtrick "business" is not "ended" as Bertram hopes (IV.iii.97); the King is not at Marseilles when the women arrive (V.i.21); Parolles is cast off but regains a position; Lavatch plans to marry but changes his mind. Helen, though dead, is "quick." The conclusion of the play is constructed as a final example of inconclusiveness in order to show marriage not as a happy ending but as an open-ended beginning. The relationships the scene focuses on, the developments it traces, the conflicts it reveals are deliberately left unresolved, unfinished—but with the potential for resolution. This open-endedness appears, for example, in Bertram's and Helen's vows, which are in the conditional and which include the possibility of "Deadly divorce" as well as perpetual love:

> *Bertram.*   If she, my liege, can make me know this
>   clearly,
>   I'll love her dearly, ever, ever dearly.
> *Helen.*   If it appear not plain and prove untrue,
>   Deadly divorce step between me and you!
>
>   [V.iii.315–18]

The King's offer of a husband to Diana is likewise couched as a conditional bargain, and one that (as revealed in the laughs or groans that it generates in productions) has the potential, in effect, to begin the play over: "If thou be'st yet a fresh uncropped flower, / Choose thou thy husband, and I'll pay thy dower" (V.iii.327–28).

The end of the play involves other beginnings, too. The realistic reference to Helen's pregnancy—"Dead though she be, she feels her young one kick" (V.iii.302)—points to another tentative beginning—one deliberately made more tentative by Shakespeare. In the source story (as in most of the analogues)[29] Beltramo demands that Giletta produce "a son in her arms begotten by me" (Bullough, p. 392). Giletta outdoes herself, producing twin sons who look exactly like their father (the fulfillment of a male fantasy prominent elsewhere in Shakespeare). In *All's Well*, however, Bertram does not specify the sex of the child, and although he does order Helen to "show me a child begotten of thy body that I am father to" (III.ii.59–60), the child remains *in utero*. This discrepancy is concealed (by Helen, Shakespeare, or both) when, claiming fulfillment of the tasks, Helen misquotes Bertram's letter, altering its original command: " 'When from my finger you can get this ring, / And are by me with child,' &c." (V.iii.312–313). The alterations of the source and of the original command emphasize potential fulfillment of the bargain—and the relationship—rather than the actualization of either.[30] Helen's visible pregnancy recalls earlier references to childbirth and childrearing which suggest that they, like marriage, are paradoxically uncertain ventures compounded of delivery's "dearest groans" (IV.v.11) and parenthood's "many quirks of joy and grief" (III.ii.49).

The deliberate irresolution of the ending of the play is underlined also by the variations on the title proverb—All's Well That Ends Well; each successive repetition increases in tentativeness both about the conclusiveness of the "end" and about its "wellness." The "end" gets pushed further and further into the future, and eventually this future follows the conclusion of the play. The play's title is first alluded to in Helen's confident assertion as she journeys with the Widow and Diana to meet the King at Marseilles in order to "perfect mine intents" (IV.iv.4):

> We must away
> Our wagon is prepared, and time revives us.
> All's well that ends well; still the fine's the crown.
> Whate'er the course, the end is the renown.
>
> [IV.iv.33–36]

Helen's second allusion to the title occurs only two scenes later when she has missed the King; it is considerably more qualified, emphasizing time's role in controlling endings: "All's well that ends well yet, / Though time seems so adverse and means unfit" (V.i.25–26). Helen herself makes no such affirmation in the last scene of the play. When the King, in ignorance of the facts, restates the adage in his concluding couplet, he is cautious about the goodness of the end and conditional regarding its attainment: "All yet seems well, and if it end so meet, / The bitter past, more welcome is the sweet" (V.iii.332–33). When the King, to conclude the play, discards his role and becomes an actor and a beggar in the epilogue, he hands over the responsibility for the successful ending of the difficult play to the audience. In his recapitulation of the play's themes, he offers to them a mutually satisfying bargain, grounded in the reversal of roles between actors and audience; the bargain mingles gain and loss, payment and receipt and pushes the "ending" still further into the future:

> The King's a beggar now the play is done.
> All is well ended if this suit be won,
> That you express content; which we will pay

With strife to please you, day exceeding day.
Ours be your patience then, and yours our parts,
Your gentle hands lend us, and take our hearts.

The spareness of *All's Well*'s ending both contributes to
our sense of its inconclusiveness and further differentiates it
from the endings of the festive comedies. They build toward
the climactic completion of nuptials, toward ritual celebration
and anticipated consummation of marriage with, for example,
Petruchio's "Come Kate, we'll to bed" (*Shr*, V.ii.186), or Duke
Senior's "We will begin these rites, / As we do trust they'll
end, in true delights" (*AYL*, V.iv.197–98). But in *All's Well*
both parts of the marriage rites have already taken place so a
conventional comic conclusion is impossible. *All's Well* likewise has none of the other adornments that embody joy and
harmony and generate release in the festive comedies: no
song, no dance, no shows, no removal of disguise (although
Helen's return provides a spectacular substitute), no Hymen,
no blessings divine or human.

Furthermore, *All's Well* does not have a number of couples
to join in a double, triple, or quadruple wedding celebration,
muting the conflicts of marriage by fragmenting or displacing
them. In *As You Like It*, for example, Touchstone and Audrey
marry reluctantly because their "poor bodies require it," Silvius and Phebe resignedly discard static romantic love and
scornful disdain for social accommodation, and Celia and Oliver precipitously climb the stairs from desire to love to marriage, representing in this way different components of marriage and freeing Rosalind and Orlando to achieve the
appearance at least of a broader and more balanced union. In
Much Ado, as we have seen, Beatrice and Benedick absorb and
transform the anxieties about marriage that are worked
through symbolically in the broken nuptials of the Hero-Clau-
dio plot and then suppressed. Uniquely, in *All's Well*, all of the
anxieties and conflicts of marriage are focused in a single couple. The clown reneges on his original plan to marry, and the
marriage of Diana remains only potential.

The continuing authority of the older generation marks

another substantial departure from the youth-generated conclusion of festive comedy.[31] The King, who presides over
the finale, is asked to ratify the union and speaks the epilogue.
The reconciliation between Helen and Bertram facilitates their
equally significant reconciliations with the older generation.
Bertram addresses his conditional vows to the King, not to
Helen: "If she, my liege, can make me know this clearly . . . ,"
and although Helen speaks her vows to Bertram, they lead to
her acknowledgment of the Countess as her mother: "O, my
dear mother, do I see you living" (V.iii.319). These two reconciliations between older and younger generations are parodied
by Lafew's with Parolles; the braggart soldier will now employ
words as Lafew's licensed fool, serving him and dependent on
his good graces: "Wait on me home, I'll make sport with thee.
Let thy curtsies alone, they are scurvy ones"(V.iii.322). The
younger generation achieves its desires by remaining under
the authority of and satisfying the needs of the older generation. It does not replace the older or circumvent its edicts as in
the festive comedies. There, social concerns were moderated to
satisfy individual desire; here desire is channeled to serve the
social needs of both generations.

The ending, like the rest of the play, bears out the first
lord's summary: "The web of our life is of a mingled yarn,
good and ill together" (IV.iii.71). The web represents the inex-
tricable blend within individuals of "virtues" and "faults" and
underlies the play's other paradoxes. Throughout *All's Well*
gains and losses are mingled: "How mightily sometimes we
make us comforts of our losses! And how mightily some other
times we drown our gain in tears" (IV.iii.65–68). Marriage, the
play suggests, participates in all the paradoxes of human life; it
is achieved through a balance of gains and losses, calls for virtues but calls up vices, and sometimes unites and sometimes
estranges the genders and generations who rely on it for personal satisfaction and social continuity. Underlying the paradoxes of life and marriage in the play is the transforming, un-
ending process of time, its giving and taking. Time is shown
bringing growth or death, summer or winter, grace or shame.
The ends toward which it moves may be bad—"And as in the

common course of all treasons we still see them reveal themselves till they attain to their abhorred ends, so he that in this action contrives against his own nobility, in his proper stream o'erflows himself" (IV.iii.21–25)—or good—"Whate'er the course, the end is the renown" (IV.iv.36). "Endings" are always unpredictable and never final. The play's inconclusive finish and the increasingly qualified reiterations of its title emphasize the time-bound and receding quality of its conclusion, which will occur only "still," "yet," "if."

All's Well That Ends Well is not, I think, an unsuccessful or incomplete festive comedy. Its deliberately stripped-down, realistic, and tentative ending dramatizes the beginning of a marriage with the potential to provide sexual satisfaction, procreation, and family continuity—and perhaps even love. Its future cannot be known. But marriage, we can know from the play, is a perilous venture—especially marriage between a brave, insecure, sexually inexperienced soldier and a bold, adoring, sexually forward daughter. Shakespeare's next play was probably *Othello*. Its irregular nuptials and delayed consummation promise greater joy and precipitate greater pain than any we can imagine being generated by the more mundane union in *All's Well*. Following *Othello* with *Measure for Measure*, Shakespeare, for the third time in a row using as his source an Italian *novella* whose plot centers on broken nuptials, reshapes his materials to exacerbate conflicts surrounding marriage almost beyond the possibility of comic reconciliation.

In *Measure for Measure*, as in *All's Well*, an irregular nuptial is at the heart of the play; a comparison of the two bedtricks clarifies important similarities between the plays and crucial differences. Whereas *All's Well*'s bedtrick is a corrupt bargain that feels like prostitution, *Measure for Measure*'s is a coercive assault that feels like rape. An examination of the contrasted enactments of these stratagems and of the different denouements to which they lead reveals the opposing attitudes toward women, sexuality, marriage, and procreation dramatized in the two plays and helps to explain why *All's Well* ends at least more "well" than *Measure for Measure* does. It suggests that although *All's Well*'s happy ending is qualified and deferred, the play's deepest affinities are with the triumphs of female resourcefulness, the united families, and the happy marriages of the romantic comedies, whereas *Measure for Measure*'s deepest connections are with the deficiencies of male authority, the anxieties about female sexuality, the broken families and destroyed marriages of the tragedies.

In both plays the bedtricks are necessary (and possible) because of the polarized attitudes toward women manifested when Bertram and Angelo reject Helen and Mariana, passionate women who wish to be their wives, and seek satisfaction with Diana and Isabella, cold virgins who are desirable because they resist or repel advances and can be seduced or despoiled and then abandoned. The men leave the women "neither maid, widow, nor wife" (*MM*, V.i.177) outside the cycle of female sexual and social roles in order to evade the roles of husband and father and the responsibilities of partriarchy. But whereas Bertram is repelled by his wife and attracted to Diana, Angelo's attitude toward sexuality is even more ambivalent and degraded; he reneges on his "precontract" to Mariana, pretending in her "discoveries of dishonor" (III.i.227) and withdraws into rigid celibacy until, his lust awakened by Isabella's purity, he craves to violate it, demanding that she "Fit thy consent to my sharp appetite" (*MM*, II.iv.160).

In each play a pair of women attempts to reconcile the men's divisions by changing places. Each pair substitutes the contracted wife for the body which is the object of sexual desire; thus the men sleep with an "imagined person" (*MM*, V.i.213)—part body, part fantasy. Each play at one level embodies male fantasies by including sharply contrasted women, the one a confirmed virgin, the other the embracer of a degraded and deceitful sexual encounter. In *Measure for Measure*, as in *All's Well*, by means of the women's names, their role reversals, the substitution, and their identifications with each other, the fragmented views of the men are countered and the reconciliation of loving wife and sexual partner in both women is affirmed. In *Measure for Measure*, however, the contrast between the two women is more extreme, their identification more painfully achieved. Isabella, a nun, at first protects her virginity ferociously, even at the expense of her brother's life; Mariana, belying the spiritual implications of her name although sharing Mary's function of intercession, leaves the protection of romantic sublimation in the moated grange to yield up her body to Angelo. Although at the end of the play Isabella joins Mariana in her humiliation and in her loving request for mercy for her husband, and although she perhaps follows her substitute into marriage, she, unlike Diana, has shown no indication of desiring marriage or sexual intimacy.

In both plays the bedtricks are employed to cure or transform male fantasy through its apparent enactment, but their different causes and arrangements contribute to their different thematic implications. In *All's Well*, as we have seen, the bedtrick is arranged and carried out by a mutually sympathetic community of women for the primary purpose of rejuvenating Helen's marriage; the protection of Diana's chastity is a fringe benefit (it, after all, could have been protected, in fact was being protected, without resort to bedtricks).[32] In *Measure for Measure*, in contrast, the bedtrick is arranged not by the woman herself but by the Duke, who urges its execution on Isabella and Mariana so that he can extricate himself from the predicament that his authority has created, can achieve the "satisfaction" he "requires" (*MM*, III.i.155) by protecting Isabella's chastity, Claudio's life, and Angelo's stewardship; the consummation of Mariana's marriage is merely a desirable side-effect: "the doubleness of the benefit defends the deceit from reproof" (III.i.257). The mutual bargaining that initiates the bedtrick in *All's Well* parallels the corrupted but mutually satisfying bargain, the symbolic prostitution of the trick itself; the Duke's coercive, authoritarian manipulation in *Measure for Measure* is analogous to the symbolic rape of the trick itself: "The maid will I frame and make fit for his attempt" (III.i.255).

The bedtrick in *Measure for Measure* is enacted, then, not as a bargain but as an assault, not as a witty "death" but as a debilitation; its shameful losses are not balanced by corresponding gains. Angelo is not merely a "wanton . . . youth" (*AWW*, V.iii.211), but a "virgin-violator" (*MM*, V.i.41) with no pretense of romance and no illusions about Isabella's possible accessibility. The description of Isabella's arduous, twice-repeated entry through the two doors into the protected garden, "circummured with brick," (*MM*, IV.i.28), a journey to be taken in earnest by Mariana, is an emblem of Angelo's need to assault and reassault Isabella's precious, closely guarded virginity, "to raze the sanctuary, / And pitch our evils there" (*MM*, II.ii.171–72). This need is likewise apparent in his vicious verbal attack on her uncomprehending virtue, as he goads her until her "sense" pursues his (II.iv.73). Angelo experiences the satisfaction of his aggressive lust solely as a degradation of Isabella and himself; instead of being "made in the unchaste composition," as Bertram was, he is left "unpregnant" (IV.iv.20).

The bedtrick does not achieve other satisfactions either. That it does not leave Mariana pregnant indicates the anomalous use here of the substitute bride motif; the bedtrick is not present in the sources and does not fulfill the usual function of the convention, which is to generate a pregnancy that proves the sexual encounter. It does not save Claudio's life (a second substitution is required to accomplish that). It does not preserve Angelo's reputation, but ruins it. Its main purpose—to protect Isabella's chastity—is accomplished, but she is then left vulnerable (in a different way than Diana) to another more subtle coercion, dependent on the first—the Duke's marriage proposal. He seems implicitly to demand marriage as *his* price for having saved Claudio's head:

> If he be like your brother, for his sake
> Is he pardoned, and for your lovely sake
> Give me your hand, and say you will be mine,
> He is my brother too.
> [V.i.493–96 Signet lines, Folio punctuation][33]

At the denouement both women testitfy explicitly to their shameful enforced compliance in a fictional or actual sexual encounter—in rape. Isabella describes giving the "gift of my chaste body / To his concupiscible, intemperate lust" (V.i.97–98), and Mariana chillingly attests to Angelo that her body "did supply thee at thy garden-house" (V.i.212).

Mariana, however, willingly acquiesces in this intended rape, transforming its character as Helen transformed the character of Bertram's intended seduction. It is Mariana's voluntary loss of maidenhead (without precedent in the sources) and Ragozine's involuntary donation of his head (with precedent) that defuse the tragedy and rescue Claudio from death, Juliet from widowhood, Isabella from sex, Angelo from lust, Mariana herself from unrequited love, and the Duke from the collapse of his fantasies of omnipotence. As Ragozine's double, Juliet's counterpart, Isabella's surrogate, Claudio's ransom, Angelo's "match" (V.i.211), and the key to the Duke's frame-up, Mariana is at the heart of the play structurally, morally, and psychologically. She experiences growth herself; for others she is the instrument that promises rejuvenation and generates the comic resolution. But an examination of her role brings into focus the lack of dramatization of those rejuvenations and the thwarting of the potential for resolution.

Mariana is the one character in the play who experiences relatively unproblematic comic growth and transformation.[34] If the Duke's tale of her is true, she has, even before the play begins, loosened her bonds to her brother and loved Angelo. She has responded to his accusations by retreating, like Hero, Helen, and, later, Hermione. But, seeking the isolated static protection of the moated grange, she maintains her "violent and unruly" passion intact (III.i.243). She does not transform this affection into the desire for death or revenge—the solutions Isabella characteristically envisages for her ("What a merit were it in death to take this poor maid from the world! What corruption in this life, that it will let this man live!" III.i.231–33). Instead she soothes her "brawling discontent" (IV.i.9) with the friar's ministrations and "please[s] her woe" (13) by sublimating the pain of Angelo's defection and the intensity of her desire into the song, "Take, O, take those lips away, / That so sweetly were forsworn" (2). When the Duke offers another remedy, she, like Helen in *All's Well*, unhesitatingly abandons romantic reverie for sexual initiation and, in the last act, faces squarely the consequences of that initiation. When she unveils herself to Angelo (as Hero and Helen and

Hermione are likewise dramatically revealed to their detractor husbands), her forthright accusations uncover what the conventional rhetoric of the song sweetened—the deceit, brutality, and dehumanization that characterize both Angelo's original transgression and their consummation:

> This is that face, thou cruel Angelo,
> Which once thou swor'st was worth the looking on;
> This is the hand which, with a vowed contract,
> Was fast belocked in thine; this is the body
> That took away the match from Isabel,
> And did supply thee at thy garden house
> In her imagined person.   [V.i.207–13]

Mariana testifies with still more painful frankness than Helen does to the dark delusion and mechanical workings of lust and the consequent fragmentation of identity. Her body, to Angelo's "cozened thoughts" (*AWW*, IV.iv.23) that of an "imagined person," supplied his lust and "took away the match from Isabel," winning the contest, keeping the appointment, fulfilling the corrupt bargain, and legitimizing the marriage.

Mariana's bold reconciliation of love, desire, and marriage makes possible the denouement of the plot. Her example might induce the other characters to achieve intimacy, accept desire, and move toward regeneration, as she has. She provides for the Duke the neat dovetailing of his own "satisfaction" and another's "benefit," an arrangement that he and the play "require" (III.i.154–55) and that reconciles his egoism and altruism. Achieving the intimacy with others that the Duke has resisted throughout, she may be the catalyst for his tentative movement out of isolation at the play's end. His paternal proposal to Isabella may be possible in part because he has already been able to establish a father-daughter relationship with Mariana; this "gentle daughter" is "bound to" the Duke (IV.i.71,25) out of affection, and he treats her more gently than he does the other characters. These others, too, are perhaps influenced by Mariana. When she saves Isabella from sexual assault and in return gains her help in pleading for Angelo's life, she may be awakening the novice's frozen emotions and teaching her a new compassion and mutuality. When she saves Angelo from the consequences of his guilty desires, she perhaps rehabilitates them. She redeems by repeating in a sanctioned way Claudio's and Juliet's sexual fall, "flourish[ing] the deceit" (IV.i.75). Her passionate, loving, faithful desires have the potential to rescue sexuality from the degradation, perversion, and repression it undergoes elsewhere in the play.

But because such transformations are not dramatized and because she remains on the periphery of the play, Mariana's participation in the bedtrick, instead of resolving problems, creates new ones. The Duke continues to remove himself from the action through his disguise and his deceits and continues to manipulate characters whom, we discover, he does not know and whose resistance to reform he underestimates. Isabella is protected by the bedtrick, but she is exposed to the Duke's manipulative proposal; her lack of response to it does not allow us to know whether she will continue her strict withdrawal from sexuality or follow Mariana into marriage. Claudio's and Juliet's affection for each other is never dramatized, and their restored marriage is not celebrated or ever acknowledged. Angelo is not transformed even in the small ways that Bertram seemed to be.[35] He reneges on his agreement more cruelly than Bertram did and hence is guilty of the "imagined" death of Claudio, his counterpart, as well as the "imagined" rape of Isabella. In the last scene, he does not merely degrade the encounter he is accused of but denies it altogether; he does not ask pardon of Mariana but only of the Duke; he desires death, not marriage: "I crave death more willingly than mercy" (V.i.478). Hence Mariana's willingness to sacrifice her virginity to him is as distasteful to us as was Isabella's refusal to sacrifice hers for Claudio's life. Isabella's self-protective chastity, Mariana's passionate sexuality, and Juliet's pregnancy cannot provide for the play or the men in it an integrated woman. Both Mariana's submission to the men's authority and Angelo's continuing repudiation of her reflect the negative attitudes toward sexuality and the polarized relations between men and women that pervade the play.

Underlying and animating the many equation/substitutions in *Measure for Measure*—of maidenhead for head, Mariana for Isabella, Ragozine for Barnardine, Angelo for Vincentio, hangman for bawd—is the equation of sexuality with death.[36] The first half of the play moves toward the substitution of death for sexuality; fornication is punished by execution, bawds become hangmen, and the Duke urges the sensual Claudio to "Be absolute for death" (III.i.5) in a speech that makes its point by draining life of all sexual reference, physical vitality, and temporal continuity, thereby denying mortal identity. But although Claudio momentarily acquiesces in the substitution, he soon makes a desperate plea for life, turning the Duke's speech upside down (and the play around) by imbuing the death he fears with violent vital sensuality.[37] Immediately following this scene, the Duke's proposal is laid out, and from then on in the play sexuality is substituted for death, marriages for executions. But these reversals do not bring joy out of pain, gains out of losses, because the equation of death with sexuality runs too deep. It is not, as in *All's Well*, merely a witty pun implying that *la petite morte* is a symbolic death and rebirth. Instead, the pervasive analogy in *Measure for Measure* implies that sexuality, like death, is corrupting—fatal.

The analogy means that men and women are in different relation to the play's substitutions. In *Measure for Measure* the men are threatened with death and the women with sex.[38] The women make the substitution of sexuality for death possible by allowing men to "take life" from female "shame"—to be "made a man" out of women's "vice" (III.i.137–39) in a number of senses, all rooted in the sexual pun. Women conceive and bear men in a "plenteous womb" (I.iv.43); they initiate men into sexual experience, "putting on the destined livery" (II.iv.137) as Mariana and Juliet do; they have the potential to confer social respectability on men by marrying them and bearing their children, as Juliet and Kate Keepdown do; they metaphorically regenerate them by forgiving them their faults, as Mariana and Isabella do. But the regenerative process is incomplete; the substitution of sex for death does not quite work, because sexuality, the "downright way of creation" (III.ii.106), is desirable and contaminated, a "saucy sweetness," or "sweet

uncleanness" (II.iv.44,53). Women are paradoxically loved and
loathed for both their chastity and their sexuality. Elbow "de-
tests" his wife for her (questionable) "honesty" (II.i.67–76);
Lucio fathers a child but views marriage to its mother as an
execution; Angelo "desires" Isabella "foully for those things /
That make her good" (II.ii.175). Hence, Angelo is undone, not
regenerated, by his sexual initiation—"This deed unshapes
me quite, makes me unpregnant / And dull to all proceedings"
(IV.iv.20–21)—and Claudio repudiates even his loving union
with Juliet—"Our natures do pursue / Like rats that ravin
down their proper bane, / A thirsty evil, and when we drink,
we die" (I.ii.131–33).

Procreation, which in the romantic comedies and in *All's
Well* legitimizes sexuality and connects it with nature's
rhythms and the creation of new life, is in *Measure for Measure*
repeatedly associated with death. Angelo, in the course of his
sexual coercion of Isabella, callously identifies illegitimate procreation with murder: "'tis all as easy / Falsely to take away a
life true made, / As to put metal in restrainèd means / To make
a false one" (II.iv.45–48). The Duke uses children as part of his
argument against life, seeing them as "thine own bowels, . . .
the mere effusion of thy proper loins" (III.i.29–30), a threat
to paternal authority and a confirmation of debility. For Lucio
and for Claudio children are a punishment for lechery, a grotesque embarrassment: "But it chances / The stealth of our most
mutual entertainment / With character too gross is writ on Juliet" (I.ii.156–58).[39] Whereas Lavatch in *All's Well* saw children, legitimate or illegitimate, as "blessings" or financial as-
sets, Lucio does not acknowledge his illegitimate child but
leaves it to be raised by Mistress Overdone. Degenerate,
"warped" children may further demean paternity—as Isabella
suggests in her rant to Claudio (III.i.141–43)—by attesting to
the father's corruption (if the child is seen as like the father) or
to his cuckolding (if the connection with the father is dis-
claimed).[40] The repeated association of procreation and children with death degrades sexuality further. Children are the
potential link between sexuality and the law which the play
needs, for they both necessitate and facilitate the law's regula-

tion of sex. But no character in the play—not Juliet, not Claudio, not Isabella, not even the Duke—voices any hint of concern for the soon-to-be-born child who is responsible for the initial crisis. And there is only the possible innuendo of the Duke's remark—"if the encounter acknowledge itself hereafter" (III.i.251)—to suggest that the bedtrick could leave Mariana, like other substitute brides, pregnant. Only a pregnancy, however, would provide a sure distinction between the "imagined" body and the actual one.

The women in the play can requite their reputed sexual frailty and contaminated procreative capacity only by taking shame upon themselves. Juliet accepts the larger share of guilt for her mutual union with Claudio; Isabella exposes herself to public defamation by confessing the gift of her body to Angelo; Mariana must suffer Angelo's "discoveries of dishonor," the private shame of the bedtrick, the public humiliation of its revelation, and the ignominy of marriage to a man who does not want her. Embracing this shame willingly, Mariana accepts that "best men are molded out of faults" (V.i.441: i.e., sexual sins, female genitalia, wombs); she does not claim to have found Angelo "wondrous kind." But men cannot bear the knowledge of their own sexual frailty; instead they insist that women put on the "destined livery" which constitutes their femaleness (II.iv.137), "condemn" women alone for the "fault" (II.i.40), and desire punishment for their participation in women's faults. Since they continue to prefer death to sex, the Duke's substitution fails to satisfy the characters or the audience. Pompey would as soon be hangman as bawd. Claudio, though unmuffled and—in effect—reborn, seems to extend his acquiescence in death by virtue of his unbroken silence at the conclusion. Angelo explicitly "craves" death. The Duke's earlier apology for death is far more compelling than his last act commands to love, marry, and reform. At the last, Lucio wittily collapses altogether the distinction between death and sexuality: "Marrying a punk, my lord, is pressing to death, whipping, and hanging" (V.i.524–25).

Although the Duke urges restoration, joy, mercy, and marriage on all the characters, there are only faint hints of the possible coalescence of love, sexual fulfillment, fertility, and social regeneration which is celebrated in the romantic comedies and is viewed as potential in *All's Well That Ends Well*. The "quick'ning" in Angelo's eye may imply that Mariana, by delivering him from guilt and punishment, has conferred on him new life, her "worth, worth [his]." The Duke's slightly suggestive "motion" to Isabella may find in her a "willing ear" (V.i.497, 499, 537, 538). Neither movement, neither establishment of intimacy, is verbally dramatized (although productions are free to do so visually). Mariana's passionate willingness has generated no response in Angelo, no acknowledged transformation of his attitudes toward women. Her resolute growth, instead of engendering his, emphasizes the lack of dramatized development in the characters who play more prominent roles. Her vigorous, straightforward responses to the events of the last scene make the evasions and silences of the others more apparent. Her passionate, unambiguous choice of sexuality over death reveals their ambivalent blurring of distinctions between the two.

At the conclusion of *All's Well That Ends Well* marriage was presented as an open-ended bargain, a socially legitimized version of the prostitution of the bedtrick with the possibility for reform and future gains. In the last scene of *Measure for Measure*, however, marriage is a social punishment for sexual sins. So the broken nuptials in *All's Well* and *Measure for Measure*, though they lead to completed marriages, engender contrasted denouements. *All's Well* takes a more realistic look at love, desire, and social necessity than did the romantic comedies but affirms their possible reconciliation in marriage. The enforced marriages at the end of *Measure for Measure*, however, embody not merely a realistic but a painfully negative attitude toward marriage. Its marriages do not recall those of the festive comedies but have affinities with unions broken by social obstacles, sexual anxieties, and, ultimately, by death in the tragedies: Hamlet's declaration of love for Ophelia in her grave; Othello's death "upon a kiss" (V.ii.357); Edmund "marr[ied] in an instant" (V.iii.231) in death with Goneril and Regan. The rupture of marriages and of men's intimacy with women begins in

Julius Caesar with Caesar's refusal to heed Calpurnia's dream and Brutus's failure to confide in Portia; in *Hamlet*, relations are shattered between Hamlet and Ophelia early in the play. Whereas at the end of the comedies, women submit willingly to marriages that solidify a relatively benign patriarchy, at the beginning of *Hamlet* women are already involuntarily subordinate.

Ophelia's movement from submissive daughter to mad prophet reveals the combination of powerlessness and freedom that women in the tragedies achieve by virtue of their isolation from men and their position partly implicated in, partly outside of the violent conflicts of patriarchy. At first she is the object of male admonition, manipulation, and brutal control. Her father and brother lecture her on maintaining her chastity and regulate her behavior toward Hamlet; Claudius and Polonius set her up as a decoy. Reinforcing earlier lessons about her appropriate role as a chaste sex object, Hamlet calls her whore and orders her to a nunnery, projecting onto her his anxiety about his mother's sexuality. Until her madness, Ophelia scarcely exists outside of men's use of her. She is not simply driven to this madness but freed for it by her father's death, Laertes's and Hamlet's absence, Claudius's indifference. The madness incorporates and allows expression of the earlier pressures on her: the desired and forbidden loss of chastity, the virtues hypocritically enjoined, the corruption perceived. And even if not fully comprehended by the other characters, her madness influences them. It magnifies Laertes's obsession with revenge, driving him to become Claudius's tool as Ophelia was before him. It draws from Gertrude an uncoerced acknowledgment of her own guilt. The death in which Ophelia's madness culminates repurifies her for Hamlet, freeing him to love her and to achieve his own revenge.

This solitary death by drowning, outside the castle walls, mermaidlike at home in the water, completes Ophelia's separation from her roles as daughter, sweetheart, subject, and from the literal and metaphorical poison which kills the others in the play. The borderline suicide prefigures Gertrude's later death when, disobeying Claudius's command, she drinks from the poisoned cup, thus withdrawing from the wifely role she has acquiesced in throughout. The two women break their ties with the corrupt roles and values of Elsinore as Laertes and Hamlet, returning to the castle to seek revenge, move toward accommodation with these values. Killing each other, they bring to the throne—with Hamlet's explicit approval—Fortinbras, the strong man, whose passionate, simplistic embrace of violence and of his father's quarrels throughout the play suggests that, while the chain of "casual slaughters" that began with the murder of Hamlet senior may be given a veneer of military heroism, it will not be ended. And the womanless world of the end of *Hamlet*, perhaps cleansed, but more obviously debilitated, has affinities with the similarly all-male, similarly shrunken worlds that survive at the conclusions of *Othello*, *Macbeth*, *King Lear*, and *Antony and Cleopatra*.

CHAPTER THREE

Women and Men in *Othello*

What should such a fool
Do with so good a woman?

ELATIONS between love, sexuality, and marriage are under scrutiny in *Othello*, as in the comedies, problem plays, and *Hamlet*. In more extreme form than in the problem plays, we see here the idealization and degradation of sexuality, the disintegration of male authority and the loss of female power, the isolation of men and women, and the association of sexual consummation with death. The festive comedies conclude with the anticipation of fertile marriage beds. The problem comedies achieve their resolutions with the help of midpoint bedtricks. The marriage bed is at the very heart of the tragedy of *Othello*; offstage but dramatically the center of attention in the first scene and again in the first scene of the second act, it is literally and symbolically at the center of the last scene and is explicitly hidden from sight at the conclusion. Whether the marriage is consummated, when it is consummated, and what the significance of this consummation is for Othello and Desdemona have all been an important source of debate about the play. Throughout its critical history, *Othello*, like the other problem plays, has generated passionate and radically conflicting responses—responses that are invariably tied to the critics'

emotional responses to the characters and to the gender relations in the play. Othello, Iago, and Desdemona have been loved and loathed, defended and attacked, judged and exonerated by critics just as they are by characters within the play.

"Almost damned in a fair wife" is Leslie Fiedler's alternate title for his chapter on *Othello* in *The Stranger in Shakespeare*. In it he asserts of the women in the play: "Three out of four, then, [are] weak, or treacherous, or both."[1] Thus he seconds Iago's misogyny and broadens the attack on what Leavis has called "The sentimentalist's *Othello*," the traditional view of the play held by Coleridge, Bradley, Granville-Barker, Knight, Bayley, Gardner, and many others.[2] These "Othello critics," as I shall call them, accept Othello at his own high estimate. They are enamored of his "heroic music," affirm his love, and, like him, are overwhelmed by Iago's diabolism, to which they devote much of their analysis.[3] Like Othello, they do not always argue rationally or rigorously for their views and so are vulnerable to attacks on their romanticism or sentimentality. Reacting against these traditionalists, "Iago critics" (Eliot, Empson, Kirschbaum, Rossiter, and Mason, as well as Fiedler and Leavis)[4] take their cues from Iago. Like him, they are attracted to Othello, unmoved by his rhetoric, and eager to "set down the pegs that make this music."[5] They attack Othello at his most vulnerable point, his love. They support their case by quoting Iago's estimates of Othello; they emphasize Iago's realism and "honesty"[6] while priding themselves on their own. Their realism or cynicism gives them, with Iago, an apparent invulnerability. But, like "Othello critics," they share the bias and blindness of the character whose perspective they adopt. Most damagingly, both groups of critics, like both Othello and Iago, badly misunderstand and misrepresent the women in the play.

Iago critics implicitly demean Desdemona, for if Othello's character and love are called into question, then her love for him loses its justification and validity. Explicitly they have little to say about her. Othello critics idealize her along with the hero, but, like him, they have a tendency to see her as an object. The source of her sainthood seems a passivity verging on catatonia: "Desdemona is helplessly passive. She can do nothing whatever. She cannot retaliate even in speech; no, not even in silent feeling. . . . She is helpless because her nature is infinitely sweet and her love absolute. . . . Desdemona's suffering is like that of the most loving of dumb creatures tortured without cause by the being he adores."[7] Iago critics, finding the same trait, condemn Desdemona for it. "But the damage to her symbolic value is greater when we see her passively *leaving everything to Heaven.* She ought in a sense to have *embodied* Heaven, given us a human equivalent that would 'make sense' of Heaven. For this task she had the wrong sort of purity."[8] When Desdemona is credited with activity, she is condemned for that, too; she is accused of being domineering, of using witchcraft, of rebelliousness, disobedience, wantonness.[9] Although discussion of her has frequently been an afterthought to the analysis of the men, recently she has been the focus of a number of studies.[10] Both Othello and Iago critics tend to see good versus evil as the play's central theme, Othello versus Iago as the play's central conflict, and hence, the major tragedies as its most important context.

A third group of "Iago-Othello critics," including Kenneth Burke, Arthur Kirsch, Stephen Greenblatt, Stanley Cavell, Edward Snow, and Richard Wheeler, elide the divisions between the first two groups and view the play from a perspective more like my own.[11] They see Othello and Iago as closely identified with each other; they are "two parts of a single motive—related not as the halves of a sphere, but each implicit in the other."[12] They find the source of the tragedy in Iago-Othello's anxieties regarding women, sexuality, and marriage—anxieties that are universal and generated by underlying social or psychological paradigms. Like Iago-Othello, these critics find the tragedy inevitable and locate its "cause" in an impersonal, implacable agency outside of the protagonists: for Burke, this "cause" is the "disequilibrium of monogamistic love" (p. 168); for Kirsch, it is "the polarization of erotic love," with its psychological and theological roots; for Greenblatt, it is ambivalent Christian views of marital sexuality as chaste and adulterous; for Snow, it is "the male order of things," the patriarchal society that represses male sexuality and suppresses female sexuality at the behest of the superego; for Cavell, it is universal (male) fears of impotence and deflowering, and of mortality; for Wheeler, it is the conflict among male autonomy, female sexuality, and nurturing femininity. These critics do not ignore or sanctify Desdemona; nor do they condemn her explicitly. All emphasize her active, loving, passionate sensuality and extol her worth. An effect of their focus is, however, that she, more than Iago, becomes the cause of Othello's destruction; it is her relaxed, frank sexuality and the passionate response it arouses in Othello which generate the tragedy.[13] These critics show how Desdemona's virtues catalyze Othello's sexual anxieties, but they fail to emphasize enough that she has the potential to provide a cure for them.

With this third group of critics, I argue that the play's central theme is love—specifically marital love—that its central conflict is between the men and the women, and that contexts as illuminating as the tragedies are its source, Cinthio's *Gli Hecatommithi* and Shakespeare's preceding comedies.[14] Within *Othello* it is Emilia who most explicitly speaks to this theme, recognizes this central conflict, and inherits from the heroines of comedy the role of potential mediator of it. She is dramatically and symbolically the play's fulcrum. It is as an Emilia critic, then, that I should like to approach the play, hoping to perceive it with something akin to her clear-sighted passion.

Gli Hecatommithi could have provided *Othello* with its theme and organizing principle as well as with its plot. The battle of the sexes in marriage is its central motif and dominates the frame, subject matter, and arrangement of the tales. In the introduction the company debates whether harmony can be achieved in marriage. Ponzio denies this, supporting his view with platitudes that Iago would relish: "Better bury a woman than marry her"; "For there to be peace between husband and wife, the husband must be deaf and the wife blind." Fabio, the group's leader, asserts instead that "the only rational love is that which has marriage as its goal, and that this is the quiet of true and wise lovers, coupled together, cooling their amorous flames with sage discourse and in legitimate union."[15] *Othello* similarly presents marriage as either potentially strife-ridden or harmonious. In *Gli Hecatommithi* the debate continues in the tales, and in the Third Decade it is intensified by the inflammatory subject matter—the infidelity of husbands and wives. The seventh tale, the source of *Othello*, is a rebuttal of the sixth, in which a husband discovers his wife's infidelity and, as the company judges, "most prudently" (*prudentissimamente*) arranges to have her "accidentally" drowned. In the eighth tale, a contrast to the two preceding it, harmony supersedes warfare. A wife forgives her unfaithful husband and wins him back, behaving with a "prudence" (*la prudenza*) exactly opposite to the behavior of the husbands in tales six and seven. *Othello* similarly rings changes on the theme of male and female in a series of parallel and contrasting couples—Desdemona/Othello, Emilia/Iago, Bianca/Cassio— along with fantasy couples—Roderigo/Desdemona, Cassio/Desdemona, Othello/Emilia. Throughout the tales of the Third Decade it is most often the men who intensify the conflicts, practicing infidelity or taking revenge on wives they suspect of infidelity; the wives, even when wronged, often succeed in mending the relationships. The men in *Othello* similarly seek revenge; the women similarly seek to secure harmonious relationships but fail to do so.

Their predecessors in this task are the heroines of Shakespearean comedy, to which *Othello* shows pervasive and profound resemblances.[16] Though it is almost always assumed that *Othello* is dominated by a tightly meshed plot, the play seems, like many of the comedies, loosely plotted, held together by theme. The conflicts introduced in the first act between Desdemona and her father and between Venetians and Turks evaporate before they are under way exactly as do those between Hermia and Egeus in *Midsummer Night's Dream* and between Duke Frederick and Duke Senior in *As You Like It*. As in the comedies, these early plot developments are presented in a flat, compressed way; they seem almost an excuse to get the characters to the woods or to Cyprus where the play's real conflicts emerge. Iago plots the remainder of the play; but his scheme is slight, repetitive, and flawed. It has been found lack-

ing in both motive (like Rosalind's plot in *As You Like It*) and
goal (like Don John's plot in *Much Ado About Nothing*), and although the play's increasing intensity is undeniable, there is
little actual plot development between the end of the first
phase of the temptation scene (III.iii.275) and the attempt on
Cassio's life in act 5. Iago's destruction of Othello, like Rosalind's education of Orlando, is not merely linear. Both are con-
tinually starting over; they are repeated variations on opposite
themes: Iago works to induce fantasy and Rosalind to dispel it.
Neither entirely succeeds. Iago's plot, like those of the comedies, rests on coincidence and absurdity. The handkerchief is
like the givens of the comedies—the fairy juice, the caskets,
the disguises, the identical twins; it is trivial and ridiculous
but, as I shall show, symbolically all-important. The play proceeds as much by a clash of attitudes, viewpoints, and sexes as
by plot developments.

Structure, too, imitates that of the pastoral comedies in its
movement from an urban center to an isolated retreat, with re-
sultant intensity, freedom, breakdown, and interaction among
disparate characters.[17] Though Othello refers to Cyprus as a
"town of war," once the threats of Turks and the storm have
lifted, it is instead Venus's isle, a place for celebration—relaxa-
tion, drinking, eating (dinner arrangements are a frequent
topic of conversation here as in Arden), flirting, sleeping, love-
making. In the comedies, the potential corruption of these activities is suggested in witty banter, songs, comic simile and
metaphor; in *Othello*, this corruption becomes literal.

The play is a terrifying completion of the comedies. In
them, realism and romanticism, lust and desire, heterosexual
and homosexual bonds, male and female power are held in
precarious balance. The men's idealism, misogyny, foolishness, and anxiety are mocked, transformed, and dispelled—
"laugh[ed] to scorn" (*AYL*, IV.ii.19)—by disguises and mock
deaths, by parodied or aborted nuptials, by delayed or deceitful consummations. The women, through their "high and
plenteous wit and invention" (IV.i.185), transform the men
from foolish lovers into—we trust—sensible husbands, and at
the end submit to their control. Although "The cuckoo then,

on every tree, / Mocks married men," (*LLL*, V.ii.896–97), the mockery grounds love without seriously threatening it. The comedies' relaxed incorporation of marital sexuality is evident in their endings, which look forward to fruitful, harmonious marital consummation—in the fairy-blessed beds of the *Midsummer Night's Dream* couples; the rewon beds of Bassanio and Portia, Gratiano and Nerissa in *Merchant of Venice*; the "well-deserved bed" of Silvius and the rest in *As You Like It*. But in *Othello*, the marriage has taken place before the play begins, and its consummation may already be under way, imaged by Iago as a theft, a violent attack. In the play, women's wit is constrained, their power over men is lost, and the men are transformed downward—"to be now a sensible man, by and by a fool, and presently a beast" (II.iii.303–04). The men's profound anxieties and murderous fantasies cannot be restrained by the women's affection, wit, and shrewishness. The play ends as it began, in a world of men—political, loveless, undomesticated.[18]

The men in *Othello* extend and darken the anxieties of the comedy heroes. They are, in Emilia's words, "murderous coxcombs" (V.ii.234). Three out of the five attempt murder; five out of the five are foolish and vain. Roderigo, most obviously a coxcomb, shows in exaggerated fashion the dangerous combination of romanticism and misogyny and the dissociation of love and sex that all the men share. He is a parody of the conventional Petrarchan lover: love is a "torment," death a "physician" (I.iii.308–09), Desdemona "full of most blest condition" (II.i.247), and consummation of their relationship securely impossible. Yet he easily accepts Desdemona's supposed adultery and the necessity of Cassio's murder; his casual cynicism comes to outdo Iago's: "'Tis but a man gone" (V.i.10). The other men have similarly divided and possessive views of women. Brabantio shifts abruptly from protective affection for the chaste Desdemona—"of spirit / So still and quiet, that her motion / Blush'd at her self" (I.iii.94–96)—to physical revulsion from the assertive sexuality revealed by her elopement—"I had rather to adopt a child than get it" (I.iii.191). Cassio's divided view is more conventionally accommodated.

He idealizes the "divine Desdemona," flirting courteously and cautiously with her and rejecting Iago's insinuations about her sexuality; this side of women is left to Bianca, who is a "monkey" and a "fitchew" and is used and degraded for it. Othello's conflict regarding women is more profound, and the other men's solutions are not open to him. Because of his marriage and his integrity, he cannot, like Roderigo, assert Desdemona's chastity and corruptibility simultaneously; like Cassio, direct his divided emotions toward different objects; or, like Brabantio, disown the problem.

Othello's shifts from the idealization of women to their degradation are "extravagant and wheeling" (I.i.136). Iago is the catalyst, but Othello makes his task easy. At the play's start, Othello's idealistic love, like that of the comedy heroes, needs some realistic grounding in the facts of sex. For Othello, sex is secondary and potentially either frivolous or debilitating and in conflict with his soldier's duty:

> no, when light-wing'd toys,
> And feather'd Cupid, foils with wanton dullness
> My speculative and active instruments,
> That my disports corrupt and taint my business,
> Let housewives make a skillet of my helm,
> And all indign and base adversities
> Make head against my reputation!   [I.iii.268–74]

Marriage and consummation naturally pose a threat to this idealistic love. Othello's greeting on Cyprus suggests his preference for a perpetually unconsummated courtship:

> If it were now to die,
> 'Twere now to be most happy, for I fear
> My soul hath her content so absolute,
> That not another comfort, like to this
> Succeeds in unknown fate.   [II.i.189–93]

In response Desdemona asserts instead quotidian joys:

> The heavens forbid
> But that our loves and comforts should increase,
> Even as our days do grow.

Perhaps she, like Rosalind or Viola or the ladies in *Love's La-bor's Lost*, might have tempered Othello's idealism, his need for absolute, unchanging love. Instead, it is nudged by Iago into its antithesis—contempt for women, disgust at sexuality, terror of cuckoldry, the preference for literal death over meta-phorical "death." The acceptance of cuckoldry and sexuality found in the comedies—"as horns are odious, they are neces-sary" (*AYL*, III.iii.49–50)—is impossible for Othello. Instead he turns Petrarchan imagery against Desdemona—"O thou black weed, why art so lovely fair?" (IV.ii.69)—praising and damn-ing her simultaneously. His conflicts are resolved, his needs to idealize and degrade her to maintain their love intact are mo-mentarily reconciled only when he kills her, performing a sac-rifice which is also a murder.[19]

Iago, though primarily the manipulator of these conflicts in the other men, is also the victim of his own. His cynical gen-eralizations are, like those of Jaques, the parody and inverse of the romantics' claims; they are self-conscious, defensive, self-aggrandizing, and divorced from reality: "My muse labours / And thus she is deliver'd" (II.i.127–28). Like the other men, he accepts generalizations—especially generalizations about women—as true, provided they are "apt and of great credit" (II.i.282), "probable, and palpable to thinking" (I.ii.76). Like the others, he is careful not to contaminate his fantasies about women with facts. Roderigo does not court Desdemona in per-son, Othello does not immediately confront Desdemona and Cassio with his suspicions, and Iago never tries to ascertain whether or not Emilia is unfaithful.

In fact—like Don John and Parolles—he has little contact with the women in the play. He is at ease in act 2 engaging Desdemona in witty banter, but he is subdued and almost speechless in act 4 when confronted with her misery and fidel-ity. Treating Emilia with casual contempt throughout, he is as-tounded by her exposure of him in the last scene. Like Braban-tio, Iago assumes that "consequence" will "approve" his "dream" (II.iii.58) and ignores evidence to the contrary.

Even protected as it is from reality, Iago's cynicism/mis-ogyny has cracks just as Othello's idealism does. He has a grudging admiration for and envy of Desdemona's "blest condition," Othello's "constant, noble loving, nature" (II.i.289), and Cassio's "daily beauty" (V.i.19). He aspires to Cassio's job and Othello's "content" and tries to identify with their love for Desdemona—"now I do love her too" (II.i.286), although this love is immediately subsumed under notions of lust and revenge. The tension between his theoretical misogyny and his awareness of Desdemona's particular virtue drives him to resolve the conflicts, to turn that virtue "into pitch" (II.iii.351), just as his verses extravagantly praise the deserving woman the better to be able to diminish her.[20] Othello's conflict has the opposite issue; he murders Desdemona to redeem her from degradation.

The women in *Othello* are not murderous, nor are they foolishly idealistic or anxiously cynical, as the men are. From the start they, like the comedy heroines, combine realism with romance, mockery with affection. Bianca comically reflects the qualities of the women as Roderigo does those of the men. The play associates her with the other two women by means of the overheard conversation about her which Othello takes to be about Desdemona and by means of her irate and essentially just response to Emilia's attack: "I am no strumpet, but of life as honest / As you, that thus abuse me" (V.i.120–21). At this point, Iago tries to fabricate evidence against her, just as Othello, in the scene immediately following, fabricates a case against Desdemona. Bianca's active, open-eyed enduring affection is similar to that of the other women. She neither romanticizes love nor degrades sex. She sees Cassio's callousness but accepts it wryly—"'Tis very good, I must be circumstanc'd" (III.iv.199). She mocks him to his face but not behind his back, as he does her. Her active pursuit of Cassio is in contrast to his indifference, to Roderigo's passivity, and to Othello's naiveté. Even when jealous, she continues to feel affection for Cassio, accusing him openly and demanding that he come to dinner on her terms. The play's humanization of her, much like, for example, that of the bourgeois characters at the end of *Love's Labor's Lost*, underlines the folly of the male characters (and critics) who see her as merely a whore.[21]

Emilia articulates the balanced view that Bianca embod-

ies—"and though we have some grace, / Yet have we some revenge" (IV.iii.92–93). She, like other Shakespearean shrews,
especially Beatrice and Paulina, combines sharp-tongued honesty with warm affection. Her views are midway between Desdemona's and Bianca's and between those of the women and
those of the men. She rejects the identification with Bianca yet
sympathizes with female promiscuity. She corrects Desdemona's occasional naiveté but defends her chastity. Although she
comprehends male jealousy and espouses sexual equality, she
seems remarkably free from jealousy herself. She wittily sees
cuckoldry and marital affection as compatible: "Who would
not make her husband a cuckold, to make him a monarch?"
(IV.iii.74–75). She understands, but tolerates, male fancy; the
dangers of such tolerance become evident in this play as they
never do in the comedies.

Desdemona's and Emilia's contrasting viewpoints in the
willow scene have led critics to think of them as opposites, but
both are strong, realistic, and compliant.[22] When we first see
them together, they encourage and participate in Iago's misogynist banter but reject his stereotypes. Desdemona here defends Emilia from Iago's insults just as Emilia will ultimately
defend Desdemona from Othello's calumny. While Desdemona is no shrew (though she might be said to approach one
in the matter of Cassio's reinstatement), her love is everywhere
tempered by realism and wit like that of the comedy heroines.
During courtship she hides, as they did, behind a sort of disguise, in this case not male dress, but a mask of docility and indifference which conceals her passion from both her father and
Othello. Like Iago's docile and deserving woman she is one
that could "think, and ne'er disclose her mind, / See suitors
following, and not look behind" (II.i.156–57). Eventually,
though, she takes the lead in the courtship as the heroines do;
she finds an excuse to be alone with Othello, mocks him by
speaking of him "dispraisingly" (III.iii.73), and traps him into
a proposal using indirection not unlike Rosalind's with
Orlando.

After marriage, as during courtship, Desdemona's love
tempers romance with realism, obedience with self-assertion.

She is indifferent to Cassio's elaborate compliments (II.i.87 ff.).
She rejects Othello's desire to stop time, instead emphasizing
love's growth.[23] Her healthy, casual acceptance of sexuality is
evident in her banter with Iago and with the clown, in her affirmation that she "did love the Moor, to live with him" (I.iii.
248), and in her refusal to postpone consummation of "the rites
for which I love him" (I.iii.257). She will not allow herself to be
idealized; nor will she romanticize Othello. She had spoken
"dispraisingly" of him during courtship, and she mocks him
gently after marriage:

> Tell me, Othello: I wonder in my soul,
> What you could ask me, that I should deny?
> Or stand so mammering on?
>
> Shall I deny you? no, farewell, my lord.
>   [III.iii.69–71, 87]

She reminds herself, in an emphatically short line:

>   nay, we must think
> Men are not gods;
> Nor of them look for such observances
> As fits the bridal.   [III.iv.145–48]

Her concise statement about her love reveals its balance and
health:

> I saw Othello's visage in his mind,
> And to his honours, and his valiant parts
> Did I my soul and fortunes consecrate.
>   [I.iii.252–54]

She loves Othello for his body and mind, for his reputation
and actions; she consecrates herself to him spiritually and
practically.

    Desdemona's spirit, clarity, and realism do not desert her
entirely in the latter half of the play as many critics and performances imply. Her inability to defend herself is partly the result of Othello's refusal to voice his suspicions directly. When
he does so in the brothel scene, she persistently questions him

to discover exactly what he is accusing her of and defends herself as "stoutly" (III.i.45) as she had earlier defended Cassio:

> If to preserve this vessel for my lord
> From any hated foul unlawful touch,
> Be not to be a strumpet, I am none.   [IV.ii.85–87]

Her naiveté and docility in the willow scene are partly a result
of her confusion and fear, but perhaps also partly a protective
facade behind which she waits, as she did during courtship,
while determining the most appropriate and fruitful reaction to
Othello's rage. The conversation and the song with its alternate last verses explore alternate responses to male perfidy
—acceptance *"Let nobody blame him, his scorn I approve"*—or
retaliation *"If I court moe women, you'll couch with moe men"*
(IV.iii.51–56). Emilia supports retaliation—"The ills we do,
their ills instruct us so" (103)—though, like Bianca, she practices acceptance. Desdemona's final couplet suggests that she
is groping for a third response, one that is midway between
"grace" and "revenge," one that would be more active than acceptance yet more loving than retaliation:

> God me such usage send,
> Not to pick bad from bad, but by bad mend!
>   [IV.iii.104–05]

The lines are a reply to Emilia and a transformation of an earlier couplet of Iago's: ". . . fairness and wit / The one's for use,
the other using it" (II.i.129–30). Desdemona will put fairness
and wit to *use* in a sense that includes and goes beyond the sexual one, acknowledging and using "bad" to heal it. Her earlier
command to have the wedding sheets put on her bed seems
one expression of this positive usage. Just before her death, as
earlier in the handkerchief and brothel scenes, Desdemona
strives to "mend" Othello's debased view of her, transforming the "sins" he accuses her of into "loves I bear to you"; a
testimony to her pure, active, humble, fertile affections. But
Othello recorrupts them: "And for that thou diest" (V.ii.40–
41).[24]

   The men's sense of identity and worth is dependent not

only on their relations with women but on their bonds with other men who guarantee their honor and reputation. Vanity, rivalry, and dependence characterize the relations among all the men in the play. Jaques's portrait of the soldier aptly sums up traits which they share: "Full of strange oaths and bearded like the pard, / Jealous in honor, sudden and quick in quarrel, / Seeking the bubble reputation / Even in the canon's mouth" (II.vii.149–52), traits which are those of coxcombs but grow murderous here. Cassio, of course, explicitly voices the men's concern with "the bubble reputation" and reveals how central their position and image are to their sense of identity: "I ha' lost my reputation! I ha' lost the immortal part, sir, of myself, and what remains is bestial" (II.iii.255). This identity is highly vulnerable because the men view reputation as detachable, external; it is a matter of rank or title, something to be conferred—or removed—by other men.[25] Hence Iago continues to care about the rank of lieutenant in spite of his continuing intimacy with Othello. Cassio equally relishes his title; "The lieutenant is to be saved before the ancient," he boasts (II.iii.103). Othello must fire Cassio for appearances' sake and because Montano "is of great fame in Cyprus" (III.i.46). Othello's dependence on others' "rich opinion" (II.iii.286) creates conflict in his love; "feather'd Cupid" potentially threatens "reputation" in the first act, and later he finds the scorn due the cuckold almost as difficult to bear as the loss of Desdemona.

Although they are neither "bearded like a pard" nor "full of strange oaths," the men in this play, in their vanity, desire the swaggering manliness which such characteristics conjure up. Iago successfully plays on the others' nervousness about this "manliness," driving them to acts of "malicious bravery" (I.i.100). He jovially calls them "man" while questioning their manhood or urging new proofs of it. He goads Cassio into "manly" drunkenness and good fellowship—"What, man, 'tis a night of revels, the gallants desire it" (II.iii.39). He urges Othello, "Good sir, be a man" (IV.i.65). He flatters Roderigo's manly pride: "if thou hast that within thee indeed, which I have greater reason to believe now than ever, I mean purpose, courage, and valour, this night show it" (IV.ii.213–16). His suggestive battle cries to Roderigo imply a connection that all the men assume between sexual and martial prowess: "Wear thy good rapier bare, and put it home. . . . fix most firm thy resolution" (V.i.2, 5); perhaps the gull's melodramatic attack on Cassio is "satisfying" even beyond Iago's "reasons," compensating him for his lack of sexual success. Inversely, cuckoldry is seen by Othello as invalidating his military glories; only the murder of Desdemona and his own suicide restore his pride in his "occupation."

Since the reputation and manliness which the men covet is achieved in competition with others, all the men are "jealous in honor, sudden and quick in quarrel." Iago's success derives largely from his ability to manipulate male rivalries, verifying his friendship with each man by shared contempt toward another. In this way, he feeds the men's need for self-esteem, insures their bond with him, and exacerbates their potential rivalries with each other.[26] He enrages Brabantio by claiming that his friend has "robbed" his daughter. He gulls Roderigo by demeaning Othello and urging that they have common cause against him: "my cause is hearted, thine has no less reason, let us be communicative in our revenge against him: if thou canst cuckold him, thou doest thyself a pleasure, and me a sport" (I.iii.366–69). He almost offhandedly belittles Othello to Cassio, Cassio to Montano, Othello to Lodovico. His entrapment of Othello begins by insinuating not Desdemona's unfaithfulness but Othello's cuckoldry, his loss of "good name." This cuckoldry triply threatens Othello: with the loss of Desdemona's love; with the supremacy of Cassio, his lieutenant, over him; and with the loss of his reputation and the scorn of other men.[27]

Iago offers to compensate for these losses with his own love—to replace Othello's other bonds with their friendship. Iago's attack is set up when Othello demands that Iago prove his love by complying with his general's wishes (he has just been threatened by Desdemona's seeming to put similar pressure on him): "If thou dost love me, / Show me thy thought" (III.iii.119–20). It concludes with Othello's attempt to replace his love for Desdemona with a vow of vengeance and a (co-

erced) bond with Iago, through which it seems he can restore
his heroism and control by regaining the love and dependence
he fears he has lost:

> *Iago.*   Witness, you ever-burning lights above,
>   You elements that clip us round about,
>   Witness that here Iago doth give up
>   The excellency of his wit, hand, heart,
>   To wrong'd Othello's service: let him command,
>   And to obey him shall be in me remorse,
>   What bloody work so ever.
> *Othello.*
>   I greet thy love;
>   Not with vain thanks, but with acceptance
>   bounteous.   [III.iii.470–78]

Iago's feigned love gives him power which Desdemona's genuine love cannot counteract; he destroys his superior by de-
stroying Othello's belief in his own superiority and the bonds
which confirm that superiority. Nowhere is his power and its
roots in Othello's fear of inferiority to other men more ruth-
lessly and painfully demonstrated than when Iago engineers
Othello's eavesdropping of his and Cassio's mockery of Bianca; here, Othello's wounded vanity, obsessive jealousy, and
competitive concern for reputation and manliness coalesce in
his terse asides with their sexual-martial double entendres:

> Do you triumph, Roman, do you triumph?
>
> So, so, so, so; laugh that wins.
>
> Ha' you scor'd me? Well.
>
> I see that nose of yours, but not that dog I shall throw 't to.
>   [IV.i.118,122,126,140][28]

Iago likewise gains power by imposing on the play,
through his bawdy, an image of heterosexuality which, like
male bonds, is seen as competitive and violent. Sexuality here
is not merely represented as an act of male assertion, as in
Much Ado, or as painful debilitation, as in *All's Well*, but as a vi-

olent, bestial overpowering of the woman by the man which degrades both: "an old black ram / Is tupping your white ewe," "you'll have your daughter cover'd with a Barbary horse," "he hath boarded a land carrack"; Desdemona is in the "gross clasps of a lascivious Moor" (I.i.88–89; 110–11; I.ii.50; I.i.126). This vision of sexuality comes to replace the tender, hallowed passion of Desdemona for Othello, her desire to participate in "the rites for which I love him" (I.iii.257), as Othello imagines that Cassio "lie[s] with her, lie[s] on her" (IV.i.38), "pluck[s] up kisses by the roots" (III.iii.429). The inevitable culmination of this fantasy occurs when Othello clasps, covers, and stifles Desdemona—"Down, strumpet. . . . Nay and you strive . . ."(V.ii.80,82), silencing her "even in the bed she hath contaminated" (IV.i.203)—and then kills himself.[29]

Although the men's aggression destroys the women, their attempts at heroic violence against each other do not completely succeed. Othello vows to kill Cassio but never does, and Roderigo's murder attempt on Cassio fails. It takes Cassio and Iago together to kill poor Roderigo, and Othello cannot kill Iago. The cowardice, clumsiness, and insecurity that belie male pretensions to valor are manifested comically—as in the *Twelfth Night* duel or in the gulling of Parolles—in the hesitation of Lodovico and Gratiano to answer Roderigo's and Cassio's cries for help: "Two or three groans; it is a heavy night, / These may be counterfeits, let's think 't unsafe / To come into the cry without more help" (V.I.42–45). Even after Iago's entrance, they still hang back, ascertaining his identity (51) but ignoring his cry (thus allowing him to murder Roderigo), introducing themselves (67), discovering Cassio's identity (70), and finally coming to his side after Bianca, who has just entered (75). They still offer no assistance but only perfunctory sympathy and an anticlimactic explanation: "I am sorry to find you thus, I have been to seek you" (81).

Male friendship, like male courage, is in this play sadly deteriorated from the Renaissance ideal. In romance and comedy, the world of male friendship in which the work opens (see, for example, the *Arcadia*, *Two Gentlemen of Verona*, *The Merchant of Venice*, *Love's Labor's Lost*) is disrupted and transcended by romantic love. In the problem comedies, male friendship is already corrupted as friends exploit and betray each other. As *Othello* begins, romantic love already dominates, but friendship is reasserted in perverted form. Iago's hypocritical friendship for all of the men, which aims to gratify his own will and gain power over them, is the model for male friendship in the play. Brabantio's "love" for Othello evaporates when his friend marries his daughter. Roderigo intends to use Iago though he is worse used by him. Othello has no hestitation in cashiering Cassio and ordering his death. The men's vanity and rivalry, their preoccupation with rank and reputation, and their cowardice render them as incapable of friendship as they are of love.

The women, in contrast, are indifferent to reputation and partially free of vanity, jealousy, and competitiveness. Desdemona's willingness "to incur a general mock" is evident in her elopement and her defense of it, and in her request to go to Cyprus. Emilia braves scorn to defend her mistress, "Let heaven, and men, and devils, let 'em all, / All, all cry shame against me, yet I'll speak" (V.ii.222–23). If Cassio's description of Bianca corresponds at all to fact, she too ignores reputation, comically, to pursue him—"she haunts me in every place . . . she falls thus about my neck; . . . so hangs, and lolls, and weeps upon me" (IV.i.131–36)—and we see her brave the confusion of the night and the ugliness of Iago's insinuations to come to Cassio's side when he is wounded. Bianca's jealousy is also in contrast to the men's; instead of corroding within, it is quickly vented and dissipates, leaving her affection for Cassio essentially unchanged. Furthermore, she makes no effort to discover her rival, to obtain "proof," or to get revenge. Likewise Emilia, though expert at noting and analyzing jealousy, seems untouched by it herself. Even her argument for the single standard is good-natured; it contains little hatred of men and no personal animosity toward Iago.

Desdemona is neither jealous nor envious nor suspicious. She is not suspicious or possessive about Othello's job, his intimacy with Iago, or his "love" for Cassio, but supports all three. She seems entirely lacking in the sense of class, race, rank, and hierarchy that concerns the men and is shared by Emilia, who refuses to be identified with Bianca. She treats her father, the Duke, Othello, Cassio, Iago, Emilia, even the clown, with precisely the same combination of politeness, generosity, openness, and firmness. Emilia's and Desdemona's lack of competitiveness, jealousy, and class consciousness facilitates their growing intimacy, which culminates in the willow scene. The scene, sandwiched between two exchanges of Iago and Roderigo, sharply contrasts the genuine intimacy of the women with the hypocritical friendship of the men, while underlining the women's isolation and powerlessness.[30] Emilia's concern for Desdemona is real, and her advice well meant, whereas Iago's concern for Roderigo is feigned, his advice deadly — "whether he kill Cassio, / Or Cassio him, or each do kill the other, / Every way makes my game" (V.i.12–14). Roderigo accepts Iago's "satisfying reasons," finding them sufficient to justify murder; Desdemona rejects Emilia's reasonable justification of wives' adultery without rejecting the concern that prompts her to offer it. In the willow scene sympathy stretches from Emilia and Desdemona to include Barbary and the protagonist of the song—all victims of male perfidy; in the Roderigo/Iago scenes, enmity reaches Cassio. In this play romantic love is destroyed by the semblance of male friendship, which itself soon disintegrates. Meanwhile, friendship between women is established and dominates the play's final scene. Othello chooses Iago's friendship over Desdemona's love temporarily and unwittingly; Emilia's choice of Desdemona over Iago is voluntary and final. Though the stakes here are higher, the friendship of Desdemona and Emilia is reminiscent of the generous, witty female friendship in the comedies, where women share their friends' hardships (Rosalind and Celia), vigorously defend their honor (Beatrice and Hero), support their stratagems (Portia and Nerissa), and sympathize with and aid even their rivals (Julia and Sylvia, Viola and Olivia, Helen and Diana, Mariana and Isabella). But in *Othello*, without the aid of disguise, bedtricks, or mock deaths, the women cannot protect each other from male animosity.

Because of the men's vanity, competitiveness, and con-

cern for honor and reputation, when they do act, they try to
exonerate themselves, persistently placing blame for their actions outside themselves. Even Cassio, while abusing himself
for his drunkenness, comes to personify that drunkenness as a
"devil," something which invades him. Roderigo blames Iago
for his failure to prosper: "Iago hurt [me]. Iago set [me] on"
(V.ii.329–30). Iago, at the last, instead of boasting about the
execution of his grand design (as, for example, Satan does in
Paradise Lost), tries to shift responsibility for it elsewhere—to
Bianca, to Emilia, and finally, even after the facts are known, to
Othello: "I told him what I thought, and told no more / Than
what he found himself was apt and true" (V.ii.177–78). Othello's longing for passivity and his denial of responsibility are intertwined throughout the play. He both sees himself as passive
and desires passivity. His narrative history before the senate,
the basis for our original impression of the heroic Othello, describes, when closely examined, what he has suffered rather
than what he has done; he speaks of "moving accidents by
flood and field; / Of hair-breadth scapes 'i th' imminent deadly
breach; / Of being taken by the insolent foe; / And sold to slavery, and my redemption hence" (I.iii.135–38), and of his subsequent enslavement by Desdemona, whom he entertained
with similar tales, for example, "of some distressed stroke /
That my youth suffer'd" (I.iii.157–58). Pity is indeed the appropriate response to his tale. His farewell to arms is, curiously, a farewell to "content," to "the tranquil mind" (III.iii.
354), and to the instruments of war; it is they who are seen as
active and heroic, not himself. His vow of revenge, likening
him to the "compulsive course" of the "Pontic sea," reveals the
longing for external control and validation which underlies the
heroic stance. In a parallel passage after his error is revealed,
he again wants to be swept along by a current: "Blow me about
in winds, roast me in sulphur, / Wash me in steep-down gulfs
of liquid fire!" (V.ii.280–81), to be consumed by hell-fire rather
than by desire. Two of his significant actions in the play—the
cashiering of Cassio and the murder of Desdemona—are, in a
sense, "compulsive," achieved, as he himself notes, only when
passion "Assays to lead the way" (II.iii.198), and he feels out of
control or seeks a false sense of being under the control of an

impersonal "cause." Even at his suicide, when he *is* in control, he sees himself as "you" rather than "I," object rather than actor, as "being wrought, / Perplex'd in the extreme . . . one whose subdued eyes, . . . Drops tears as fast as the Arabian trees / Their medicinal gum" (V.ii.346–51). In the anecdote that accompanies his suicide, Othello is actor and acted upon, hero and victim, and his action is again violent and enraged. But it is also premeditated—and gives him, at last, the command over himself he has not achieved throughout.

Desdemona's self-recriminations must be seen in the light of Othello's evasions. Critics have found them puzzling, excessive, intolerable, even neurotic;[31] perhaps they are all of these. But her unwarranted self-accusations—"beshrew me much, Emilia, / I was (unhandsome warrior as I am) / Arraigning his unkindness with my soul; / But now I find I had suborn'd the witness, / And he's indited falsely" (III.iv.148–52)—and her false assumption of responsibility for her death—"Nobody, I myself, farewell" (V.ii.125)—provide the sharpest possible contrast to the men's excuses. Her last request, "Commend me to my kind lord," not only conveys her forgiveness but is one final active effort to restore their mutual love. She is not, however, a willing victim and does not sacrifice herself to Othello, although she does not attribute guilt to him either. She defends her innocence and pleads for her life; but he murders her anyway.

Desdemona's cryptic lines after she is apparently dead give to her actual death some of the functions and the feel of Shakespearean mock deaths. Like the women who stage them, she defends her innocence—"A guiltless death I die" (V.ii.123)—assumes responsibility for the death, and seeks to transform Othello into a "kind lord." When the audience finds that the woman it has thought dead remains alive, the poignant, momentary impression that this may be a mock death intensifies the horror of the scene. Desdemona's refusal to blame and hurt Othello is at the heart of her loving virtue. Hero, Helen, and Hermione likewise do not blame their detractors directly. But this virtue coalesces in dangerous ways with Othello's need to blame and hurt her.

From the beginning, Desdemona has viewed love as risk

and challenge. She has violently uprooted herself from her father's protection and the conventional expectations of Venetian society, whereas Othello has put himself into "circumscription and confine" for her. She has initiated while Othello has responded. She is neither the "rose" or "chrysolite" of Petrarchan convention seen by Othello nor the saint extolled by critics. She sets the stage for her wooing by an extraordinarily active listening, which Othello naturally notices and describes; she would "with a greedy ear / Devour up my discourse" (I.iii.149–50). She engenders his love by her own: "She lov'd me for the dangers I had pass'd, / And I lov'd her that she did pity them" (168–69); she proposes and elopes. She is the one who challenges her father directly, who determines to go to Cyprus. She moves after marriage to bring the lovers' idiom down to earth, using all of her "plenteous wit and invention" at their reunion and in the discussion of Cassio. All the characters in the play make mention of her energizing power. Cassio, hyperbolically, attributes to her the ability to influence recalcitrant nature:

> Tempests themselves, high seas, and howling winds,
> The gutter'd rocks, and congregated sands,
> Traitors ensteep'd, to clog the guiltless keel,
> As having sense of beauty, do omit
> Their common natures, letting go safely by
> The divine Desdemona.   [II.i.68–73]

Othello is awed by her power to move man and beast—"She might lie by an emperor's side, and command him tasks . . . . O, she will sing the savageness out of a bear" (IV.i.180–81, 184–85)—testifying, late in the play, to his ineradicable love for her. Iago, in soliloquy, attributes to her unlimited power over Othello—"she may make, unmake, do what she list" (II.iii.337). And Desdemona herself, vowing support for Cassio, reveals her sense of her own persistance and controlling force:

> If I do vow a friendship, I'll perform it
> To the last article.   [III.iii.21–22]

But Desdemona's energy, assertiveness, and power are made possible by Othello's loving response to her, just as his subduing of himself to her, his "garner[ing] up" (IV.ii.58) of his heart is engendered by her love for him. Each has "thrive[d]" (I.iii.125) in the apparent security of their mutual love, but their joyous subduing of themselves to each other leaves them vulnerable. With that certainty lost, with their responses to each other mistrusted, Othello is plunged into chaos and Desdemona into helplessness. In this crisis, he seeks to be "unhoused" again, and she refuses to acknowledge the loss of her new home: "Commend me to my kind lord" (V.ii.126).

All of the women, in spite of their affection, good sense, and energy, fail to transform or to be reconciled with the men. The sexes, so sharply differentiated in the play, badly misunderstand each other.[32] The men, as we have seen, persistently misconceive the women; the women fatally overestimate the men. Each sex, trapped in its own values and attitudes, misjudges the other. Iago acts on the hypothesis that women, on the one hand, share his concern with reputation and propriety ("Be wise, and get you home" [V.ii.224], he orders Emilia) and, on the other, enact his salacious fantasies. Othello assumes, with Iago's prompting, that just as he is the stereotypical soldier, foreigner, older husband, so Desdemona will be the stereotypical mistress, Venetian, young bride. He responds to Iago's claim to knowledge about Desdemona—"knowing what I am, I know what she shall be"—with comic enthusiasm: "O thou art wise, 'tis certain" (IV.i.73–74). Likewise the women attribute their own qualities to the men. Desdemona projects her lack of jealousy onto Othello. Emilia attributes to Iago her own capacity for empathy: "I know it grieves my husband, / As if the case were his" (III.iii.3–4). Even Bianca, because she does not view herself as a whore in her relationship with Cassio, is surprised that he should treat her as one. Hence, although the women recognize the foolishness of the men's fancies, they are all too tolerant of them. Emilia steals the handkerchief for the sake of Iago's "fantasy" (III.iii.303) and thus assures the success of his plot. Desdemona's salutation to Othello in act 3 is lamentably prophetic—"Be it as your

fancies teach you, / What e'er you be, I am obedient" (III.iii.
89–90). He leaves her to be instructed in her whoredom.

The lost handkerchief becomes the emblem of the wom-
en's power and its loss. Both Othello's original description of
the handkerchief and its part in the plot reveal that it is a symbol of women's loving, civilizing, sexual power. It has passed
from female sibyl to female "charmer" to Othello's mother to
Desdemona. Othello is merely a necessary intermediary between his mother and his wife—"She dying, gave it me, / And
bid me, when my fate would have me wive, / To give it her"
(III.iv.61–63). Its creator, the sibyl, who "In her prophetic fury
sew'd the work," and its next owner, the Egyptian charmer
who "could almost read / The thoughts of people," reveal the
source of its power in women's passionate intuitive knowledge. This knowledge, it seems, enables them to use and control sexuality. The middle ground that women find between
lust and abstinence (as the men in the play cannot do) is suggested in the description of the process by which the handkerchief is made. The worms that did "breed" the silk, emblems of
death, sexuality, and procreation, are "hallow'd." The thread
they spin vitally and naturally from themselves is artificially
improved, dyed in "mummy" which is "conserve[d] from
maiden's hearts." The handkerchief then represents marital
chastity—sexuality transformed by loving fidelity. Its function
is to chasten and control men's love and desire:

> she told her, while she kept it
> 'Twould make her amiable, and subdue my father
> Entirely to her love; but if she lost it,
> Or made a gift of it, my father's eye
> Should hold her loathly, and his spirits should hunt
> After new fancies.   [56–61]

It represents women's ability to moderate men's erratic (and
erotic) "fancies," to "subdue" their promiscuity (assumed to
be the norm under the double standard outlined by Emilia),
and perhaps, by extension, their vanity, romanticism, jealousy, and rage as well. The handkerchief is the symbol of Desdemona's loving power over Othello:

Excellent wretch, perdition catch my soul,
But I do love thee, and when I love thee not,
Chaos is come again.

[III.iii.91–93]

The handkerchief is lost, literally and symbolically, not because of the failure of Desdemona's love, but because of Othello's loss of faith in that love. Once lost, the female power it
symbolizes is degraded and constrained, and comedy gives
way to tragedy.

After the handkerchief's original loss, all of the characters,
men and women alike, misuse its power and misinterpret its
symbolism, marking the disruption of all the love relationships
in the play. The abuse begins when Othello pushes it aside, rejecting Desdemona's loving attempt to heal the pain on his
forehead, and Emilia picks it up to give it to Iago, thereby making herself subservient to him and placing her loyalty to her
husband above affection for Desdemona. Her silence about its
whereabouts confirms her choice. Shakespeare's alteration of
his source—removing Iago from an active role in the theft of
the handkerchief and dramatizing its loss in these particular
circumstances—emphasizes the handkerchief's symbolism
and the active role played by Desdemona and Emilia in the
misunderstandings that follow from its loss. In Iago's hands,
its function is reversed; it is used to confirm his power over
Emilia and Othello and to induce in Othello loathing for Desdemona. Iago's first mention of it incites Othello to reject love
and embrace vengeance (III.iii.441–86). Now the hero, under
Iago's tutelage, proceeds to reinterpret the handkerchief as *his*
love token—a pledge of his love and possession of Desdemona and of her sexual fidelity—"She is protectress of her
honour too, / May she give that?" (IV.i.14–15). Hence its loss
provides "proof" of his suspicions. The reinterpretation continues in his altered description of its history in the last act. As
he uses it to support his "cause" against Desdemona, it becomes "the recognizance and pledge of love / Which *I* first
gave her . . . an antique token / *My father* gave my mother"
(V.ii.215–18; italics mine). It is now a symbol of the male con-

trol and love which Desdemona has betrayed; hence she must be punished—"Yet she must die, else she'll betray more men" (V.ii.6).[33]

Desdemona, too, alters her view of the handkerchief. Instinctively using it to cure Othello's pain, she almost succeeds. She "loves" the handkerchief (III.iii.297) and recognizes the danger of its loss. But when pressed by Othello, she rejects its significance—"Then would to God that I had never seen it!" (III.iv.75). Her rejection reflects the failure of her power. In Desdemona's earlier discussion of Cassio she was in control; now her persistence is foolish and provokes Othello's rage. Even in the early part of this scene, Desdemona deftly parries and "mends" Othello's ugly insinuations, turning his implied sexual vices into passionate virtues:

> Othello.   . . . this hand is moist, my lady.
> Desdemona.   It yet has felt no age, nor known no sorrow.
> . . . .
> Othello.   For here's a young and sweating devil here,
>   That commonly rebels: 'tis a good hand,
>   A frank one.
> Desdemona.   You may indeed say so,
>   For 'twas that hand that gave away my heart.
>   [III.iv.32–41]

But after the tale of the handkerchief she loses the initiative. She tries to regain it by—just barely—lying, and by changing the subject. But the attempt to calm and heal Othello fails. Her lie, like Ophelia's similarly well-intentioned lie to Hamlet, is generated by her love but signals the loss of her maiden's power and innocence; it confirms—Othello believes—his notions about female depravity, as Ophelia's lie confirms Hamlet's similar views. Both women, rejected by their lovers, do not regain the initiative in the relationship.

The handkerchief next creates conflict in the Iago/Emilia and Cassio/Bianca relationships. Both men use it, as Othello has done, to consolidate their power over women. When Emilia regrets its theft, Iago snatches it from her and dismisses her, "Be not you known on 't" (III.iii.324). Cassio similarly gives orders to Bianca regarding it and dismisses her (III.iv.188–89). She, though jealous, agrees to copy the work; her willingness to be "circumstanc'd" (200) is a flaw which all the women share. Later, however, she returns the handkerchief in a scene parallel and in contrast to that when the handkerchief was lost. Bianca, like Othello, is jealous. She flings down the handkerchief as he pushed it aside, and it lies on the stage ignored by the couple, who go off to a possible reconciliation. But Bianca's refusal to be used by the handkerchief or by Cassio leads to a truce and a supper engagement, whereas Othello's refusal to be healed by it opens the breach in his relationship with Desdemona that culminates in her murder.

Eventually the handkerchief's original function is reestablished; it becomes the vehicle through which civilizing control is returned to the women. The reference to it by Othello in the last scene enlightens Emilia; it ends Iago's domination of her, engenders her accusations of Othello and Iago, and enables her to prove Desdemona's faithful "amiable" love. Othello is once again "subdue[d]" to this love. Emilia, stealing the handkerchief, is catalyst for the play's crisis; revealing its theft, she is catalyst for the play's denouement.

Her reiteration of "husband" and "mistress" in the last scene emphasizes the play's central division and the "divided duty" of Emilia. When Iago's villainy is made known, she shifts her allegiance unhesitatingly. Instead of tolerating both Iago's "fancy" and Desdemona's virtue, she denounces the one and affirms the other. She questions Iago's manliness: "Disprove this villain, if thou be'st a man: / He said thou told'st him that his wife was false, / I know thou didst not, thou art not such a villain" (V.ii.173–75). Then she rejects the wifely virtues of silence, obedience, and prudence that are demanded of her, "unhousing" herself:

> I will not charm my tongue, I am bound to speak:
> . . . .
> 'Tis proper I obey him, but not now:
> Perchance, Iago, I will ne'er go home.   [185, 197–98]

Her epithet just before she is stabbed appropriately refers to all the men in the play: Iago, to whose taunts it is a response; Othello, who responds to it; and Cassio, Roderigo, and Brabantio as well:

> O murderous coxcomb! what should such a fool
> Do with so good a woman?   [234–35]

Emilia, another "good woman," dies without self-justifications or calls for revenge; instead she testifies to Desdemona's innocence and love just as her mistress had done at her own death. Her request to be laid by her mistress, her reiteration of the willow song, and her own attempts to "by bad mend" complete her identification with Desdemona.

Emilia's story has utterly destroyed Iago's bond with Othello and foiled his attempt to "make up [his] will," (I.iii.393), to complete himself by compensating for his own misshapenness through the stories that allow him to shape others.[34] He and his fantasies are repudiated by Roderigo, by Othello, and by Emilia. Her refusal of obedience destroys Iago's plot and refutes his philosophy, which requires that she act in her own self-interest. Iago's final, Othello-like attempt to deny his wife's betrayal is to call her "villainous whore" and stab her, thus validating her confession and her epitaph for him. But this act, like all of the other events of the night, "fordoes" Iago instead of "mak[ing]" him (V.i.128). He has not eradicated Othello's love for Desdemona or turned her virtue into pitch. The deaths of Roderigo, Desdemona, Emilia, and Othello destroy the power over others which is the source of his self-engendering and identity. His final silence—"Demand me nothing, what you know, you know, / From this time forth I never will speak word" (V.ii.304–05)—is, for him, the equivalent of suicide.[35] Iago's silence, his imperviousness, his unmade-upness, his refusal to suffer, all mitigate his scapegoat function throughout the last scene, emphasizing instead his role as catalyst to Othello's tragedy. It is Othello's speech, his pain, his recreation of a self to which we attend.

While the division between Iago and Emilia is absolute after he kills her, some connections between Othello and Desdemona are reestablished in the last act. Desdemona, as we have seen, continues to affirm their relationship up to the moment of her death, and Othello in the last scene does move away from the men and toward the women. Othello, like Desdemona and Emilia, dies in pain testifying to love, whereas Iago lives, silent; Othello, like the women, stays to acknowledge at least partial responsibility for his actions, while Iago flees, accepting none. But Othello cannot abandon his masculine identity by asserting a new one: "That's he that was Othello; here I am" (285). Instead of applying Emilia's accusation to himself, he stabs Iago; the two men are one in their desire to place guilt elsewhere and eliminate its bearer. With Iago's exit, Othello turns his attention, characteristically, to his honor and a suicide weapon. Emilia's death, though it reenacts Desdemona's, is a mere parenthesis in his search, scarcely noticed by him. Although male bombast is virtually silenced at the end of this play, as it is in the comedies—Iago "never will speak word" (305) and the terseness and precision of Roderigo's dying epithet for Iago ("O inhuman dog") are equaled in Cassio's epitaph for the dead Othello ("For he was great of heart")—Othello's rhetoric continues unchecked.[36] Throughout the scene, he persists in seeing himself and Desdemona as ill-fated, "unlucky," as victims of Iago who has "ensnar'd" (303) him. Desdemona is still imagined as the remote, passive, perfect object of romantic love. She is "cold, cold" as her "chastity" (276–77), associated with "monumental alabaster" (5), with an "entire and perfect chrysolite" (146), and with a "pearl" (348). In his last speeches, his own brand of Iago's "motive-hunting," he strives to reconstitute his heroic reputation. He leaves the play exactly as he had entered it, affirming his services to the state (cf. I.ii.17), confessing, asking for justice and judgment (cf. I.iii.122–25), telling stories about his past, and putting his "unhoused free condition" into its ultimate "confine" for love of Desdemona. His suicide both punishes himself as an Iago-like "dog" and reasserts his identity as a decisive, just commander and a passionate lover of Desdemona: "I kiss'd thee ere I kill'd thee, no way but this, / Killing myself, to die upon a kiss" (359–60). His love remains idealistic, anxious, self-justifying—consummated "no way" but in death.

Indeed, most of the characters remain where they started —or return there. Here there is not even the tentative movement beyond folly that we find in the comedy heroes. Roderigo was upbraiding Iago in the play's first lines and is still doing so in the letter that is his last communication. Cassio has again received a promotion and is again caught up in events he does not comprehend. Brabantio, had he lived, likely would have responded to Desdemona's death exactly as he did to her elopement: "This sight would make him do a desperate turn" (208). Iago, like Jaques, Malvolio, and Shylock, the villains of the comedies, is opaque and static. His cryptic last words, "What you know, you know," (304) reveal no more about him than did his overexplanatory soliloquies. Desdemona, just before her death, challenges Othello as she had challenged her father and defends herself with the same straightforward precision she used before the senate:

> And have you mercy too! I never did
> Offend you in my life, . . . never lov'd Cassio,
> But with such general warranty of heaven,
> As I might love: I never gave him token.   [59–62]

Bianca comes forth to seek Cassio at her last appearance as at her first; both times she frankly declares her affection and is brusquely dismissed. Emilia's function and attitudes do change, however, though her character perhaps does not. She moves from tolerating men's fancies to exploding them and from prudent acceptance to courageous repudiation. She ceases to function as reconciler of the views of the men and the women, and the separation between them widens.

The play's ending is tragic; but it is also cankered comedy. The final speech effects a disengagement even greater than that which is usual at the end of the tragedies. Avoiding mention of the love of Othello and Desdemona and direct reference to Othello's murder and suicide, it focuses on the "state matters" (III.iv.153) which the lovers themselves earlier sought refuge in and on the punishment of Iago, who does, at this point, become a scapegoat. Lodovico asks us to see the tragedy as Iago's "work," to look forward with relish to his torture, and to avert our gaze from the bed and its significance. But the restoration of military order provides little satisfaction here. The speech does not look back over the events of the play, creating a sense of completion and exhaustion as in *Romeo and Juliet* and *King Lear*; it does not look forward to a new beginning, however equivocally, as do *Hamlet* and *Macbeth*. The conflict between the men and the women has not been eliminated or resolved. The men have been unable to turn the women's virtue into pitch, but the women have been unable to mend male fantasies. The comic resolution of male with female, idealism with realism, love with sex, the individual with society is aborted. The play concludes, not with symmetrical pairings off and a movement toward marriage beds, but with one final triangle: Emilia, Desdemona, and Othello dead on wedding sheets. We are made to look with Iago, ominously a survivor, at the "tragic lodging of this bed"; *lodging* here, with its resonance from other Shakespearean uses, concludes the play on a note of arrested growth, devastated fertility.[37] "The object poisons sight"; it signifies destruction without catharsis, release without resolution.[38] The pain and division of the ending are unmitigated, and the clarification it offers is intolerable. "Let it be hid" is our inevitable response.

CHAPTER FOUR

Gender and Genre in
Antony and Cleopatra

Here I am Antony
Yet cannot hold this visible shape.

No more but e'en a woman . . .

It is shaped, sir, like itself.

C RITICS have long found *Antony and Cleopatra* a peculiar play whose genre is problematic. It has been viewed as an anomaly among the tragedies, a Roman play, a problem play, a precursor of the romances, and, most commonly, a blend of comedy and tragedy.[1] Recently, psychoanalytic and feminist critics have likewise found in the play the dissolution of gender boundaries, a dissolution variously interpreted—as a regression to infantile modes of awareness in which self and other are undifferentiated; as a transcendence of gender oppositions allowing for interpenetration and metamorphosis; as Antony's terrified feminization at the hands of a powerful Cleopatra; or as Antony's achievement of an "alternative masculinity" through his acceptance of feminine aspects of himself.[2] Underlying these studies is the assumption that the dissolving of gender roles is in some way connected with the amorphousness of the play's generic structure, that genre is determined by the nature of the psychological conflicts explored and the nature of the resolution to them. But the relationship is not specifically explicated.[3]

This chapter provides a detailed consideration of the interaction between gender and genre in *Antony and Cleopatra*. Its purpose is to show that, in this play, gender roles are not exchanged or transcended, but are played out in more variety than in the other tragedies. In consequence, the generic boundaries of *Antony and Cleopatra* are expanded to include motifs, roles, and themes found in Shakespeare's comedies, histories, problem plays, and romances. This examination illuminates both the gender relations characteristic of different Shakespearean genres and the unique generic mix of *Antony and Cleopatra*, a play which, like Egypt's crocodile, is shaped only like "itself."

Antony at first evades full commitment to Cleopatra by playing the romantic lover, and she responds by playing the mocking, realistic beloved; both roles are familiar from the comedies. Then, like the protagonists of the history plays, especially the Roman histories, Antony turns for self-definition to a public, political realm; he leaves Cleopatra behind to commit himself to Roman politics, male alliance, and a marriage with Octavia designed to cement that alliance. As the bond with Caesar engenders new conflicts, Antony ruptures marriage and alliance together. He returns to Cleopatra and achieves with her the synthesis of love and heroism, authority and sexuality, autonomy and mutuality sought in the problem plays and early tragedies by Romeo, Troilus, Hamlet, Bertram, and Othello. But this synthesis engenders its own dissolution. When Antony succumbs to the enraged misogyny of the tragic heroes, Cleopatra defends herself by accommodation and a strategic mock death. Enobarbus, caught between Antony and Cleopatra, Roman power and Egyptian desire, comedy and tragedy, dies embodying the play's oppositions. Through their own deaths, Antony and Cleopatra resolve these conflicts and achieve the self-realization and reunion that will be more fully achieved in the romances through the diminishing of tragic conflict and tragic scope. But unlike the romances, *Antony and Cleopatra* does not conclude with reunion; the deaths are framed and distanced by Caesar, whose commentary reduces the lovers' story from myth to stereotype and exploits it to enhance his power. Antony's and Cleopatra's symbolic marriage, although it affirms their sexual union and mutual commitment, does not reconcile them to the social order, ensure family continuity, or rejuvenate the political order as do the marriages in the comedies, histories, and romances; their deaths, like those of other tragic protagonists, transcend rather than transform the social order.

Throughout the variety of Antony's and Cleopatra's roles, gender divisions remain constant—as they do, I think, throughout the Shakespearean canon. Gender roles are polarized sexually, emotionally, and socially within a patriarchal framework. Men's roles are more varied, undergo more development, and are often experienced as dangerously unstable. Women's roles and identity are less varied, change less, and are more secure; but, paradoxically, because women so often act in response to the fluctuations of the men, they are perceived as stereotypically mutable and untrustworthy.[4] Cleopatra's "See where he is, who's with him, what he does: / . . . If you find him sad, / Say I am dancing; if in mirth, report / That I am sudden sick" (I.iii.2–5) is merely a subtle, self-conscious, and inverted example of the responsiveness that is characteristic of Shakespeare's women.[5] Antony, like men in other plays, experiences anxiety about his identity, his masculinity, his relations to love and war. His assertions and Cleopatra's that he *is* Antony only emphasize his difficulty in maintaining his "shape" (IV.xiv.13–14).[6] He experiences perpetual conflict between self-realization as a soldier and a lover, between male bonds and heterosexual ones, between his own autonomy and his commitment to Cleopatra. He is both threatened and enhanced by Cleopatra's sexuality, her difference from him, her responsiveness to him.

Cleopatra, like other Shakespearean women, assumes more effortlessly her own identity and sexuality. She finds no conflict between her roles as queen and lover, between friendship with her women and love of Antony, between self-realization and union. Her desire for Antony affirms rather than threatens her identity;[7] even when his death frees her from playing in response to him, she settles easily into a self defined entirely by its female "passion": a self, "No more but e'en a woman, and commanded / By such poor passion as the maid that milks / And does the meanest chores" (IV.xv.76–78). Her project, like that of other heroines, comic and tragic alike, is to absorb Antony's conflicts and to validate his heroic manhood for him so that he may allow her to become herself by satisfying her passion: "But since my lord / Is Antony again, I will be Cleopatra" (III.xiii.186–87).

Indeed, the moments of apparent gender reversal on which critics base their assumptions of the dissolution of gender boundaries seem to me only to confirm the profound polarization of gender roles in the play. Caesar's accusation that Antony is "not more manlike / Than Cleopatra, nor the Queen of Ptolemy / More womanly than he" (I.iv.5–7), like many of the judgments in the play, is biased, limited, and contradicted—both by the preceding scene, which ends with Cleopatra's acquiescing in Antony's departure and wishing him honor and victory, and by those following it, which show Cleopatra in Egypt, languishing with desire for Antony and Antony's return to Rome and his successful negotiations with Caesar. Cleopatra's exuberant memory of hers and Antony's unique drunken exchange of clothes: "I drunk him to his bed; / Then put my tires and mantles on him, whilst / I wore his sword Philippan" (II.v.21–23) is given its joyous point by the secure and satisfying gender roles in which the two ordinarily exist. These are suggestively revealed in Cleopatra's very next line to the messenger from Rome: "O, from Italy! / Ram thou thy fruitful tidings in mine ears, / That long time have been barren" (23–25). Both of these descriptions of gender role reversals are given their ironic point by the fact that they are not characteristic of the couple. This play seems different from the others, not because it overcomes gender dichotomies, but because it incorporates the greatest variety of gender relations, conflicts, assumptions, accommodations; because in it, Antony and Cleopatra have equal prominence, eloquence, complexity, and power, although the central conflicts and development are Antony's; and because it embodies the fullest mutual acceptance and self-realization of any of the plays. But this mutuality is neither complete nor symmetrical, and its price is death.

In the opening of the play, Cleopatra, like the heroines of

comedy, mocks her lover's romantic hyperbole and his heroic poses to educate him to a more honest expression of his own passion, a more realistic view of his heroic posture, a less stereotyped view of her, and a fuller sexual commitment. She plays "the fool she is not" so that Antony can become "himself" (I.1.42–43). Her first line, "If it be love indeed, tell me how much," jokingly calls into question, even as it provokes, Antony's romantic affirmation of a love that transcends all other claims on him: "let Rome in Tiber melt, and the wide arch / Of the ranged empire fall!" (I.i.33–34). She counters throughout his "excellent falsehood[s]" (I.i.40)—that his "Full heart / Remains in use" with her (I.iii.43–44), that he is her "soldier-servant, making peace or war / as thou affects" (I.iii.70–71), that their separation is not really one (103–05) —by harping on the fact of his marriage, the claims of Rome represented by its ambassadors, the callousness of his response to Fulvia's death. She mocks the empty posturing of the "Herculean Roman," as well as the hyperbole of the lover, refusing to let Antony swear by his aggressive "sword" without adding to it a gynocentric and defensive "target" (I. iii.82–85), and taunting him with his subservience to Caesar and Fulvia. She expresses her own desires bluntly:

> O happy horse to bear the weight of Antony!
>
> [I.v.21]

> My music playing far off, I will betray
> Tawny-finned fishes. My bended hook shall pierce
> Their slimy jaws; and as I draw them up,
> I'll think them every one an Antony,
> And say, "Ah, ha! y'are caught."
>
> [II.v.11–15]

Impatient with his rhetoric of sublimation, she imagines him expressing his desires for her: imagines him "murmuring, 'Where's my serpent of old Nile'" (I.v.25). When Cleopatra tries to articulate the magnitude of their love and its loss in unconventional terms, she fails; but she does intimate that both love and its loss involve reciprocity or fusion:

Sir, you and I must part, but that's not it:
Sir, you and I have loved, but there's not it:
That you know well. Something it is I would—
O, my oblivion is a very Antony,
And I am all forgotten.

[I.iii.87–91]

Forgotten by Antony, Cleopatra forgets simultaneously him, herself, and the means to express their love; but even with the past, present, and future of their love obliterated, unarticulated, Antony fills up the void.[8]

Antony's refusal to commit himself fully to the sexual aspect of the relationship is apparent in the Petrarchan idealization of his rhetoric, in his anger at Enobarbus's sexual innuendos, and in his fear of sexual entrapment and debilitation: "These strong Egyptian fetters I must break / Or lose myself in dotage" (I.ii.117–18). The contrast between Antony's attempt to conventionalize and idealize their relationship and Cleopatra's desire to enter into a concrete, sexual intimacy with him is summed up in their contrasting communications during their separation. Antony sends a formal, romantic message: " 'Say the firm Roman to great Egypt sends / This treasure of an oyster; at whose foot, / To mend the petty present, I will piece / Her opulent throne with kingdoms' " (I.v.42–46). Cleopatra seeks to penetrate the stilted rhetoric of the messenger to make contact with the actual varied Antony beneath it: "What was he, sad or merry? . . . Be'st thou sad or merry, / The violence of either thee becomes, / So does it no man else" (I.v.50, 59–61). The "sweating labor" (I.iii.93) in the relationship is all Cleopatra's, and Antony misunderstands its nature and its purpose. She has wrested from him a commitment to the concrete and variable self she is, to the "wrangling queen! / Whom everything becomes—to chide, to laugh, / To weep, whose every passion fully strives / To make itself in thee, fair and admired" (I.i.48–51). But her mockery does not lead to a comic reconciliation. At their parting, when her "becomings" fail to please, she ceases to mock his "excellent dissembling" and confirms his heroic self-image: "Upon your sword / Sit laurel victory" (I.iii.99–100), accepting the separation it imposes. But he must abandon the relationship entirely, seeking military glory and political power and a pragmatic marriage in Rome before he is ready to return to Egypt to enter a new union with Cleopatra.

Antony finds that Rome does not enable him to achieve his identity either; it offers no scope for his courage, his honor, his generosity. Personal heroism is no longer possible or useful; it is dead with Pompey's and Caesar's fathers. Battles are now won by shrewd calculation, by exploiting the enemy's weakness as at Actium, or by having him assassinated like Pompey. Displays of heroic endurance like Antony's at Modena are no longer called for. Hal, defeating Hotspur in personal combat, incorporates some of his rival's archaic glory. Caesar, who will refuse personal combat and defeat Antony through strategy, eliminates the need for and the possibility of such glory. Roman politics render honor likewise superfluous. In Rome, Antony is reduced to emulating the hypocrisy of Caesar, Lepidus, Menas, and the others. He weasels out of Caesar's accusations by blaming his lapses on the dead, defenseless Fulvia; he marries Octavia to consolidate his power; he and Caesar buy off Pompey rather than fight him and then have him liquidated. Male friendship no longer exists; it is merely simulated in the strained, drunken feast on Pompey's barge. Caesar has subordinates or rivals, not friends. As Antony's rich-hued, generous heroism emphasizes Caesar's colorlessness, Caesar's political power insures Antony's powerlessness; his "Noble, courageous, high, unmatchable" spirit is "o'erpow'red" by Caesar, as the soothsayer says (II.iii.18–21).

There is in the play no image of Rome or of empire that transcends the corruption of its current leaders. Rome is no longer an ideal inspiring loyalty as it was in *Julius Caesar*; its republican values, Pompey reminds us, have been lost. Nor is Rome embodied as a presence calling up devotion as England does in the English history plays, largely through the pervasive imagery of the bleeding land, which compels identification and sympathy. In Caesar's reference to "universal peace," even peace lacks the emotional charge that it has in both tetral-

ogies, in which the brutality of war and the exhaustion and depletion of the war-torn country are experienced. With no alliance he can contribute to and no ideal he can serve, Antony
eventually flees the Roman fetters of politics and marriage to
Octavia as he earlier fled "Egyptian fetters" (I.ii.117).[9]

The institution of marriage serves in the comedies to qualify romance, to incorporate sexuality, and to reconcile individual passion with the social order. In the tragedies, where it
provides an alternative to heroic self-assertion, sexual and political anxieties are exacerbated by it. In *Antony and Cleopatra*
marriage is stripped of its comic purpose as a ritual for reconciliation and rejuvenation and of its tragic status as a catalyst to
self-knowledge and self-destruction. The marriage of Antony
and Octavia, even more than those between Henry and Kate
and Richmond and Elizabeth at the conclusions of the two te-
tralogies, exaggerates the sociopolitical function of marriage to
secure male alliances and eliminates its sexual and emotional
purposes. The marriage is proposed by Caesar's subordinate,
presumably at his master's behest, to solidify the renewed alliance between Antony and Caesar. In Octavia's absence the
two men enact an Elizabethan betrothal ceremony; parodying
the customary form for spousals, they take hands, deny "impediment," and vow love and fidelity to each other: ". . . from
this hour / The heart of brothers govern in our loves / And
sway our great designs" . . . "Let her live / To join our kingdoms and our hearts; and never / Fly off our loves again"
(II.ii.147–54). This betrothal embodies the purpose of the marriage, which is, as Agrippa tells the two triumvers, "To hold
you in perpetual amity, / To make you brothers, and to knit
your hearts / With an unslipping knot" (II.ii.126–28). Because
this marriage is entirely subsumed under the political order, it
is hardly surprising that it fails to engender either personal or
political harmony.[10]

The marriage is made possible by Caesar's "power unto
Octavia" (II.ii.144) and by her perfect obedience to him, her
willessness and docility. But this docility engenders the self-
division that eventually exacerbates the men's rivalry. Octavia's inability to transfer her love and loyalty from Caesar to

Antony as marriage requires of her is emphasized at each of her appearances. The Folio stage direction for her first entrance in act 2, scene 3 encapsulates her dilemma: "Enter Antony, Caesar, Octavia between them." At her parting from Caesar, Octavia is paralyzed by her divided love as a "swansdown feather / That stands upon the swell at the full of tide, / And neither way inclines" (III.ii.49–51). At her third appearance Caesar and Antony have fallen out, and Octavia, finding "no midway / Twixt these extremes at all" (III.iv.19–20) in effect chooses brother over husband, returning to Rome to magnify Caesar's rage and catalyze Antony's return to Egypt.[11] Enobarbus's prediction proves exact: ". . . the band that seems to tie their friendship together will be the very strangler of their amity" (II.vi.120–22).

Just as the men victimize Octavia, so the play exploits her to ignite the men's rivalry, compel admiration for Cleopatra even at her worst, and justify Antony's return to Egypt. Each of Octavia's brief, timorous appearances is juxtaposed to a vignette of Cleopatra's self-assertive vitality. Octavia's first entrance is preceded by Enobarbus's hyperbolic portrait of Cleopatra. Octavia's tearful farewell to Caesar is followed by the scene in which Cleopatra extracts from the messenger a derogatory description of her rival. Octavia's parting from Antony is followed directly by Caesar's description of Cleopatra and Antony extravagantly ruling in Egypt. Although Octavia's "beauty, wisdom, and modesty" (II.ii.243) are praised, they are given meager representation. Her stereotypical wifely virtues are repeatedly reduced to lifelessness by their contrast with Cleopatra's "infinite variety" (II.ii.238).[12] Her marriage and the play demand that she become the messenger's caricature:

> She creeps:
> Her motion and her station are as one.
> She shows a body rather than a life,
> A statue than a breather.   [III.iii.21–24]

The lack of identity that makes possible Octavia's marriage also subverts it. Its political and personal bankruptcy serves to legitimize for the play's audience Antony's return to a union with Cleopatra that exists outside of the institutions of marriage, the family, and the state.[13]

But the reestablished union seeks to appropriate these dimensions, as is first evident in Caesar's enraged tableau:

> Contemning Rome, he has done all this and more . . .
> I' th' marketplace on a tribunal silvered,
> Cleopatra and himself on chairs of gold
> Were publicly enthroned; at the feet sat
> Caesarion, whom they call my father's son,
> And all the unlawful issue that their lust
> Since then hath made between them. Unto her
> He gave the stablishment of Egypt; made her
> Of lower Syria, Cyprus, Lydia,
> Absolute queen.   [III.vi.1–11]

No longer fixed in the comic roles of romantic soldier-servant and worshiped beloved (as Antony imagined) or of mocking heroine and exasperated hero (as Cleopatra contrived), Antony and Cleopatra now play more mutual roles. Loving and fighting together, their union is political, erotic, dynastic. Antony delegates power to Cleopatra, and she rules, gives audience, and fights (not well). She, in turn, now that Antony is fighting on her side, wholeheartedly supports his political and military goals instead of mocking them.[14] The issues of their desire are legitimized as kings and heirs. As Plutarch describes: "They have made an order betwene them which they called Amimetobion (as much as to say, no life comparable and matcheable with it)" (Bullough 5:275), an order that unites power and desire.

As Caesar's unintended tribute suggests, this union defies temporarily the antithesis of love and heroism which is common to all the plays in this study. Philo opens *Antony and Cleopatra* by introducing the terms of the conventional dichotomy: Antony's eyes, which once "glowed like plated Mars, now bend, now turn / The office and devotion of their view / Upon a tawny front.   His captain's heart, / Which in the scuffles of great fights hath burst / The buckles on his breast, reneges all temper / And is become the bellows and the fan / To cool a gypsy's lust" (I.i.4–10). The oppositions of hard/soft, rigid/tempered, glowing/bending express, in terms familiar from earlier plays, the mutually exclusive claims and effects of war and love. Masculine energy is imagined as single-minded and limited, so that redirection of it into sexual passion inevitably diminishes heroic activity. Claudio waits until the "rougher tasks" of war are done before making room for "soft and delicate desires" (*Ado*, I.i.292–96); Parolles warns Bertram against spending "manly marrow in her arms, / Which should sustain the bound and high curvet / Of Mars's fiery steed" (*AWW*, II.iii.284–86); Romeo claims of Juliet, "Thy beauty hath made me effeminate / And in my temper soft'ned valor's steel" (*Rom*,III.i.116–17); Othello promises that "light-wing'd toys, / And feathered Cupid" will not "foil with wanton dullness / My speculative and active instruments" (I.iii.268–70); and Enobarbus argues that union with Cleopatra must deplete Antony: "Take from his heart, take from his brain, from's time, / What should not then be spared" (III.vii.11–12). Coriolanus—"thing of blood" (II.ii.109)—will be the fullest embodiment of the heroic drive toward absolute autonomy and perfect invulnerability.

But at the midpoint of *Antony and Cleopatra* these antitheses merge. Passion becomes for Antony a source of heroism, and heroism becomes for Cleopatra a source of passion. As love is merged with and expressed through war, heroic activity becomes personal, erotic, de-Romanized (but not, I think, feminized). No longer a matter of abstinence and self-control as in Rome's past, nor of impersonal strategy as for Caesar, it is, instead, a passionate ritual of self-realization and communal rejuvenation. Because Caesar "dares us to 't," Antony determines to fight at sea, forgoing "assurance" and "knowledge" and giving himself up to "chance" and "hazard" (III.vii.29, 45–47). He challenges Caesar, with moving futility, to single combat. He goes into battle from Cleopatra's bed, armed by her, and eager to "make death love me" (III.xiii.194). Returning from battle, he celebrates his victory with his boldest declaration of passion in the play, radically transforming the heart imagery, which has earlier been used by Philo to mock Antony's decline and by Antony to keep desire at bay, into a fantasy of erotic vigor and emotional openness:

> Leap thou, attire and all,
> Through proof of harness to my heart, and there
> Ride on the pants triumphing.   [IV.viii.14–16][15]

His men, emulating him, have likewise fought heroically, embracing his cause as their own; they are urged to return, like him, to intimate reunions that validate their heroism, celebrate their courage, and acknowledge their vulnerability and dependence on family and community:

> Enter the city, clip your wives, your friends,
> Tell them your feats, whilst they with joyful tears
> Wash the congealment from your wounds, and kiss
> The honored gashes whole.   [IV.viii.8–11]

Intimacy here generates and restores heroism instead of depleting it.

But this union of heroic activity and love poses threats to both. Calling out new strengths in the protagonists, it also makes them vulnerable in new ways. The reckless courage that enables Antony to win the second battle causes his loss at Actium. His deepening dependence on Cleopatra allows him to brush off this dishonor and go on to win a victory, but it makes him fearful of his powerlessness and of her infidelity. Although Cleopatra has gained political power and Antony's sexual commitment, she is forced into an increasingly submissive posture by Antony's degradation of her. In the series of scenes from Actium through Antony's death, love and heroic activity renew and destroy each other as they begin to do in the problem plays, in which Bertram, Troilus, and Othello are sometimes energized but more often depleted by their relations to women. But unlike those other protagonists, Antony endures military defeat as well as emotional loss; his love is threatened not only from within but from without by the constraining context of Caesar's power.

After his retreat at Actium, Antony first takes responsibility for his own loss: "I have fled myself, and have instructed cowards / To run and show their shoulders" (III.xi.7–8), but at Cleopatra's entrance he transfers the blame: "O whither hast thou led me, Egypt? See / How I convey my shame out of thine eyes / By looking back what I have left behind / 'Stroyed in dishonor" (III.xi.51–54), "conveying" his shame to her. He claims that she is to blame for his flight as well as her own, excusing his actions by a declaration of romantic dependence: "Egypt, thou knew'st too well / My heart was to thy rudder tied by th' strings, / And thou should'st tow me after" (III.xi.56–58). Cleopatra's (unjustified) acceptance of full responsibility,[16] her request for pardon, and the tears that confirm her fault are necessary to erase Antony's loss and shame. By giving over to Cleopatra the maintenance of his honor and identity, Antony decreases his vulnerability to military defeat but increases his dependence on her sexual fidelity. He also initiates a pattern of male attack and female submission, a pattern familiar from the other tragedies, in which the tragic male protagonists, to assuage the sense of powerlessness they derive from their dependence on women,[17] insist that these women accept blame and subordination. The pattern is repeated twice more in *Antony and Cleopatra*.

Antony's new vulnerability is apparent when, in the messenger scene, he is more enraged and humiliated by Caesar's imagined indirect sexual triumph than he was by his actual military one. Viewing Caesar as a sexual rival—"To the boy Caesar send this grizzled head, / And he will fill thy wishes to the brim / With principalities" (III.xiii.17–19)—Antony believes Enobarbus's dubious reading of Cleopatra's rhetoric as seductive and compliant. Belatedly longing for the legitimacy of marriage and the family, Antony assumes this legitimacy in a curious way by imagining that he (ironically, the adulterer) is a cuckold like other husbands: "O, that I were / Upon the hill of Basan to outroar / The hornèd herd!" (III.xiii.126–28). Whereas after Actium Cleopatra had to absorb and transform Antony's shame, now she must deflect his attack on her promiscuity, his degradation of her as a "morsel," a "fragment," a "boggler" (III.xiii.116, 117, 110). Finding that Antony does not

yet "know" her, Cleopatra caricatures his
heartedness in order to counter it. In her
fertile sexuality with which she has been i
into a poisonous hail which "dissolve[s]
her first son, her other children, her "
(III.xiii.164), until they, "By the discand
storm, / Lie graveless, till the flies and gnats of Nile / Have
buried them for prey!" (III.xiii.165–67). By magnifying the effects of Antony's failure to credit her love and to attain the
knowledge on which her generative erotic power depends,
and by providing images of the effects of the deprivation of it,
she proves her love and "satisfies" and revitalizes Antony. "I
will be treble-sinewed, hearted, breathed" (III.xiii.178), he
vouches, and is triumphant in the next day's battle. Cleopatra
absorbed Antony's military loss by taking responsibility for it.
She now counters his imagined sexual loss by fantasizing her
own destruction through her failure to love. In the third battle,
Cleopatra's defection is imagined as both political and sexual;
afterward she can only prove her love by pretending to acqui-
esce in Antony's demand for her death.

In this battle Antony assumes that the Egyptian fleet, tied
to her as he was earlier, has made peace with Caesar at her behest and that she is a, "triple- turned whore" (IV.xii.13) whose
promiscuous sexuality is inseparable from political treachery.
His double defeat is experienced as a loss of authority, honor,
and manhood, and as a loss of the followers who guarantee
these attributes but whose defection castrates Antony to en-
large Caesar: now they "do discandy, melt their sweets / On
blossoming Caesar; and this pine is barked, / That overtopped
them all" (IV.xii.22–24). Cleopatra's apparent defection engenders in Antony an emptiness more profound than the "oblivion" his departure had created in her: she "Whose bosom
was my crownet, my chief end, / Like a right gypsy hath at
fast and loose / Beguiled me to the very heart of loss"
(IV.xii.27–29). This loss of love, of heroism, of identity can be
compensated only by the death of Cleopatra: "The witch shall
die" (IV.xii.47). Cleopatra responds with a mock death (suggested first by Charmian) which, like her other performances

like the mock deaths of Hero, Helen, and Hermione, is carefully staged to prove her love and to test and transform Antony's. Her mock death, like her real one later, is both active and defensive, both for her own sake and for his: "Mardian, go tell him I have slain myself: / Say that the last I spoke was 'Antony' / And word it, prithee, piteously. Hence, Mardian, / And bring me how he takes my death" (IV.xiii.7–10).

He takes it magnanimously, accepting it as confirmation of her love and courage, and hence of the validity of his love. Like Claudio, Bertram, Othello, and Leontes, Antony's intimacy with Cleopatra is restored, although, unlike the other men, he has received no proof of her fidelity. His desire to kill her is transformed into a desire to kill himself. His love for and dependence on her are acknowledged when he affirms his heart stronger through vulnerability to love than when apparently protected by soldier's armor:

Off, pluck off:
The sevenfold shield of Ajax cannot keep
The battery from my heart. O, cleave, my sides!
Heart, once be stronger than thy continent,
Crack thy frail case!   [IV.xiv.37–41]

He prepares to die not as a defeated soldier but as a desirous lover, affirming not Cleopatra's idealized perfection but the regenerative sexual aspects of their union, imagined now as a marriage in death: "I will be / A bridegroom in my death, and run into 't / As to a lover's bed" (IV.xiv.99–101)—"With a wound I must be cured" (78). His subsequent suicide, however inept and incomplete, ratifies their love and prepares him to accept without anger or recrimination one more betrayal, her last gigantic mockery of his final grand gesture—the message that she is alive.

Antony is unlike the other tragic heroes, not because he takes on a more feminine role than they do, but because he can accept more fully Cleopatra's sexuality, duplicity, and difference from him and find them compatible with his manhood. Cleopatra is unlike most of the women in tragedy in that she, like the women in comedy and romance, fights to save both her love and her life. Her suicide is accomplished on her own terms and in her own good time. The full function and meaning of the deaths of Antony and Cleopatra can be explicated only by looking at both halves of the two-part death scenes of each: her mock and real deaths, his suicide attempt and death in Cleopatra's arms.

First, their deaths can be illuminated by their contrasts and similarities to that of Enobarbus, whose ambivalence in both life and death highlights their conflicts and their resolution of them. Enobarbus's death aptly concludes the life of this divided figure with mixed roots in comedy and tragedy. On the one hand, his role is that of the hero's friend in comedy, who, whether he is a misogynist like Benedick and Parolles or a lover of the hero like the two Antonios, is in rivalry with and must be subordinated to the marriage bond. On the other hand, Enobarbus's role is that of the friends who, in the tragedies, represent the narrow values of assertive manhood, which the hero partly transcends for a wider commitment to love and honor and partly remains bound to. Such characters either contribute to the rupture of the heterosexual bond (inadvertently, as in Mercutio's case, or maliciously, as in Iago's) or else outlast it (as when Horatio lives to tell Hamlet's story). In *Antony and Cleopatra*, Enobarbus is at first the witty, detached misogynist, most familiar from comedy, who degrades Cleopatra and mocks Antony's attachment to her. But even his mockery hints at Cleopatra's compelling power, and in Rome, Enobarbus idealizes her and turns his cynicism against Roman pretensions to honor and the practice of realpolitik. After his return to Egypt, Enobarbus first leaves Antony, protesting his loss of Roman virtues, then dies affirming his love for Antony, his master's nobility, and Cleopatra's power. His movement from the detached misogynist of comedy to the loyal friend of tragedy parallels Antony's deepening commitment to Cleopatra. But his ambivalent and ambiguous suicide—on behalf of the Roman Antony who exists no longer—contrasts with Antony's more single-minded death.

Enobarbus's ambivalence toward Cleopatra is dramatized in his first appearance. We hear him order a feast with "wine enough / Cleopatra's health to drink" (I.ii.13) and then mock her when alone with Antony. His mockery, however, is double-edged. His sarcasm manages to suggest the splendor of her self-dramatizing passions: "We cannot call her winds and waters sighs and tears; they are greater storms and tempests than almanacs can report" (I.ii.148–50). His bawdy innuendo about her "celerity in dying" (145) describes her courage as well as her lasciviousness. She is, his banter implies, a "wonderful piece of work" (155) in more than the sexual sense; she is never merely degraded, as is Fulvia, whom he smuttily reduces to a "cut," a "case to be lamented," an "old smock" (I.ii.168–69).

This scene has a function similar to that of early scenes in other plays in which the hero's friend—Parolles, Iago, Polixenes—engages the woman who is or who will become his rival—Helen, Desdemona, Hermione—in misogynist sexual banter. The friend degrades female sexuality while acknowledging its power; the scenes assert the woman's healthy desires and acquit her of the friend's misogynist imputations, but these will infect the hero and hurt her. Parolles, in the dialogue on virginity, reveals his anxiety about women's capacity to "blow up" and "blow down" men (I.i.127); when Helen has taken his advice and married Bertram, he urges his friend's flight, aids his infidelity, and woos Diana for himself. Iago's banter with Desdemona more sinisterly reduces all the virtues of good women to counters for trivial sexual use and procreation—"To suckle fools, and chronicle small beer" (II.i.160). The scene foreshadows Iago's compulsion to turn Desdemona's "virtues into pitch" (II.iii.351), and Othello will come to accept these commonplaces as truth, degrading Desdemona as adulterer and "procreant" (IV.ii.28). In his dialogue with Hermione, Polixenes is charmingly guileless but no less explicit about the threat posed by female sexuality. He claims that Hermione and his wife are responsible for his and his friend's sexual falls: "Temptations have since then been born to's" (I.ii.77). Polixenes and Hermione, like Desdemona and Cassio, will be falsely accused of the infidelity that Parolles seeks to contrive with Diana and that the fair friend of the sonnets engages in with the dark lady. Although Enobarbus's dia-

logue is with the friend, not the woman,[18] the woman's vexed
relation to male bonds is implied. Male bonds are confirmed
through degradation of women, but they are infected by rivalry over the possession of women which ruptures all the relations in the triangle. These early scenes foreshadow disruptions of heterosexual bonds by male friendship, as well as the
eventual accommodation of male bonds to heterosexual union
that takes place in all of the plays discussed.

Just as Antony's and Cleopatra's separation is foreshadowed in Enobarbus's jokes about Cleopatra in Egypt, so their
reunion is predicted in his extravagant praise of her in Rome.
There, in Cleopatra's absence, Enobarbus can idealize her
—for himself, for Antony, for his audience, for the play—
while indirectly acknowledging her sexual power. His set piece
defends Antony by impressing his Roman audience and protecting Cleopatra from their degrading alehouse innuendos
and by sublimating his desire. In the crucial central image of
the encomium, Cleopatra is described by indirection; she is a
static, indescribable artwork: "For her own person / It beg-
gered all description she did lie / In her pavilion, cloth-of-gold
of tissue, / O'er picturing that Venus where we see / The fancy
outwork nature" (II.ii.199–203). Her eroticism and the desire
it arouses are first displaced onto her fluid, rhythmic, mutually responsive surroundings: "Purple the sails, and so per-
fumèd that / The winds were lovesick with them; the oars
were silver / . . . and made / The water which they beat to
follow faster, / As amorous of their strokes. . . . The silken
tackle / Swell with the touches of those flower-soft hands, /
That yarely frame the office" (II.ii.195–99, 211–13). These surroundings radiate and invite desire but are kept separate from
Cleopatra and Antony. The power of her sexuality is also implied—abstractly—by the "gap in nature" (220) that her presence creates and by her capacity to "make defect perfection"
(233); it is expressed more concretely when Enobarbus counters Agrippa's cheerfully reductive bawdy, "He ploughed her,
and she cropped" (230), with a description that is energetically
physical, but not yet specifically sexual: "I saw her once /
Hop forty paces through the public street; / And having lost

her breath, she spoke and panted" (230–32). Both this anecdote and that of Antony going to meet her, "barbered ten times o'er" (226), comically distance her seductiveness. When Enobarbus finally affirms Cleopatra's compelling sexual power more directly, he still renders it as unthreatening as possible:

Age cannot wither her, nor custom stale
Her infinite variety: other women cloy
The appetites they feed, but she makes hungry
Where most she satisfies; for vilest things
Become themselves in her, that the holy priests
Bless her when she is riggish.   [II.ii.237–42]

Her mutability is translated into the "infinite variety" that guarantees perpetual pleasure; the connection of her sexuality with corruption, transience, and mortality is denied by this infiniteness and by the priests who sanction her wantonness.

But whereas, in Rome, Enobarbus mocked Roman strategy and defended Cleopatra, when back in Egypt, he supports the Roman values of reason and honor that generate opposition to Cleopatra and to Antony. In the second movement of the play, Cleopatra's opening challenge to Enobarbus, "I will be even with thee, doubt it not" (III.vii.1), signals their new relationship to each other and to Antony and prophesies her eventual victory, which Enobarbus fights to avert. He tries to sever the union by urging her to give up her part in the wars, by attempting to prove her politically unfaithful, and by exposing Antony's weaknesses to her. When his strategies fail and the union persists, Enobarbus's ambivalence is transferred from Cleopatra to Antony. Witnessing what seems to him the disintegration of the heroic Antony he loves, Enobarbus experiences a parallel division between love and reason: "my reason / Sits in the wind against me" (III.x.35–36)—"Mine honesty and I begin to square" (III.xiii.41). He rejects his master's claim of rejuvenated commitment to love and war on the eve of his triumphant battle. Instead, he views Antony's love as a self-destructive depletion of reason: "I see still / A diminuation in our captain's brain / Restores his heart. When valor preys on reason / It eats the sword it fights with" (III.xiii.197–200).

He deserts to escape the self-division he finds in Antony and cannot endure in himself.

The parallels between the two men are, however, intensified when Enobarbus, like Antony before him, flees the Egyptian side for the Roman; his self-division increases and is embodied in his death. When Antony, by forgiving Enobarbus and sending his treasure after him, demonstrates his undiminished magnanimity and the union in him of heroism and love, Enobarbus, like Antony, abandons the security of reason for the fragility of the heart's affection. But whereas Antony, at his death, is reinvigorated by his love for Cleopatra, Enobarbus's heart, dry and brittle from his denial of love, shatters: "Throw my heart / Against the flint and hardness of my fault, / Which, being dried with grief, will break to powder, / And finish all foul thoughts" (IV.ix.15–18). The painfully thwarted and self-directed violence of Enobarbus's death reflects his trammeled, self-destructive passion. He can resolve his ambivalence toward Antony only by his suicide, debasing himself to ennoble his flawed master, like the poet of the sonnets, "Myself corrupting, salving thy amiss" (35). By becoming "the villain of the earth," Enobarbus affirms that Antony is a "mine of bounty" (IV.vi.30, 32); Enobarbus's epithet, "master-leaver" (IV.ix.22), demonstrates the incomparable generosity of the master who forgives his defection.

The circumstances of the death likewise express Enobarbus's continuing ambivalence toward Cleopatra and his acknowledgment of her power. His invocation to Cleopatra's planet, the moon—"O sovereign mistress of true melancholy, / The poisonous damp of night disponge upon me" (IV.ix.12–13)—recalls the "discandying" of the poisonous hail in Cleopatra's fantasy. The "ditch" in which he dies—"the foul'st best fits / My latter part of life" (IV.vi.38–39)—embodies and punishes his shame and has associations with that "ditch in Egypt" that Cleopatra will defiantly choose as a "gentle grave" (V.ii.57–58). The ditch and his wish to be inundated by the moon's "damp" hint that Enobarbus's death is experienced not just as self-abasement before Antony's nobility, but as an ironic and inadvertent capitulation to the "abode" of fe-

male sexuality which he had hitherto mocked. The suicide itself is surrounded with ambiguity. Enobarbus does not explicitly kill himself but expires so mysteriously that the only
observers, the indifferent watch, do not know if he has fallen
asleep, swooned, or died, and do not acknowledge his death
as final: "he may recover yet" (IV.ix.33).

As the limitations of Antony's marriage to Octavia emphasize the fullness of his union with Cleopatra, so the self-abasement and self-division of Enobarbus's suicide heighten the
self-affirming unity of Antony's death.[19] Like the separation
of friends in the comedies, Enobarbus's death represents the
freeing of the heterosexual union from one kind of competing
bond. Antonio becomes a "surety" to the marriage of Portia
and Bassanio. Benedick challenges Claudio on Beatrice's behalf. Parolles joins Helen and Diana in exposing Bertram. In
Antony and Cleopatra the actual departure of Enobarbus and the
symbolic one of Hercules (IV.iii.15) represent the purging of
Antony's excessively rational and excessively heroic aspects.
As Cleopatra and Eros (significantly, the replacement for Enobarbus) lovingly arm Antony for battle, he takes on a fuller
identity without discarding the virtues of the old. The deaths
of rational Roman Enobarbus and passionate Egyptian Cleopatra are, taken together, an affirmation of the potential of this
larger self. The first part of Antony's death scene echoes
Enobarbus's divided, self-defeated death. As Antony prepares
to die, he enacts the sense of disintegration and paralysis—"all
labor / Mars what it does; yea, very force entangles / Itself
with strength" (IV.xiv.47–49)—engendered by Cleopatra's
apparent death. In his reunion with Cleopatra he anticipates
her triumphant suicide.

Reunited with Cleopatra, Antony completes his death in
another key, and "the play begins to live up to itself."[20] He
submits himself to the full range of Cleopatra's "becomings"
and achieves his own heroic identity.[21] By dying for Cleopatra
and ignoring her deceit, he makes restitution for his former
fantasy of her betrayal. Unlike Romeo, Hamlet, and Othello,
who idealize dead beloveds, Antony acknowledges Cleopatra's sexual power, her love and selfishness, her fidelity and

infidelity, while she is still alive. By urging her to stay alive, even at the price of her fidelity to him, he confirms his magnanimity. He happily allows her to turn his tragic death into farcical comedy. She is cowardly, refusing to leave the monument; domineering, as she tries to steal the scene from him—"No, let me speak and let me rail so high" (IV.xv.42); wistfully selfish—"Noblest of men, woo't die? / Hast thou no care of me?" (59–60). As the helpless Antony is, like those "Tawney-finned fishes," slowly and laboriously (somehow) "drawn up"[22] into the enclosed space of Cleopatra's monument, his longed-for sexual weight now dead weight, the scene becomes a comic and visually suggestive enactment of Antony's ennobling submission to Cleopatra's seductive power and a staged antidote to the "fall" of his botched suicide.

Relinquishing himself to this Egyptian enfettering, Antony dies the heroic death he has sought, "a Roman by a Roman, valiantly vanquished" (IV.xv.57–58), but with his Roman manhood achieved through Cleopatra and pledged to her. At his death he recalls his heroic past, not to restore his public honor or to cheer himself up, but for Cleopatra's sake: "please your thoughts / In feeding them with those my former fortunes" (52–53). Her suggestive epitaph, correspondingly, joins the sexual and military aspects of this manhood. She laments the loss of his heroism and of erotic mutuality, seeing his death as the climax and end of female desire and male power: "The crown o' th' earth doth melt. My lord! / O, withered is the garland of the war, / The soldier's pole is fall'n; / young boys and girls / Are level now with men" (IV.xv.63–66).

In the last act Cleopatra must, as Antony did earlier, define her relation to Rome and Caesar; she must test her fidelity to Antony, achieve her own identity apart from her response to him, recreate his identity, and then die a death complementing his and transforming its comical tragedy into tragic comedy.[23] Cleopatra's dealings with Caesar show her newly submissive in a more narrowly stereotypical gender role than heretofore. In place of her usually unabashed affirmation of her own gender, she admits, playing up to Caesar's misogyny, to "like frailties which before / Have often shamed our sex" (V.ii.123–24). She begs a kingdom from him as she never did from Antony. Her calculatedly false acquiescence to Caesar's unctuous hypocrisy reveals, in retrospect, the emotional honesty and self-realization that informed the roles she played for and with Antony. With him, Cleopatra could become herself, but with Caesar she can only play false. Acting for Caesar, in the absence of Antony, Cleopatra becomes more elusive than formerly. (Similarly, Antony's motives are most opaque when he is apart from Cleopatra.) We cannot be sure whether she genuinely seeks the "briefest end" (IV.xv.99), as she claims at the end of act 4, or whether she stalls to bargain for acceptable terms. We cannot tell whether her suicide attempt as the monument is seized is faked or authentic. We are not allowed to know whether Seleucus betrays her in the matter of the treasure, whether they conspire, whether he is an accident who furthers or ruins her game.[24] Although Cleopatra can "word" Caesar (V.ii.191) as well as he "words" her, in doing so she must play a role as narrow, fixed, and deceitful as his; her "sweet dependency" is as false as his "bounty" (V.ii.26, 43). Each assumes a role to deceive rather than to change the other; and each recognizes the other's deceit; he wishes to keep her alive for display in his triumph; she, to evade it.

The image of this triumph dominates the end of the play. It reveals the limits of the power of all three protagonists, but especially the limits of Caesar's. Although he has won a military victory, his urgent need to display Antony and Cleopatra in Rome reveals the hollowness and vulnerability of his domination of the world. The threats to his order represented by Antony's personal heroism and Cleopatra's passionate sexuality remain unconquered by the military defeat. The triumph will enable Caesar to humiliate Antony, to appropriate his rival's valor for himself, and to degrade Cleopatra, vulgarizing and hence controlling her.[25] As they imagine their parts, they imagine Caesar taking from both that which is most their own. Antony pictures his humiliation as a suppression of his physical valor and autonomy designed to transfer vital energy to his political rival; he pictures himself "with pleached arms, bending down / His corrigible neck, his face subdued / To penetrative shame, whilst the wheeled seat / Of fortunate Caesar, drawn before him, branded / His baseness that ensued" (IV.xiv.73–77). Cleopatra's role in the triumph is pictured differently from Antony's. Instead of being subdued, she will be caricatured; instead of "bending down," she will be "hoisted up" to sexual display. (Antony's threatening reference to the event and two of Cleopatra's defiant statements make use of this metaphor: IV.xii.34; V.ii.55; V.ii.211.) She will be exhibited as a degraded sex object, "brooch[ing]" (IV.xv.25) the triumph with her whoredom, "chastized" (V.ii.54) by *her* vindicated rival, Octavia, and mocked by the vulgar mob, "the shouting varletry / Of censuring Rome" (V.ii.56–57). She understands, too, that her degradation will be eternal, reiterated in endlessly reductive reenactments: "Antony / Shall be brought drunken forth, and I shall see / Some squeaking Cleopatra boy my greatness / I' the posture of a whore" (V.ii.218–21). To escape Caesar's appropriation of his heroism, Antony chooses a suicide that affirms and protects it. To escape the debasement of her sexuality, Cleopatra would choose the most abhorrent bodily degeneration: "Rather on Nilus' mud / Lay me stark naked and let the waterflies / Blow me into abhorring" (V.ii.58–60). Instead, she counters Caesar's planned degradation with alternate stagings of herself and her love.

First, Cleopatra's dream of Antony rescues him from defeat. It enlarges and reconciles his sexuality and heroism, satisfies her desire for him, and makes him worthy to die for. (More practically, it moves Dolabella to reveal Caesar's plans to her.) Like Enobarbus's vision of her, which it parallels and complements, the dream defends Antony to a disbelieving Roman audience by sublimating his sexuality and mythologizing him as a heroic ideal. Instead of being "subdued," bent, and penetrated as he would have been in Caesar's triumph, Antony is massive, upright, and in control: "His legs bestrid the ocean: his reared arm / Crested the world: his voice was propertied / As all the tunèd spheres, and that to friends; / But when he meant to quail and shake the orb, / He was as rattling thunder" (V.ii.82–86). In the protected space of the dream, Antony's conflicts become rich paradoxes; his vacillation, the embracing of positive extremes; and his disintegration, comic fluidity: "His delights / Were dolphinlike, they showed his back above / The element they lived in" (V.ii.88–90). Roman heroism, purged of its associations with calculation, rigidity, and greed, becomes one with personal generosity and sexual largesse: "For his bounty, / There was no winter in't: an autumn 'twas / That grew the more by reaping. . . . In his livery / Walked crowns and crownets: realms and islands were / As plates dropped from his pocket" (86–88, 90–92). Cleopatra's desire-suffused dream of a perpetually satisfying Antony completes Enobarbus's vision of a Cleopatra who "makes hungry where most she satisfies" (II.ii.239–40). In the two visions, female and male sexuality are seen as reciprocal opposites: infinite variety and eternal bounty, magnetic power and hyperbolic fruitfulness, stasis and motion, art and nature. In Enobarbus's idealized picture of Cleopatra, "fancy out-work[s] nature" (II.ii.203); in Cleopatra's desire-suffused dream, Antony is, she claims, "Nature's piece 'gainst fancy" (V.ii.98).

As Cleopatra's dream completes Enobarbus's vision of her, her death complements and completes Antony's. Like his, it is partly a mockery, partly an expansion, partly a transformation of the roles she has played all along. Antony's flawed suicide is redeemed by his generosity to Cleopatra, and her vacillation is redeemed when she grows "marble-constant" (V.ii.240). Both look forward to reunion. Antony imagines a gentle literary idyll "where souls do couch on flowers" (IV.xiv.51) and a marital consummation: "I will be / A bridegroom in my death, and run into't / As to a lover's bed" (IV.xiv.99–101); "I come my queen" (IV.xiv.50). Cleopatra likewise views death as a "lover's pinch, / Which hurts and is desired" (V.ii. 295–96). Characteristically, she also imagines its concrete human details, creating Antony's response to her—"Methinks I hear Antony call: I see him rouse himself / To praise my noble act"—and acting in response to him—"Husband, I come: / Now to that name my courage prove my title!" (V.ii.283–85, 287–89). Antony turned his phallic sword comically against himself. Cleopatra, "the serpent of old Nile," makes herself a morsel for asps, embodying the poisonous as well as the renewing aspects of her sexuality. At her death she assumes a variety of female roles: she is queen and goddess but also "no more but e'en a woman" (IV.xv.76), identified with the ordinary and archetypal woman of the clown's commentary—"a very honest woman, but something given to lie as a woman should not do but in the way of honesty" (V.ii.252–54). She is longing mistress, eager wife, satisfied mother: "Dost thou not see my baby at my breast, / That sucks the nurse asleep" (309–10). Her "Immortal longings" (281) are not only hopes for immortality but perpetual female desires. The scene, with its fluid images, its panting rhythms, and its identification of Antony with the asp, embodies the pun on *die* which has pervaded the language of the play.[26] The painful, pleasurable tension of the scene builds through imagery of melting and disintegrating—"Dissolve, thick cloud . . . O, break! O, break!" to the ecstatic release of Cleopatra's mid-sentence death: "As sweet as balm, as soft as air, as gentle— / O Antony! Nay, I will take thee too: What, should I stay—." The asp is lover and child, phallic and gynocentric, death-bringing and immortality-conferring: "with thy sharp teeth this knot intrinsicate / Of life at once untie" (V.ii.299–313). Fulfilling the asps' desires, Cleopatra, in one last achievement of perfect mutuality, fulfills her own.

In *Romeo and Juliet* the love death is painfully poignant, and in *Othello* it is perversely terrible; here it is profoundly satisfying.[27] In *Othello*, Desdemona was desexualized at the last; here Cleopatra is allowed the fullest expression of her sexuality in the play. The elegant staging and ecstatic eroticism of the scene detach death from its connections with decay, corruption, pain, and lifelessness; the affirmation of future union mitigates its finality. Sexuality mystifies death, and death renders female sexuality benign. Its frank expression can be accommodated by the play and its audience because female sexuality here is tender, not violent; because it is autoerotic, expressed in the absence of men; because it is associated with conventional female roles; and because Cleopatra is dying of it, in it, for it. Even Caesar, after her death, can acknowledge not only her courage—"Bravest at the last, / She leveled at our purposes, and being royal, / Took her own way" (V.ii.334–36)—but also her seductiveness—"She looks like sleep, / As she would catch another Antony / In her strong toil of grace" (345–47). He can do so because he is safe now—she has not caught him. But neither does he catch her. His attempt to diminish and exploit Antony's and Cleopatra's deaths is not entirely successful. While his victory elicits the resignation to order characteristic of the history plays, this dimension does not eradicate the sense of joyous fulfillment characteristic of comedy or the experience of irretrievable loss characteristic of tragedy.

The complex gender relations played out by Antony and Cleopatra lead to an ending that blends the dynamics of comedy, history, tragedy, and romance. Cleopatra, like the heroines of comedy, dominates the play to its end. Like them, she has, by her love and flexibility, transformed the hero and made possible their union. Like Portia, she loosens the bonds of friendship, tempers romanticism, and counters her lover's "betrayal"; like Viola, she would die for her lover "most jocund, apt, and willingly" (*TN*, V.i.131); like Helen, she transforms sexual degradation into sexual fulfillment. She must also, like earlier heroines, effect some submission of her power and control to the prevailing patriarchal order. Just as Kate vows subordination, Titania discards the changeling child and her fantasies to achieve amity with Oberon on his terms, Hero and Helen undergo mock death, and Helen and Mariana the erotic humiliation of the bedtrick, so Cleopatra must endure Antony's vilification of her, endorse Antony's values, negotiate with Caesar on his terms, and die. But, like the other heroines, she engineers this submission to her own benefit, bringing Antony to participate with her in a loving union and in a love death that symbolizes joyous marital consummation.

Consummation, however, occurs only in death, and the play is not a comedy. Cleopatra is not, like the comedy heroines, a chaste maid whose sexuality is only potential; her sexualilty is fully expressed, its threat fully acknowledged. Nor is

Antony a boyish, pliant comic hero, but a mature warrior whose confrontations with passion and defeat are disintegrating. In Shakespearean comedy the concluding marriages are emblems of the reconciliation of the individual with the social order, of sexuality with love, family, and procreation. In contrast, Antony's and Cleopatra's symbolic marriage is a liberation of sexuality from family, society, and history, a consummation in death, not a movement into the world's future; "it is the conclusion and apotheosis of a union, not its beginning."[28] Because it is divorced from the family, sexuality can be more fully admitted into the play and can withstand more extravagant degradation than in the comedies.

Antony's and Cleopatra's love is anomalous; it does not regenerate Rome. Egypt and the values it represents must be conquered, exorcised, appropriated. As in the other history plays, political order is secured by the elimination of rebellious individualism. The self-indulgently weak Richard II is deposed; the flamboyantly villainous Richard III is killed. In *Henry IV* the rebels are defeated, and Falstaff, whose joyous contempt for morality and politics anticipates Cleopatra's, is banished. In this play Caesar not only eliminates the lovers; he attempts to demythologize them. He drains Cleopatra's death of its symbolic splendor by his literal-minded search for its physiological explanation. He sharply constricts the huge space that Antony claimed for his love and that Cleopatra so lavishly ceded to her lover in her dream: "No grave upon the earth shall clip in it / A pair so famous" (V.ii.358–59). He exploits them, although not in the way he had first hoped, to confirm his success by their pathos: "their story is / No less in pity, than his glory which / Brought them to be lamented" (360–62).

In the history plays such exclusions are made tolerable by the positive values of the new dispensations they make way for. The new orders at the end of the histories establish peace, promise future prosperity, justice, good rule, the end of tyranny. They are solidified by dynastic marriage, which, it is hinted, will bring individual happiness as well as political harmony and the continuity of heirs:

O now let Richmond and Elizabeth,
The true succeeders of each royal house,
By God's fair ordinance conjoin together!
And let their heirs, God, if thy will be so,
Enrich the time to come with smooth-faced peace,
With smiling plenty and fair prosperous days!
                                        [*R3*,V.v.29–34]

Take her, fair son, and from her blood raise up
Issue to me, that the contending kingdoms
Of France and England, whose very shores look pale
With envy of each other's happiness,
May cease their hatred, and this dear conjunction
Plant neighborhood and Christian-like accord
In their sweet bosoms.   [*H5*,V.ii.348–354]

But in *Antony and Cleopatra* Roman order is never fully endorsed; there is no gaze outward toward a prosperous, blessed future for family and land. The "High order" which Dolabella is urged to "see" in the last line of the play is not that of the future empire but of Antony's and Cleopatra's funeral. This emphasis on what has been lost is characteristic of tragedy, not history.

Caesar's order is, like those which take over at the ends of the other tragedies, narrowly political, male, and barren. It achieves its control, like those others, through a purging of women, marriage, family, sexuality, and the conflicts they generate, conflicts eliminated in the tragedies through marriages that are aborted, perverted, broken. Hamlet declares his love for Ophelia only in the grave strewn with the flowers that should have decked her bride-bed, and Fortinbras takes over, free of the conflicts which paralyzed Hamlet. *Othello* concludes with a focus on the "tragic lodging" of the marriage bed, and power passes into the hands of "unwived" Cassio and "proper" Lodovico. Edmund, Goneril, and Regan "now marry in an instant," consummating their love triangle in violent death; Lear joins Cordelia in death, and Kent joins Lear and Cordelia, the triangle of fidelity complementing that of infidelity. The last lines in the play are spoken by a man (whether Edgar or Albany) who is without family and disgusted by sexuality, aware of the new order as a falling off from the old. Lady Macbeth uses her sexuality to incite Macbeth to frenzied manhood and then loses him to a diabolical marriage with the witches;[29] Malcolm, the new king, has a dead father and a dead saintly mother and presents his chastity as a qualification for the throne.[30]

Similarly, Antony's and Cleopatra's marriage is consummated in death, and the puritanical "boy" Caesar, in a departure from Plutarch, is without wife or children. But this order seems both pettier and more powerful than those at the end of the other tragedies; Caesar seems to have learned little, to be less chastened by his contact with Antony and Cleopatra than the other survivors of the tragic cataclysms. And here the exclusions matter more. Hence Antony's and Cleopatra's deaths seem less a defeat, more a fulfillment than those of the other tragic heroes. The play's ending thus holds in solution the marital celebration of comedy, the political achievement of the history play, and the self-realizing individual defeat of tragedy; no one element is precipitated out. Later, in the romances, these elements will be joined, not merely juxtaposed, as the endings involve transformed sexuality and regenerated relationships that rejuvenate the family and promise political order as well.

In *Antony and Cleopatra* genre boundaries are not dissolved but enlarged. Motifs, themes, and characterization from comedy, tragedy, and history are included. Gender distinctions, too, are not dissolved but are explored, magnified, and ratified. And male and female roles are not equal—not even here. Cleopatra, like the heroines of comedy, engenders Antony's growth and her own, controlling the ending to glorify her submission to him. Like the heroines of the problem comedies, she endures sexual degradation and uses sexuality fruitfully. Like the heroines of tragedy, she dies, though her death is more self-willed and self-fulfilling than theirs. This death, however, serves Caesar's political needs, confirming his historical control; serves Antony's emotional needs, reaffirming the nobleness of his "shape"; and serves Shakespeare's aesthetic needs, allowing him to make Cleopatra's death, like her life, "eternal in [his] triumph" (V.i.66).

CHAPTER FIVE

ıncest and Issue in the Romances:
The Winter's Tale

N the romantic comedies, broken nuptials release and exorcise external and internal threats to marital union, and the endings celebrate marriages; wider family, social, and political harmonies are usually assumed or ignored. In the tragedies, nuptials are permanently shattered and families destroyed; the restored political order of the conclusions is achieved— most emphatically in *Antony and Cleopatra*—by the absence of women, family, and sexuality. In the romances, as in the problem comedies, sexual/marital anxieties are intertwined with family and political conflicts; nuptials, families, and states are shattered. In the tour-de-force denouements, marriage, the family, and (usually less importantly) the state are restored together, assuring sexual health, procreative fertility, and political order. But the endings of the romances are more satisfying than those of the problem comedies because they are generated and justified by the strategies and structures of the plays.

The huge scope of the romances allows marital, familial, and political conflicts to be diffused into two generations and dispersed geographically and temporally. Their numerous plot strands provide room for threats to be displaced onto comic or grotesque doubles or onto parodic subplots. Anxieties are distanced or contained by manipulation of tone: by detachment and self-referentiality, allegory or parody, local infusions of comic relief.[1] Conflicts are absorbed into the apparently unpredictable but ultimately secure designs of nature, time, fate, and the gods.

The whole structure of the plays works toward thematic resolutions embodied in the comfortably happy endings. The excessive power of the men is expressed, blunted, and transmuted into benign forms, while threatening female sexuality is chastened through women's defended chastity, disguise, separation, confinement, or death. These transformations are made possible by the birth of children, the absence or death of mothers, the deemphasis on marriage, and the alternative focus on the father-daughter bond—a relationship which, while allowing the father to exercise his power, also enables him to learn its limits. Antiochus's incest opens *Pericles* with an emblem of paternal tyranny. The blessings that the romance fathers eventually bestow on their daughters' nuptials embody the tempering of paternal power. In consequence, Cymbeline and Prospero achieve political reconciliations with rivals, and Pericles and Leontes are reunited with their wives.

INCEST AND ISSUE

The incest shockingly encountered at the beginning of *Pericles* and decisively eschewed at the conclusion of *The Tempest* is the antithesis of this healthy father-daughter union and of the other relations flowing from it. The incest of Antiochus and his daughter is an emblem of extreme and interconnected perversions of patriarchal control. Antiochus, a husband, father, and "mighty king" (II.i.1), abuses his marital, paternal, sexual, and political power.[2] He defiles his marriage vows and the memory of his dead wife. He "provoke[s]" (I.Cho.26–27) his daughter to eat "her mother's flesh" and to corrupt her own. The riddle itself—

> I am no viper, yet I feed
> On mother's flesh, which did me breed.

I sought a husband, in which labor
I found that kindness in a father.
He's father, son, and husband mild;
I mother, wife, and yet his child.
How they may be, and yet in two,
As you will live, resolve it you—   [I.i.65–72]

also emphasizes the daughter's seductiveness and complicity. It embodies the confusion of generations and kinship roles, the perversion of sexuality, and the destructive collapse of the family that are the consequences of incest. Because the father contrives to keep her "still" (Cho.I.36), the daughter is deprived of growth, normal sexuality, and her place in the scheme of generations. So is Antiochus himself, who is left essentially wifeless, daughterless, and heirless. His "law" (Cho. I.35) to enable him to retain possession of his daughter and behead her suitors is a tyrannical exercise of his political power: "Kings are earth's gods; in vice their law's their will" (I.i.104). Further, in "pride of all his glory" (II.iv.6), Antiochus arrogantly flaunts his crime, soliciting suitors and deliberately revealing his secret through the obvious riddle and presentation of his daughter, "clothèd like a bride, / For the embracements even of Jove himself" (I.i.7–8). Antiochus's perverse assumption of Jove's power and the resulting contamination and collapse of the family are fittingly avenged by the "fire from heaven" that consumes the pair "shrivel[ing] up their bodies, even to loathing" (II.iv.10).[3]

Shakespeare altered the incest riddle he found in his sources, making it both easier and harder to answer; his changes, like his unique inclusion of the daughter onstage when Pericles is tested, emphasize its effects on her. In earlier versions of the riddle such as the one in Laurence Twine's *The Patterne of Painefull Adventures*—"I am carried with mischief, I eat my mother's flesh: I seek my brother my mother's husband and I cannot find him" (Bullough, 6:428)—the riddle's hidden referent and correct answer is Antiochus himself. He can be said to eat his mother's flesh because the incest makes his daughter his "mother" (i.e., mother-in-law): "As wife, she becomes the mother-in-law of her husband as daughter."[4] The riddle's second hidden referent is the suitor, the daughter's potential husband, who would become, as a result of the incest, both "brother" (i.e., brother-in-law) to Antiochus (since his daughter is also his wife) and "husband" to Antiochus's "mother" (i.e., his mother-in-law, since his daughter is also his mother). The father cannot "find" this future husband because he prohibits his daughter's marriage. The focus of this very difficult riddle is on the father and on his rivalry with his daughter's suitors. In Shakespeare's altered riddle the answer is the daughter; its focus is on her acquiescence in corruption (it is now she who "feed[s] on mother's flesh") and on the confusion of her roles as well as her father's: "He's father, son, and husband mild / I mother, wife, and yet his child." The *Pericles* riddle, unlike that in the sources, is technically unanswerable since Antiochus's daughter has no name and has been deprived of a clear-cut role by which she can be designated.[5] In Shakespeare's version, Antiochus's destruction of his daughter is at the heart of his tyranny.

The vicious potentials of male power which Antiochus's incest manifests—violent aggression, sexual degradation, possessiveness, jealousy, tyranny—are released and then mitigated, dispelled, or transmuted in the subsequent action of *Pericles* and of the other romances. Incest's two-tiered disruption of marriage and family relations is reiterated in modified ways in the other plays when nuptials or marriages are impeded or broken in two generations. The incest of Antiochus grotesquely caricatures the concatenation of marital, familial, and political ties and their potential for mutual corruption. But the potential for mutual restoration is also present. In *Pericles* it is embodied in Pericles himself, the "benign lord" (II.Cho.3), who is the antithesis of Antiochus and who undoes the tyrant's incest. Losing wife and daughter, he regains them by his withdrawal into patient, passive mourning. In this play, Marina's resemblance to her mother becomes the catalyst, not to incest, but to a recognition scene which, much altered from the sources, reverses the dynamics of the play's opening. Marina's riddling remarks, which suggest her mysterious birth and submerged identity—"No, nor of any shores. / Yet I was mortally brought forth, and am / No other than I appear" (V.i.106–08) —*can* be explicated; they lead to wondrous clarification for her and for Pericles. This is possible because Marina knows her identity—her name and her parentage—can announce that she is "Called Marina / For I was born at sea" (V.i.159–60), that she is "the daughter to King Pericles" (183), and that her "mother's name was Thaisa" (214). Marina's answerable riddles enable her to become Pericles' mother—"Thou that beget'st him"—not through the verbal and sexual confusions of the incest riddle but through her father's symbolic regaining of his identity, his symbolic rejuvenation. In *Cymbeline, The Winter's Tale*, and *The Tempest*, the protagonists themselves, like Pericles' antithesis, Antiochus, exercise their power to corrupt family or social bonds. But instead of being destroyed, they are preserved, like Pericles, to cooperate in the restoration of the bonds that they themselves have helped to shatter.

Childbirth makes possible incest and is its antithesis. It is present in the romances in dramatic episodes and pervasive metaphors—as a psychological crisis and as a resonant symbol. The moment of birth alters the family constellation, extending it and anticipating its division and proliferation instead of consuming it. Childbirth is ultimately regenerative but at first traumatic for mother, child, and father. As wife becomes mother in the romances, her power and vulnerability are heightened; she is both fulfilled and divided, and the sexual power that is confirmed by the birth of her child seems to require nullification. When husband becomes father, he gains an emblem of his potency and an extension of his powers. But he is also made to confront his wife's sexual power and his own decline and mortality. The child, "freed and enfranchised" (*WT*, II.ii.60) from the womb, experiences violent separation from parents and is threatened with confinement, banishment, or death. These subsequent painful separations, reiterating that of parturition, permit growth and lead to the reformation of the old family and the creation of a new one.

BIRTH AND THE DEATH OF MOTHERS

The puzzling absence of mothers in many Shakespeare plays (where, as in *The Taming of the Shrew, Love's Labor's Lost, Midsummer Night's Dream, The Merchant of Venice, Much Ado About Nothing, As You Like It, Troilus and Cressida, Othello, King Lear, Cymbeline, The Tempest*, there are children with fathers but no mothers present or accounted for) has often been noted, and a variety of explanations offered. The rarity of mothers may reflect or confirm demographic data showing that Renaissance women frequently died in childbirth.[6] It may embody the social reality that patriarchal culture vested all authority in the male parent, making it both logical and fitting that he alone should represent that authority in the drama. It may derive, on the other hand, from generic conventions: the uncommonness of mature women as protagonists in the genres of comedy, history play, and tragedy. Or it may result from a scarcity of boy actors capable of playing mature women in Shakespeare's company.[7] The nature and the significance of this phenomenon and the relative significance of the factors accounting for it probably vary from genre to genre or even from play to play. The scarcity of mothers in comedy, which probably derives from the father's authority to negotiate marriages in the period, serves to highlight the oedipal conflicts that are traditional to the genre. In the romances, however, mothers are not merely absent but are dead or else die or apparently die in the course of the play. If the death occurs before the play's action, it is noted and remembered. These deaths and mock deaths are prominent determinants of plot and theme. The absence of mothers in the romances causes broken nuptials in the older generation, allows female sexuality to be represented by the chaste innocence of young daughters, and shifts emotional and dramatic emphasis to father-daughter bonds. Mock deaths in the romances symbolize separation and engender reconciliation not only in the heterosexual bond but in the mother-child bond as well.

Like Titania's votress in *Midsummer Night's Dream*, who, "being mortal, of that boy did die" (II.i.135), several mothers in the romances die in childbirth or closely following the birth of a child. These concomitant births and deaths exaggerate the trauma of birth and manifest its physical and psychological consequences for the mother. The frighteningly liminal nature of childbirth is dramatized in Thaisa's "blusterous" (III.i.28) delivery in a tempest at sea exactly midway between her father's and her husband's kingdoms: "Their vessel shakes / On Neptune's billow; half the flood / Hath their keel cut" (III. Cho. 44–46).[8] The mother experiences physical and emotional division and a transformation of role and identity. The location of Thaisa's delivery symbolizes how her position as daughter becomes attenuated as she takes on the new role of mother to a child who is first connected to her, then violently separated from her. The vulnerability of the mother and the violence of this separation of one body into two are implied when Marina is seen as "a piece / Of [the] dead queen" (III.i.17–18), Posthumus is "ripped" (V.iv.37) from the dead body of his mother, and Perdita is from Hermione's "breast, / The innocent milk in its most innocent mouth, / Haled out to murder" (III.ii.97–99). These three mothers die or seem to die in childbirth or immediately afterward. Miranda's mother also seems to have died soon after her birth, since the daughter, two when she was exiled from Milan, remembers her waiting woman but not her mother. Belarius, who steals Cymbeline's two sons when the oldest is three, makes no mention of their mother. Caliban's mother, Sycorax, and Antiochus's wife likewise die leaving children behind, though the exact timing of their deaths is unspecified.

When they survive the physical division of childbirth, mothers remain emotionally bound to their children and fatally vulnerable to the loss of them. In the tragedies mothers die ambiguously in connection with the loss or death of children. At the end of *Romeo and Juliet*, Lady Montague dies, her husband tells us, because "grief of my son's exile hath stopped her breath" (V.iii.212), and Lady Capulet, looking on Juliet's body predicts her own death: "O me, this sight of death is as a bell / That warns my old age to a sepulcher" (V.iii.207–08). Gertrude dies saluting the dying Hamlet with the poison intended for him. In the romances, too, mothers' deaths are the consequence of the loss of children. Posthumus's mother's death in childbirth results from grief at the death of her two sons. Hermione, already grieving over her violent separation from Perdita, "dies" at the announcement of Mamillius's death; his name connotes the intimate physical bond between mother and child, which extends beyond birth and makes the loss of a child a kind of death. Even the wicked Queen in *Cymbeline* develops "a fever with the absence of her son, / A madness, of which her life's in danger" (IV.iii.2–3) and dies although unaware that Cloten has died arrogantly identifying himself as "the queen's son" (IV.ii.93).

Cymbeline's Queen is "cruel to the world" as well as "cruel to herself" (V.v.32–33); she brings about her son's death as well as her own. Birth and the fierce bonds between mother and child can be destructive for children and stepchildren as well as for mothers. Marina's stormy birth is imaged as an assault; it prefigures other assaults and losses that the children of romance must endure:

Thou hast as chiding a nativity
As fire, air, water, earth, and heaven can make
To herald thee from the womb. Even at the first
Thy loss is more than can thy portage quit,
With all thou canst find here.   [III.i.32–36]

After Marina's abrupt separation from her mother's womb and loss of her mother, her father leaves her behind, and years later, Dionyza, the stepmother who has raised her, plots her death. The Queen in *Cymbeline* likewise plots Imogen's death. Both stepmothers act out of their love for their own children. Perdita is taken away from her mother, and Mamillius dies of grief at his mother's loss of honor and his separation from her. Cloten dies in consequence of the arrogance bred in him by his aggressive mother. Even Euriphile is accused, at the end of *Cymbeline*, of stealing the King's sons. The destructive potential in mothers' and surrogate mothers' intimate bonds with their children, dramatized in the margins of the romances, is embodied in two striking images. One is of Dionyza, who "like the harpy / Which, to betray, dost, with thine angel's face, / Seize with thine eagle's talents" (IV.iii.46–48). The other describes as one of the consequences of famine, "Those mothers who, to nuzzle up their babes, / Thought nought too curious, are ready now / To eat those little darlings whom they loved" (I.iv.42–44). Behind these mutilating mothers looms the image of Volumnia, whose separation from and reconciliation with her son, Coriolanus, prove "most mortal to him" (V.iii.189).

In the romances, the death of bad mothers protects fathers and children from their destructive power. The death of good mothers allows their sexual and procreative power to be appropriated and idealized. Idealization is effected when dead mothers are ritually buried and mourned and their memory cherished. Thaisa's sea burial associates her with a nature which, in contrast to that of the storm, is benign. She receives a "priestly farewell" (III.i.70); in her sea grave, where "e'er remaining lamps, the belching whale / And humming water must o'erwhelm thy corpse, / Lying with simple shells" (III.i.63–65), she is absorbed into the tranquil rhythms of nature in preparation for her regeneration within its cycles: "nature awakes; a warmth / Breathes out of her. . . . See how she 'gins to blow / Into life's flower again!" (III.ii.94–97). Euriphile, the surrogate mother to Cymbeline's sons, is buried with a beautiful dirge that imagines her similarly removed from nature's destructive excesses—"Fear no more the heat o' th' sun / Nor the furious winter's rages" (IV.ii.258–59)—and that imagines death as protection and consummation. Her grave is honored daily by Guiderius and Aviragus as Hermione's "grave" is visited daily by Leontes. The old shepherd in *The Winter's Tale* vividly calls up the memory of his dead wife as a model for Perdita. Through their deaths into nature and the cherishing of their memory, the desexualization and sanctification of good mothers is achieved. It is achieved also by mothers' mock deaths—by the long, chaste seclusions of Thaisa as a vestal virgin in the Temple of Diana (a curious denial of her sexual initiation and motherhood) and of Hermione as, in effect, a statue in the house of Paulina.

Paulina is the only mother in the romances who does not

undergo a real or apparent death, and the fact that her sexuality and her motherhood are dramatically invisible confirms the romances' requirement that mothers be dead. It is not Paulina, but her husband, Antigonus, who refers to having three daughters. With his death they too vanish from the play, leaving Paulina free to be solely a chaste nurturer of Leontes and Hermione for sixteen years, educating them for remarriage instead of raising her own daughters for marriage. Like Thaisa and Hermione, she can assume a sexual role again only at the point of children's nuptials and her charges' reunion; then she is granted Camillo as a substitute husband. Mothers' sexuality, necessary for conception and childbirth, is eliminated from the romances until the moment when they can bequeath it to marriageable daughters.[9]

As a result of the mother's deaths and other losses, the fathers, too, withdraw, deny their sexuality, and, in the absence of wives, learn to take on nurturing roles. The fathers' sexuality and their part in generation are minimized—most explicitly when Gower deftly and comfortingly removes Pericles entirely from his idealized description of defloration and conception: "Hymen hath brought the bride to bed, / Where by loss of maidenhead / A babe is molded" (III.Cho.9–11). The fathers endure withdrawals that parallel in some ways the seclusion of wives. Pericles, after the death of Thaisa, vows not to shave his hair until his daughter's marriage, and after Marina's apparent death, he suffers a deathlike mourning. Leontes also withdraws from life, eschewing the possibility of heirs who might revive his kingdom. Prospero's involuntary seclusion is likewise characterized by sexual abstinence, penance, and transformation. He, Belarius in *Cymbeline*, and the old Shepherd in *Winter's Tale* nurture children and surrogate children, taking them up "for pity" (*WT*, III.iii.75), educating or trying to educate them, and preparing for the moment when they will reach maturity.[10]

In each of the plays, the children's being "ripe for marriage" (*Per*, IV. Cho. 17) ends the fathers' withdrawal and leads to the revival of the wife and/or to other reunions. The reestablishment of the bond between parent and child and the acknowledgment of the powerful physical connection between them overshadows in the romances the sexual union—or reunion—of husband and wife, who are "one flesh" only symbolically and by means of their children; oddly, even the villainous Aaron in *Titus Andronicus* testifies to this priority: "My mistress is my mistress, this my self, / The vigor and the picture of my youth" (IV.ii.107–08). Pericles' recovery of his wife gives way to Thaisa's acknowledgment of the daughter whose existence she only now realizes.

> *Marina.*   My heart
>   Leaps to be gone into my mother's bosom.
>   [*Kneels*]
> *Pericles.*   Look who kneels here: flesh of thy flesh,
>   Thaisa;
>   Thy burden at the sea, and called Marina,
>   For she was yielded there.
> *Thaisa.*   Blest, and mine own!
>   [V.iii.44–47]

Imogen's and Posthumus's embrace is likewise interrupted —by Cymbeline's desire for recognition by his daughter:

> *Cymbeline.*   How now, my flesh, my child?
>   What, mak'st thou me a dullard in this act?
>   Wilt thou not speak to me?
> *Imogen.*   [*Kneeling*]   Your blessing, sir.
>   [V.v.264–66]

Hermione is called from her embrace of Leontes to bless the daughter for whom she has preserved herself:

> *Paulina.*   kneel,
>   And pray your mother's blessing; turn, good lady,
>   Our Perdita is found.
> *Hermione.*   You gods look down,
>   And from your sacred vials pour your graces
>   Upon my daughter's head! Tell me, mine own,
>   Where hast thou been preserved?
>   [V.iii.119–24]

Even in *The Tempest*, where the central family is not reunited
—where the mother remains absent, and Prospero's and Miranda's separation is yet to come—the final reunion of the play,
that of Alonso with the son he believes dead, recapitulates the
earlier parent/child reunions:

> *Ferdinand.* Though the seas threaten, they are
> merciful
> I have cursed them without cause. [*Kneels*]
> *Alonso.*   Now all the blessings
> Of a glad father compass thee about.
>   [V.i.178–80]

COURTSHIP AND MARRIAGE:
FATHERS AND SUITORS, HUSBANDS AND WIVES

The dynamics of these moments of reunion are one manifestation of the fact that courtship and marriage, so often at the center of Shakespeare's plays, are subordinated to other concerns
in the romances. The prominent couples are seen together only
at the time of courtships enacted or remembered, at the moments of their separation, and at their final reunion. The courtships in the romances, as well as some of the secondary marriages, exorcise anxieties and obstructions that impeded
nuptials more absolutely in earlier plays by recapitulating them
in an abbreviated or comic way.

In the courtships dramatized in the romances, the father-
suitor rivalry that proved deadly in the story of Antiochus is attenuated or merely simulated. When Cymbeline banishes
Posthumus, berates Imogen, and sends her to her room, she
talks back to her father. No one much heeds him, since his
blustering does not seem to give him the power to enforce an
estrangement; the marriage in fact will be finally ruptured only
by Posthumus's jealousy. Polixenes, too, plays the heavy father; commanding the "divorce" of Perdita and Florizel, he becomes a kind of rival of his son for the affections of the "low-
born lass" he had formerly praised (IV.iv.156). But his threats

feel empty and prove so as other characters and other forces cooperate to bring about the couple's marriage. Thaisa's father, Simonides, in his first aside connects himself with Jove as Antiochus did and seems to imply possessive jealousy in the presence of a potential rival—"By Jove I wonder, that is king of thoughts, / These cates resist me, he but thought upon" (II.iii.28–29). Pericles, remembering Antioch, fears this rivalry and denies any claims on Thaisa: "'Tis the king's subtlety to have my life" (II.v.43). But Simonides' possessiveness, like that of Prospero later, is dispelled through merely feigned obstructions to the match. In the romances the jealous rage of Antiochus and of a long line of Shakespearean fathers against their daughters' suitors is diminished to a joke, a trick, or a comic turn.

Another stereotype, the shrewish wife, is likewise rendered less threatening in the romances. Dionyza in *Pericles*, Cymbeline's Queen, and Paulina (in part) are conventionally domineering, aggressive, and emasculating; but they are also secondary, flat, or comic, partly because they are stock figures. Dionyza plots the murder of Marina and taunts her husband, Cleon (as Goneril does Albany), with cowardice, childishness, and impotence when he upbraids her. The Queen is a wicked stepmother who tries to poison her stepchild. Her aggressiveness, like that of the other romance witch, Sycorax, is projected onto her son: Cloten, like Caliban, is uncontrollable. Paulina verbally assaults Leontes, Antigonus, and the courtiers and is accused of being a "mankind witch" (II.iii.67), although she breaks the boundaries of the stereotype. The power of all of these women is turned back on themselves or proves beneficial. Marina's murder is interrupted, and the wickedness of Dionyza is avenged by the incineration of her whole family. The Queen destroys only herself and her son, ends "with horror, madly dying, like her life, / Which being cruel to the world, concluded / Most cruel to herself" (V.v.31–33). In contrast, Paulina's shrewishness is used for the positive ends of defending Perdita and Hermione and reforming Leontes. With the elimination or transformation of domineering wives, the plays can focus on the courtships of modest daughters and on reunions with good wives.

But even good wives, in the romances as in earlier plays, must endure slander and estrangement. The disrupted marriages in *Cymbeline* and *The Winter's Tale* reiterate old conflicts and use new strategies to achieve their resolution. Imogen is the only wife in the romances (besides Claribel) who is a wife but not a mother or surrogate mother; her situation, her plot, and her character associate her with the soon-to-be or recently married wives of the comedies, problem comedies, and early tragedies. Like Hero[11] and Desdemona, Imogen is idealized by her husband as more "fair, virtuous, wise, chaste, constant, qualified, and less attemptable" (I.iv.62–63) than other women. Like these women and Helen, she is violently repudiated by her husband. Posthumus, like Claudio, Bertram, Othello, and Leontes, is insecure, uneasy about sex, and caught up in rivalry with other men. Hence he wagers on Imogen's chastity, believes she has been seduced by Iachimo on the basis of his "ocular proof," and orders her killed; like Claudio, Bertram, Antony, and Leontes, he believes his wife dead and holds himself responsible.

Among these earlier plays, it is *All's Well* that *Cymbeline* most closely resembles. In both there is a weak but disruptive father figure whose control of family and state is ineffectual. The King in *All's Well* endangers his ward's marriage by commanding it; Cymbeline, his daughter's, by condemning it. Bertram's revulsion from marriage to an adopted sister and from his wife's sexuality is echoed by Posthumus when he believes Imogen unfaithful. Each escapes to a military world in which he is wonderfully successful. The reviled women withdraw to a peripheral community: Helen to a supportive female enclave; Imogen, in disguise, to a nurturing male retreat. The plays' resolutions are also assisted by the scapegoating of the heroes' doubles, Parolles and Cloten. The abridged reunions in both plays emphasize the potential fruitfulness of the couples' relationships.

But crucial differences in the relative weight of the elements, the treatment of the characters, and the paths to resolution reveal distinctions between problem comedy and romance. In *All's Well*, the father/daughterlike relation of the King and Helen, rendered symbolically incestuous by the erotic resonances of her cure of the King, and the mother-son relation of Bertram and the Countess are submerged by the marriage plot.[12] Bertram's and Helen's reestablished marriage is the sole focus of the end of the play. In *Cymbeline*, by contrast, the original emphasis on the marriage plot is dissipated in the conclusion, where the marital reunion becomes only one of the multiple concerns of the final scene.[13] The situation of the central couple in *Cymbeline* is also the reverse of that in *All's Well*. As we have seen, Helen is at the center of the problem play. She achieves the recovery of Bertram and is allowed explicit manifestation of her sexuality through the bedtrick, her articulated response to it, and her pregnancy. Bertram, however, is given little opportunity for growth or rehabilitation. In *Cymbeline*, Imogen, who is exposed to more threats and challenges than Helen, is not permitted to take the initiative in meeting them or to remain central. Nor is she enabled by the play to give full expression to her sexuality. Posthumus, however, is protected by his doubles and given the opportunity to change and repent, to act heroically, to have his family restored to him.

Helen's multiple roles—she is her father's daughter, the Countess's ward, the King's restorer, Bertram's sister and wife, Diana's friend and double—allow her to grow and absorb threats to her, whereas Imogen's roles increase her liability to attack. Her father and stepmother try to destroy her secret marriage, whereas the Countess and the King support Helen's aspirations to marry Bertram. As Cymbeline's heir, Imogen is the object of the Queen's cruelty and of Cloten's political/sexual aggression. Her marriage and fidelity make her the target of Iachimo's wager and cynical attempt at seduction. Like Helen, Imogen at first vigorously defends herself. She retorts to her father with sharp anger, to the Queen with sarcastic disgust, to Cloten with devastating contempt. She shrewdly sees through Iachimo. Unlike other slandered women, she first responds to Posthumus's accusations in a counterattack which accuses *him* of "incontinency": "Men's vows are women's traitors" (III.iv.47, 54).

But Imogen's eventual response to Posthumus's accusations, like Helen's original one to Bertram's revulsion, is to desire death, and the play gives her no means to recover and to move back toward a reunion. She expresses no wish to find Posthumus and clear herself. Although Pisanio contrives a mock death to protect her, in this play the strategy is only defensive and is not envisaged as a cure for Posthumus. Her death averted, Imogen puts aside her marriage, her sexuality, and even her sharp tongue, and passively acquiesces in the life of the curiously undifferentiated family in the Welsh mountains. Her actual but unrecognized brothers, Guiderius and Aviragus, responding to her female self, her male disguise, and the sensed kinship bonds, accept her as a brother but at the same time adore her as a sister, wife, and mother. They call her "angel," would "woo hard" if she were a woman (III.vi.42, 69), admire her singing and cooking, mourn her with the dirge they sang for their mother, and would sacrifice their father for her. Imogen is relieved to participate in this asexual family: "I'ld change my sex to be companion with them, / Since Leonatus false" (III.vi.87–88). This confusion of gender and generational roles seems an odd and benign transformation of Antiochus's incest (although it too does not allow growth). Asexual, unhierarchical, and gender neutral, this family is a welcome escape from the tyranny of Imogen's father, the cruelty of the Queen, and the degraded sexuality of her stepbrother, Cloten, Iachimo, and Posthumus.[14]

The ambiguity of gender roles in the Welsh retreat is only one of a number of ways in which Imogen's sexuality is both denied and made uneasily provocative in *Cymbeline*. Her desires and desires for her are thwarted or degraded. Her husband declares himself "her adorer, not her friend" (I.iv.72) and seems to deny the consummation of their marriage, attacking her titillating modesty: "Me of my lawful pleasure she restrained / And prayed me oft forbearance—did it with / A pudency so rosy, the sweet view on't / Might well have warmed old Saturn" (II.v.9–12). The sublimated desires of Iachimo and the unsublimated ones of Cloten also have the effect of degrading her. Whereas in the problem plays the bedtricks, however deceitful, provided the women the means to commit them-

selves to and satisfy their desires for their husbands, the parodic versions of these encounters in *Cymbeline* degrade
Imogen, who is an unwitting participant in them. In Iachimo's
verbal violation of the sleeping Imogen, his salacious desires
contaminate their object. Her inert chastity, as he describes it,
invites assault: "That I might touch! / But kiss, one kiss! . . .
The flame o' th' taper / Bows toward her and would under-
peep her lids / To see th' enclosèd lights, now canopied /
Under these windows" (II.ii.16–17, 19–22). When she wakes
and embraces the corpse, her passionate idealization is under-
mined by the fact that the body is dead, headless, and Cloten's. Iachimo's desires corrupted their object; here her desires
are degraded by the inappropriateness of their object: "I know
the shape of's leg; this is his hand, / His foot Mercurial, his
Martial thigh, / The brawns of Hercules; but his Jovial face—
/ Murder in heaven? How? 'Tis gone" (IV.ii.309–12).[15] Yet
this is Imogen's fullest expression of passion. Otherwise her
desires are expressed primarily in her eroticized death wish:

> I draw the sword myself. Take it and hit
> The innocent mansion of my love, my heart.
> Fear not, 'tis empty of all things but grief.
> Thy master is not there, who was indeed
> The riches of it.   [III.iv.67–71]

And unlike other chaste heroines—Hero, Helen, Isabella, Desdemona, and Hermione—Imogen has no female friend and
double. She has no one who can express the desires that she
cannot as Beatrice and Mariana do. She has no one to defend to
the hero her passionate chastity as Beatrice, Emilia, and Paulina do. She has no one to absorb her degradation as Diana and
Mariana do. She has no protection from the degraded desire
that pervades the play.

Posthumus, however, is given every opportunity to separate himself from it, to do penance, to reform and be forgiven.
His character is protected by his doubles, Cloten and Iachimo,
who express aggression and sexual degradation in more extreme and pernicious forms than he does.[16] The brutality of

Cloten's plan to kill Posthumus and rape Imogen to achieve "valor" (III.v.139), and the salacious combination of extravagant praise and obscene degradation of women expressed in Iachimo's attempted prostitution of Imogen and his bedchamber violation, make Posthumus's misogyny in his diatribe against, "the woman's part" (II.v.19–35) seem merely the conventional textbook variety. "I'll write against them" (II.v.32) seems a more expected response to infidelity for him than does murder. Posthumus's heroism in battle further contributes to his transformation. It is active, not passive, like his flight and loss of the wager. It is less flamboyant, more solid and patriotic, and more important to the plot than Bertram's showy exploits in the insignificant Italian wars. Most important, we are made to witness Posthumus experiencing the guilt, penitence, and forgiveness that other disillusioned husbands only mouth. Unlike his counterparts in the source versions of the wager plot, and unlike all other husbands in Shakespeare, he forgives his wife for "wrying but a little" (V.i.5), reasserts her nobility, and repents of her death *before* her innocence is proved.[17] Finally, his family is restored to him in a dream vision in which they, with Jupiter, bless him and lend him protection.[18] As in the other romances, but here only symbolically, the original family is restored before the new family reunites.

Although Posthumus feels guilt, does penance, and comes to love Imogen again, the manifest sexual anxieties of the play never seem fully resolved. Posthumus, though protected by the punishments of his doubles—the castrating death of Cloten and the unmanning of Iachimo by guilt— seems similarly unmanned himself. Whereas in *All's Well* Helen's visible pregnancy embodies the potential fruitfulness of the union, in *Cymbeline*, Imogen is still in male disguise at the end of the play. Posthumus does not recognize her in wonder, but throws her on the ground, reiterating in his gesture and language the source of their rupture—his need to destroy Imogen for her apparently corrupt sexual parts: "There lie thy part" (V.v.229). "You ne'er killed Imogen till now" (V.v.231), declares Pisanio, calling attention to the repetition. Posthumus's recognition of Imogen is then delayed by that of other characters. When it finally occurs, their beautiful, cryptic exchange

> *Imogen.*   Why did you throw your wedded lady from
> you?
> Think that you are upon a rock, and now
> Throw me again.
> *Posthumus.*   Hang there like fruit, my soul,
> Till the tree die!   [V.v.261–64]

only hints at Imogen's fierce anger and loyalty and Posthumus's still sublimated, still passive adoration. Their union is imaged as fruitful, bodiless, and mortal, and it is interrupted, as we have seen, by the reunion of Cymbeline with the daughter who is his flesh. Whereas at the end of *All's Well* the King's offer of a husband to Diana is a prominent reminder of the anxieties that separated the couple, in *Cymbeline* the still problematic marriage moves into the background as subsequent reunions and the celebration of wider harmonies take over the play. In *The Winter's Tale*, as we will see, the rejuvenated marriage will receive more dramatic space and weight but will still be only one among many reconciliations. The contrasting emphases of *All's Well* and *Cymbeline* show how the problems of the problem comedies are redistributed and absorbed by the shape of the romances.

DAUGHTERS AND FATHERS: CHASTITY AND
SELF-RESTRAINT

Imogen's position in *Cymbeline* is perhaps especially under strain because she is simultaneously a wife and a daughter, and because both relationships are disrupted and neither becomes dominant. As a result, she is doubly under attack. Like other wives in romance and elsewhere, her fidelity is doubted; she is threatened by her husband with mutilating murder: "O that I had her here, to tear her limb-meal! / I will go there and do 't i' th' court before / Her father" (II.iv.147–49). Like the other romance daughters, she is threatened with violent sexual assault, which is associated, in Cloten's mind, with murder: "With that suit upon my back will I ravish her; first kill him [Posthumus], and in her eyes. . . . and when my lust hath dined . . . to the court I'll knock her back, foot her home again" (III.v.137–44). In both attackers the desire to violate Imogen is intertwined with the desire to triumph over their rival and her father. These attacks are, however, thwarted, as are others in the romances, by the daughters' vehement protection of their chastity and by restraints on violence.

The daughters in romance must embody both innocent purity (necessary for their protection) and healthy sexuality (which will gain them suitors and impel them toward marriage). In the absence of parents or parental support (with the notable exception of Prospero), daughters are responsible both for protecting their chastity and choosing their own husbands. Each achieves a different balance of purity and desire which in part depends on the seriousness and extensiveness of the attacks made on them. As we have seen, Imogen, already a wife, is the most persistently and degradingly assaulted, and her own sexuality is consequently minimized. Likewise Marina, endangered when her maidenhead is put up for sale in the brothel, must vehemently defend her virginity and integrity and is in fact able to quench the desires that her virginity ignites, as her potential customers testify: "I'll do anything now that is virtuous; but I am out of the road of rutting forever" (IV.v.8–9); "She's able to freeze the god Priapus, and undo a whole generation" (IV.vi.3–4). Her need to defend the "glass of her virginity" (IV.vi.147) precludes any dramatization of her sexuality; her betrothal to Lysimachus is conventionally sketched in with no hint of either sexual anxiety or sexual commitment on either side. Indeed, Lysimachus himself is inexplicably transformed from a jovial brothel-frequenter and virgin-violator who jokes at his first appearance, "How a dozen of virginities" (IV.vi.20), to a decorous governer who observes proprieties by asking for Marina's hand only when he has learned her origins. Miranda and Perdita, under the protection of father and surrogate father and respected by their chaste suitors, are in less danger and are allowed some manifestations

of their desires. Miranda's is indirect and restrained by her ignorance and innocence. However, she does, like Juliet and
Desdemona, offer herself frankly, though riddlingly, to Ferdinand against (as she thinks) her father's will, weeping, "At
mine unworthiness, that dare not offer / What I desire to give,
and much less take / What I shall die to want. . . . I am your
wife if you will marry me; / If not, I'll die your maid" (III.i.
77–84). Although Perdita withholds herself from the sexual license of the Bohemian countryside and rejects seductive artifice, her expressions of desire and Florizel's acknowledgment
of them are the frankest and fullest in any of the romances.

The daughters must assert themselves against their father
or choose a mate without him, but his acceptance of their
choice is necessary before they can be married or reunited with
spouse.[19] When each of the daughters in the first three romances kneels to receive her father's or parents' blessing, she
expresses both her love for her father and her subordination to
him. The father is able, as a result of the reunion with his
daughter and her confirmation of his power, to relinquish her
to a son-in-law.[20] Miranda's subordination is still more complete. She is silent as her father gives her away to Ferdinand,
and his gesture affirms his control of her even in the process
of relinquishing it: "Then, as my gift, and thine own acquisi-
tion / Worthily purchased, take my daughter" (IV.i.13–14). In
spite of the fathers' gestures and the daughters' impending
marriages, the separation of the pair is not completed dramatically or emotionally within the romances, for no weddings
take place and the focus remains on the father-daughter bond
and the reformation of the original family. The resonance of
Pericles' reunions with Marina and Thaisa is much greater than
that of the conventionalized betrothal of Marina and Lysimachus. Imogen's reunion with Posthumus is displaced by other
recognitions. Perdita's and Florizel's romance becomes secondary in the last scenes of *The Winter's Tale*, and, at the end of
The Tempest, Prospero's losses assume more importance than
Miranda's and Ferdinand's nuptials. The chastened sexuality
of the daughters and the subordination of their nuptials are
also apparent in the comparative dearth of references to their

future fertility, references that were common in the romantic comedies.[21]

Although the fathers retain their primacy at the conclusions of the romances, their power has been blunted and tempered. Unlike Antiochus, they learn that they cannot have absolute control over family and subjects, over time and sexuality. The plays dramatize both external and internal restraints on their power. First, unlike the tragic heroes, none of the protagonists of romance kills anyone directly, although Leontes is indirectly responsible for the deaths of Mamillius and Antigonus. The murderous impulses of rulers and others are deflected by good servants who (unlike Thailand, who tries to murder Pericles lest he himself be murdered by his master, Antiochus) speak out against tyranny and, when deputized to do violence, mitigate its force. Pisanio refuses to kill Imogen, as Camillo does Polixenes; instead, each servant helps the intended victim to flee. Antigonus, along with the other courtiers, persuades Leontes to banish, not murder, Perdita and leaves her safely on the Bohemian shore. Gonzalo, ordered to cast away Prospero and Miranda, provides them with provisions. More sensationally and coincidentally, Leonine's deputized murder of Marina is halted when she is abducted by pirates.

Violent excesses of power are also curbed by being rendered comic and thwarted or by the elimination of the aggressor or his servant in such a way that the chain of violence does not continue. Antiochus and his daughter are conveniently destroyed by the gods; Dionyza and Cleon, by their subjects. Antigonus and the ship that brings him to Bohemia are just as conveniently eliminated by a bear and a storm; the force of these deaths is absorbed by the comic narration of them. The other deaths are also distanced by being narrated. Cloten's aggression is so untrammeled and inept that it is comic; his death at the hands of the innocent, courageous Guiderius is as untroubling and satisfying as that of a cartoon "bad guy."

When their abuses of power are mitigated by others, the father/rulers learn through loss and suffering to temper their own power. Pericles, Leontes, and Prospero withdraw voluntarily or involuntarily from rule; like Thaisa and Hermione, they reassume chastity, do penance, and learn patience. All are returned to more benign rule through the restoration of the family they have lost and the extension of family through their daughters. Pericles breaks his mourning and plans to extend the family's rule through his son-in-law. Cymbeline's reunion with his sons, daughter, and son-in-law generates his decision to renew the tribute payments and grant pardons to all. Leontes' reunion allows him to provide his kingdom with an heir. Somewhat differently, Prospero, who has been separated from country, not daughter, can make use of Miranda's acknowledged readiness for marriage as the catalyst to confrontation and reconciliation with his old enemies and to his return to rule in Milan: "I have done nothing but in care of thee, / Of thee my dear one, thee my daughter" (I.ii.16–17).

The transformations of the rulers' power are most fully explored in *The Tempest*. In its opening scene, a final renunciation of the incest of Antiochus, Prospero gives to Miranda a past so that she will be prepared for a future marriage: "'Tis time / I should inform thee farther" (I.ii.22–23). His primary concern in the play is to bring her together with Ferdinand; he feigns opposition to the match so that it will prosper. Having achieved this, he reconciles himself with his old enemies, including her suitor's father, and sympathizes with him in his "like loss" (V.i.143–44). His altered exercise of his power is embodied in the contrast between the remembered violence of the "potent art" that he renounces—

> I have bedimmed
> The noontide sun, called forth the mutinous winds,
> And 'twixt the green sea and the azured vault
> Set roaring war; to the dread rattling thunder
> Have I given fire and rifted Jove's stout oak
> With his own bolt; the strong-based promontory
> Have I made shake and by the spurs plucked up
> The pine and cedar—   [V.i.41–48]

and the masque of Ceres, which he produces to "enact / My present fancies" (IV.i.121–22) and which, narrated by female deities, presents images of harmonious, domesticated, bountiful nature: "Earth's increase, foison plenty, / Barns and garners never empty, / Vines with clust'ring bunches growing, / plants with goodly burden bowing; / Spring come to you at the farthest / In the very end of harvest" (IV.i.110–15). In the first vision, Prospero incites and appropriates nature's violence; in the second, he invokes and cooperates with nature's controlled beneficence to bless his daughter's marriage and enjoin the couple's fertility.

Having exchanged thunderbolts for pastoral plenty, his control of the isle for his daughter's nuptials, Prospero can also give up more. He chooses virtue over vengeance. He frees Ariel, whom he loves and whose exquisite service he will miss. He acknowledges his kinship with Caliban and his inability to control him, with or without magic powers: "This thing of darkness I / Acknowledge mine" (V.i.275–76). Finally, he relinquishes his power not only as a magician, a ruler, and a father, but in the epilogue acknowledges that power's limits, as character, as actor, and perhaps as playwright: "Now my charms are all o'erthrown, / And what strength I have's mine own, / Which is most faint."

But in a way Prospero's self-curtailment is too easy. Because the political conflicts in the play are distanced in the past, parodied in the conspiracy of Stephano, Trinculo, and Caliban, and controlled in the present, Prospero's renunciations of revenge are not made difficult for him. Indeed, his rage at Antonio and Sebastian almost seems excessive, considering that they are now in his power and that he, in effect, ceded authority before it was seized. Since he would seem to have preferred the seclusion of the isle to rule in Milan, vengeance under the circumstances would seem gratuitous.[22] Prospero is also kept removed from the profound anxieties about female sexuality that have troubled so many of the men in the plays examined. His wife is but a "piece of virtue" who existed to produce Miranda (I.ii.56). Miranda's purity is flawless. The dead witch, Sycorax, provides him with a useful scapegoat on which to project the possibility of female evil. Furthermore, Prospero's repeated claims to be relinquishing

his power are something of a sham; he continues to control everything and everyone in the play up to his epilogue, which
extends his manipulations to the audience. But however qualified Prospero's transformation is, and however easy it is made
for him to accomplish it, strikingly in this, the last of the romances, our attention is no longer focused on the destructive
excesses of paternal power but on the cost of relinquishing it,
on the pain of losing a daughter to marriage and thereby con-
fronting one's "frail mortality": "and so to Naples, / Where I
have hope to see the nuptial / Of these our dear-beloved sol-
emnizèd; / And thence retire me to my Milan, where / Every
third thought shall be my grave" (V.i.308–12).

In the romances, all the fathers are brought to acknowledge the sexuality, maturity, and independence of daughters
and wives. Each must, that is, relinquish the desire for a
woman who will be "Mother, wife, and yet his child," a
woman who can be both pure and sexual, both possessed and
nurturing, both unchanging and rejuvenating. Through their
rejection of this fantasy, incest's deadly confusion of family
and sexual roles is transformed into an affirmation of the symbolically regenerative power of family ties. Recovering Marina,
Pericles finds not just an "heir of kingdoms" but "another life"
(V.i.211): "O, come hither, / Thou that beget'st him that did
thee beget" (V.1.198–99). Cymbeline likewise feels himself
newly generative upon recovering his children—"O, what am
I? / A mother to the birth of three? Ne'er mother / Rejoiced de-
liverance more" (V.v.368–70). At their banishment, Miranda,
an infant, "preserve[d]" and comforted her weeping father:
"Thou didst smile, / Infusèd with a fortitude from heaven, /
When I have decked the sea with drops full salt, / Under my
burden groaned; which raised in me / An undergoing stomach, to bear up / Against what should ensue" (I.ii.153–58).
Most miraculously, Leontes' and Perdita's desire for Hermione
and her love for Perdita enable Hermione to "Bequeath to
death [her] numbness" (V.iii.102) and experience a painful
birth back into life. Through the structure of the romances,
birth's painful separations are symbolically transmuted into
ecstatic rebirth, and incest's destructive inversions of family

bonds are metamorphosed into mutually regenerating intimacies.

THE WINTER'S TALE: WOMEN AND ISSUE

Most critics have seen the final reconciliations in *The Winter's Tale* as the triumph of nature, art, the gods, time: these large extrapersonal forces inform every aspect of the play, as of the other romances. But the play's central miracle—birth—is human, personal, physical, and female, and its restorations are achieved by the rich presence and compelling actions of its women, Hermione, Paulina, and Perdita. They are more active, central, and fully developed than the women in the other romances. Through their acceptance of "issue" and of all that this central idea implies—sexuality and delivery, separation and change, growth and decay—they bring the play's men and the play's audience to embrace life's rhythms fully. In this romance, incest is most extensively and fruitfully transformed and the ruptures in marriage most fully manifested and healed.

Childbirth is the literal and symbolic center of the play. Hermione's pregnancy, delivery, recovery, and nursing receive close attention. Pervasive imagery of breeding, pregnancy, and delivery transforms many actions and scenes into analogues of birth with emotional and symbolic ties to the literal birth of Perdita:

> The child was prisoner to the womb and is
> By law and process of great Nature thence
> Freed, and enfranchised.   [II.ii.58–60]

Submerged metaphorical references are everywhere: "What may chance / Or breed upon our absence" (I.ii.11–12); "Temptations have since then been born to 's" (I.ii.77). Birth is proscribed in Antigonus's threat to geld his daughters so they will not "bring false generations" (II.i.149), parodied when the Shepherd and Clown become "gentlemen born" in the last act, and corrupted in the gestation of jealousy in Leontes' "Affection! Thy intention stabs the center" speech (I.ii.138–46).

Images of birth likewise resonate through other significant speeches and crucial scenes: the messengers' return from Delphos with the wish that "something rare / Even then will rush to knowledge. . . / And gracious be the issue" (III.i.20–22); the penance that is Leontes' "recreation"; the old shepherd's central line—"Thou met'st with things dying, / I with things new born" (III.iii.110–11); Time's description of his role as father-creator; Polixenes' grafting scheme for the purpose of conceiving new stock; the narrated reunion where, in spite of the "broken delivery," "Truth [is] pregnant by circumstance" (V.ii.32–33), and "every wink of an eye some new grace will be born" (V.ii.112–13); and the reanimation of the statue which imitates the labor of birth. The metaphors emphasize the fundamental components of the process of reproduction: union and fullness, labor and separation, creation and loss, risk and fulfillment, enclosure and enfranchisment.

In spite of this imagery, *The Winter's Tale* begins in a static, barren masculine world that appears determinedly self-sufficient, capable of sustaining itself without the violent trauma of birth. It purports to control time and space through the unchanged boyhood friendship of Leontes and Polixenes and through Leontes' son, Mamillius, who "makes old hearts fresh" and will perpetuate Leontes' kingdom. Women are strikingly absent from the idyllic picture. When Hermione enters in scene 2, visibly very pregnant and her condition emphasized by insistent innuendo ("Nine changes," "burden filled up," "perpetuity," "multiply," "breed"),[23] she becomes the "matter" that "alters" the brittle harmony and, after catastrophe ensues, one source of less fragile unions at the end of the play.

The possessive misogyny that fuels Leontes' jealousy reveals itself first in a sour memory of their courtship, when Hermione hesitated before declaring, " 'I am yours forever' " (I.ii.105). It develops as Leontes corrupts her "open[ing]" of her "white hand" to declare herself his possession into a fantasy of her "paddling palms and pinching fingers" with Polixenes (I.ii.103, 115). It erupts finally with debased imagery of intercourse and gestation to "prove" her infidelity and his cuckoldry.

Affection! Thy intention stabs the center.
Thou dost make possible things not so held,
Communicat'st with dreams—how can this be?—
With what's unreal thou coactive art,
And fellow'st nothing. Then 'tis very credent
Thou mayst co-join with something, and thou dost,
And that beyond commission, and I find it,
And that to the infection of my brains,
And hardening of my brows.   [I.ii.138–46][24]

The pseudologic and metaphoric substratum of this speech
connect Leontes' jealousy both with the self-conscious conventionality and folly of Posthumus and the comedy heroes and
with the profound sexual revulsion of the heroes of tragedy.[25]
His "weak-hinged fancy" (II.iii.118) creates the objects of jealousy as the comedy lovers created the objects of their love, and
he, like Theseus, recognizes the mechanics of this process:
"With what's unreal thou coactive art, / And fellow'st nothing" (I.ii.141–42). As the lovers conventionalized the objects of
their love into ideal Petrarchan mistresses, so in his jealousy
Leontes transforms Hermione into an abstract "hobbyhorse,"
(I.ii.276) a "thing" (II.i.82). He adopts the conventional gestures and responses of the cuckold with as much relish as the
lovers adopted their roles: "Go play, boy, play: thy mother
plays, and I / Play too—but so disgraced a part, whose issue /
Will hiss me to my grave" (I.ii.187–89). He creates extravagantly out of nothing the promiscuity of the adulterers and the
gossip of the court. Then he allegorizes his predicament into a
comfortingly commonplace drama ("Should all despair, / That
have revolted wives, the tenth of mankind / Would hang
themselves" (I.ii.198–200). At the root of Leontes' conventionalized folly is his divorce of sexuality from love, his pernicious
swerve—resembling Hamlet's, Othello's, and Antony's—
from the idealization of women to their degradation. The sexual disgust that leads Leontes to imprison and condemn Hermione corrupts and destroys his relations with Polixenes and
Mamillius as well.

     These latter relationships had been his protection against

full participation in his marriage. Both Leontes and Polixenes are nostalgic for their innocent presexual boyhood when each had a "dagger muzzled, / Lest it should bite its master" (I.ii. 156–57), and their "weak spirits" were not yet "higher reared / With stronger blood" (I.ii.72–73). Both blame their "fall" into sexuality on women who are "devils" (I.ii.82), seductive and corrupting. Both wish to remain "boy eternal," preserving their brotherhood as identical, innocent, "twinned lambs." The boyhood friendship, continued unchanged across time and space, is a protection against women, sex, change, and difference.[26] It is no wonder Leontes wants Polixenes to stay longer in Sicily! But the fantasy of Hermione's infidelity contaminates the friendship, and Leontes orders Polixenes killed.[27]

If the kings' friendship with each other takes precedence over any relationship to wives, so too does their intimacy with their sons. But this relationship is likewise defensive. The fathers' love for their sons is as stiflingly incestuous as is their affection for each other. They see their children as copies of themselves, extensions of their own egos, guarantees of their own innocence. Just as Polixenes describes the friends as "twinned lambs" (I.ii.67), so Leontes repeatedly insists that his son is "like me" (I.ii.129). Polixenes' description of the self-justifying use he makes of his son sums up the attitudes of both toward their children:

> He's all my exercise, my mirth, my matter;
> Now my sworn friend, and then mine enemy;
> My parasite, my soldier, statesman, all.
> He makes a July's day short as December,
> And with his varying childness, cures in me
> Thoughts that would thick my blood.   [I.ii.166–71]

Despite Polixenes' claim, the children cannot "cure" their fathers, for the men's corrupted views of sexuality are projected onto their children. Mamillius, since he was not created by some variety of male parthenogenesis, as Leontes would seem to prefer, is declared infected by his physical link with Hermione:

> I am glad you did not nurse him;
> Though he does bear some signs of me, yet you
> Have too much blood in him.   [II.i.56–58]

His death, like Leontes' jealousy, is from "mere conceit and fear / Of the Queen's speed," and his "cleft" heart mirrors his father's (III.ii.141–42, 194). He dies not only because of his connection with his threatened mother but because of the power of Leontes' projections of corruption onto him and because of the father's repudiation of the physical integrity of mother and son: "Conceiving the dishonor of his mother, / He straight declined, drooped, took it deeply, / Fastened, and fixed the shame on 't himself: / Threw off his spirit, his appetite, his sleep, / And downright languished" (II.iii.13–17). Leontes cannot both repudiate Hermione and retain his son.[28] Mamillius's death and the concomitant death of Hermione deprive Leontes of the possibility of recapturing childhood innocence or regenerating himself. And he misreads this death as a punishment for his delusion instead of a consequence of it.

Later in Bohemia, Polixenes—astonishingly—views his son's rebelliousness as a loss comparable to Mamillius's death: "Kings are no less unhappy, their issue not being gracious, than they are in losing them when they have approved their virtues" (IV.ii.26–28). His tirade just before he reveals himself at the sheepshearing feast suggests that he views his son's achievement of a sexual maturity that is beyond his control and not identified with him as a confirmation of his own impotence, and experiences it as deterioration into a second, now unwelcome childhood. ("Is not your father grown incapable / Of reasonable affairs? Is he not stupid / With age and alt'ring rheums? . . . Lies he not bed-rid? And again does nothing / But what he did being childish?" IV.iv.400–05.) His vicious, suggestive attack on Perdita (whom up to this moment he had openly admired) reveals nakedly the generalized distaste for women wittily apparent in his tales of boyhood and pompously implicit in his discussion of grafting to "make conceive a bark of baser kind / By bud of nobler race" (IV.iv.94–95). It reveals as well the threat which her innocent seductiveness poses to him as to his son. She, like Hermione before her, is seen as a whore, "the angle that plucks our son thither" (IV.ii.47). Polixenes now worries about the infection of *his* blood and threatens to eliminate Florizel from it as Leontes has already eliminated Hermione, Perdita, and Mamillius. Ironically, by denying their children freedom, difference, and sexual maturity, the two men deny themselves the potency, regeneration, and continuity that they need and desire but which cannot be achieved by their own return, through their children, to incestuous ideals of childhood innocence and father-son symbiosis.

The three women in the play, who, unlike the women in the other romances, are fully developed characters, serve, along with the pastoral scenes, as the "cure" for the "thoughts" that "thick" the men's "blood" (I.ii.170–71). They are witty and realistic whereas the men are solemnly fantastic; they are at ease with sex whereas the kings are uneasy about it; and they, like the old shepherd, assert their differences from children, spouses, parents. They take for granted change, difference, separation.

The extraordinary dignity and subdued control with which Hermione responds to Leontes' accusations have obscured for critics her earlier vivacity. In the opening scene she is remarkable for her wit, sexual frankness, and deflating banter. She takes pleasure in competing verbally with men—"A lady's 'Verily' is / As potent as a lord's" (I.ii.50–51), she remarks to Polixenes (and the play will more than bear this out). But, though quick and forthright, her wit is inevitably good-natured and affectionate. She uses her persuasion of Polixenes as occasion to emphasize her love for Leontes: "yet, good deed, Leontes, / I love thee not a jar o' th' clock behind / What lady she her lord" (I.ii.42–44). And after talking Polixenes into staying, she diplomatically pacifies him by drawing him out on his favorite topic—his friendship with Leontes—but insists, jokingly, on her preference for Leontes, "the verier wag o' th' two" (I.ii.66). She denies the notion that marital sex implies "offenses" (I.ii.83), and goes on to counsel Leontes in the appropriately tender management of it—"you may ride's / With one soft kiss a thousand furlongs, ere / With spur we heat an acre" (I.ii.94–96).

Her relationship to her children is similarly realistic in its acknowledgment of physical ties and emotional differences. She affirms her physical connection with them: Mamillius is the "first fruits of my body" (III.ii.95), and Perdita, her babe, is "from my breast, / The innocent milk in its most innocent mouth / Haled out to murder" (III.ii.97–99). But she does not identify herself with her children or assume their perpetual innocence. At the beginning of act 2, scene 1, in one of the most apt of the play's numerous realistic touches, she is quite simply tired of Mamillius: "he so troubles me, / 'Tis past enduring" (II.i.1–2). Mamillius's flirtatious banter with the waiting women shows his precosity, not his innocence, and he himself protests being treated like a baby. Later, when Hermione is "for [him] again" (22), she asks *him* to tell *her* a tale rather than imposing her stories on him as Leontes does.

Hermione, "killed" by Leontes' horror story, is absent from the play until the last scene and does not speak until the last few lines. Her mock death is the most extended and powerful version of the motif. Like other mock deaths, it is, we eventually discover, engineered by the woman and her confidante for the purpose of self-protection and self-preservation as well as for the punishment and rehabilitation of the man. But Shakespeare—uniquely—withholds information of the deception from the audience until the last scene of the play; even then Hermione comes alive as gradually for the audience as she does for Leontes. The belief that the death is actual enhances the sanctification of Hermione as ideal wife and mother, enabling her to acquire near mythic status. In her absence, her power is extended through Paulina's defense of her and through Perdita's recreation of her. Indeed, through Antigonus's dream of her, she becomes the play's very human deity.

Northrop Frye defines the dream visions of Diana in *Pericles* and of Jupiter in *Cymbeline* as "an emblematic recognition scene, in which we are shown the power that brings about the comic resolution" and in which "the controlling deity appears

with an announcement of what is to conclude the action."[29]
Similarly, Hermione appears to Antigonus in a dream vision in
which she is transformed into an emblematic figure, a chaste,
grieving victim, "In pure white robes, / Like very sanctity"
(III.iii.21–22). Alive, she was not "prone to weeping" (II.i.108),
but in the vision, "her eyes / Became two spouts"; alive, she
was never at a loss for words, but here she is "gasping to begin
some speech" (III.iii.24–25). She instructs Antigonus as Diana
instructs Pericles, and she narrates the conclusion of the first
part of the play as Jupiter does the conclusion of *Cymbeline*.
Like Posthumus's family in his dream, the figure's aim is to
protect her child and ensure its future. The wedding masque in
the *Tempest*, the counterpart of these dreams, is likewise a
prayer for the prophecy of future happiness for the children,
Miranda and Ferdinand. All three visions eventually restore
parents to each other and/or children to parents. The wedding
masque, however, is broken off; Posthumus cannot understand his dream or his prophecy; and Antigonus misinterprets
his vision. Although he takes it to mean that Hermione is
guilty and dead, it is emblematic, rather, of her persistent,
fierce love and grief for her daughter. In this play, through
Antigonus's dream, the sanctified dead mother is given mythic
status and power.

A maternal deity, Hermione resembles most closely the
goddess of fertility, Ceres, with whom she is explicitly linked
when Perdita associates herself with Ceres' daughter, Proserpina. Critics who have noted the relevance of the myth's cycli-
cal motif to the play have paid little attention to the narrative
parallels between the two works. Ovid's tale focuses on Ceres'
desperate grief and on her frantic efforts to be reunited with
the lost Proserpina. Unable to find her, Ceres takes vengeance
on the land, especially on Sicily, where the rape occurred:

> Therefore there shee brake
> The furrowing plough; the Oxe and owner strake
> Both with one death; then, bade the fields beguile
> The trust impos'd, shrunk seed corrupts. That soile,
> So celebrated for fertilitie,

Now barren grew: corne in the blade doth die.
Now, too much drouth annoy's; now lodging showres:
Stars smitch, winds blast. The greedy fowle devoures
The new-sowne graine.[30]

Having learned that Proserpina was stolen by Pluto, "Stone-
like stood Ceres at this heavy newes; / And, staring, long continued in this muse" (510–11). (Perhaps this story, as well as
that of Pygmalion, suggested the statue scene to Shakespeare.)
Because of the consummation of the rape,[31] Proserpina cannot
become fully a daughter again but is returned to her mother for
six months of the year, suggesting both the inevitable separation of mother and daughter when the child reaches sexual maturity and their continuing bond. When reunited with her
daughter, Ceres is rejuvenated and regenerates the earth, just
as when Perdita returns to Sicily, its barren winter ends, its air
is purged of "infection" (V.i.169), and Hermione is brought
back to life. Proserpina, Sandys says, represents "the fertility
of the seed" (p. 254); in the play as in the myth, Sicily's "fail of
issue" (V.i.27) is the direct result of the absence of Hermione
and Perdita.

During this absence Paulina is present as the heroine's
double, defender, and surrogate, a role familiar from the comedies, problem comedies, and tragedies, but one not found in
the other romances. Paulina's role is crucial to the transformations enacted in the play. Like Beatrice and Emilia, she is
Hermione's shrewishly outspoken and vehement defender,
asserting her mistress's chastity more vociferously than the
slandered woman can. She likewise absorbs the most brutal of
the verbal and physical expressions of Leontes' repudiation of
Hermione and his daughter, as Diana absorbs Bertram's scorn.
Like Emilia, she expresses the audience's rage at the heroine's
"death." And like her, Paulina is a mediator both dramatically
and psychologically. Her role shifts from that of comic shrew
to wise counselor as she engineers the penance that will transform Leontes' tragic actions to a comic conclusion. She also
mediates more fruitfully than Emilia can between her mistress
and her mistress's husband. Loving Hermione, she believes

Leontes is salvageable—and worth saving for her. So, unlike Camillo, she stays around to reform him and preserve Hermione.

Her attacks on Leontes, unlike those of Antigonus, are calculated, judicious, positive. While castigating Leontes' folly, she offers him alternatives to it. She first urges him to accept and bless Perdita, using the argument, designed to please him and to dispel his suspicions, that the child is "the whole matter / And copy of the father" (II.iii.97–98). After her tirade against Leontes following Hermione's "death," Paulina offers him one last chance to "see" Hermione—"if you can bring / Tincture or luster in her lip, her eye, / Heat outwardly or breath within, I'll serve you / As I would do the gods" (III.ii. 202–05). Finally, she presents him with an image of penance that will rehabilitate Hermione's image for him more thoroughly than did those penances arranged for Claudio and Bertram.

The penance is fruitful in part because Paulina, who shares many of Hermione's qualities and is present when she is absent, is a surrogate for her mistress. She can lead Leontes toward a reunion with Hermione as Hermione herself cannot because she assumes an unthreatening, asexual role. We are reminded of the literal disguises that freed Julia, Rosalind, and Viola to educate their beloveds. At first, Paulina takes on an explicitly masculine identity. Bringing Perdita to Leontes, she substitutes for the "minister of honor" (II.ii.49) Hermione feared to approach. Arriving, she urges the timid lords to "be second" (II.iii.26) to her and later makes explicit her warrior's role—"[I] would by combat make her good, so were I / A man, the worst about you" (II.iii.59–60). But after Leontes has accepted Hermione's innocence and Paulina's tutelage, Paulina changes her strategy. She professes to drop her loquaciousness ("I'll say nothing" [III.ii.230]) and identifies herself as a woman subordinate to Leontes—"Now, good my liege, / Sir, royal sir, forgive a foolish woman" (III.ii.224–25). She is now no longer the "mankind witch" (II.iii.66) of her first scene with Leontes but a "good lady" (III.ii.172) who closely resembles Hermione in her articulateness and affection for Leontes. By act

5, scene 1, Paulina and Leontes have achieved understanding and reciprocity; their long, intimate, chaste friendship is a transformation and vindication of that of Hermione and Polixenes.

As Hermione's virtues are regenerated for Leontes by Paulina, they are regenerated for the audience in Perdita. In her flower speeches with their embrace of change and pity for maidenhood, in her image of Florizel as "a bank for Love to lie and play on" (IV.iv.130), and in her easy assumption that he should "Desire to breed by me" (IV.iv.103), Perdita expresses a frank and whole-hearted acceptance of sexuality that recalls Hermione's in the opening scenes. She also shares with her mother and Paulina what Tillyard calls her "ruthless common sense"[32] and employs it as wittily and adeptly as they to deflate men's exaggerated rhetoric and vapid generalizations— whether Camillo's about "affliction" (IV.iv.579) or Polixenes' about art and nature. She recognizes the risk she runs in loving the son of the king and embraces it boldly, but she is not very surprised or "much afeard" (IV.iv.446) when their betrothal is interrupted by Polixenes in a comic replay of Leontes' wrath.

Perdita is important not only as a character and as Hermione's double but also for the healthy relationships in which she participates, transformations of the infected ones in Sicily. Florizel, in comparison with the heroes of the comedies, even with Othello, but specifically with Leontes, is a remarkable lover. His courtship, unlike Leontes' "crabbèd" one (I.ii.102) is joyous and confident. He acknowledges Perdita's sexuality and his own, identifying himself with the gods, who have "taken / The shapes of beasts upon them" (IV.iv.26–27) but controlling his burning "lusts" (34). He delights in Perdita's frankness, her beauty, her wit, in her "blood" which "look[s] out" (IV.iv.160). He praises her unconventionally:

> When you speak, sweet,
> I'd have you do it ever; when you sing,
> I'd have you buy and sell so; so give alms,
> Pray so; and for the ord'ring your affairs,
> To sing them too. . . .

> Each your doing,
> So singular in each particular,
> Crowns what you are doing in the present deeds,
> That all your acts are queens.   [IV.iv.135–46]

His blazon admires not her looks but her particular "deeds," each one of them, thus reversing Leontes' disgust at Hermione's second "good deed" and his need to turn Hermione's "actions" into his "dreams."

As Florizel is a transformation of Leontes as lover, so the old shepherd is a transformation of Leontes as father. His attitudes toward his children are at every point contrasted with Leontes' need to identify with and possess his. Believing, like Leontes, that Perdita is a bastard (although not, of course, his), he takes her up "for pity" (III.iii.75) as well as for gold. He does not treat his children as possessions but rather as friends whose independence he respects and whose innocence he knows better than to count on. He makes Perdita mistress of the feast and urges her to "lay it on" (IV.iii.41–42), to behave with the boldness, warmth, and flirtatiousness embodied in his remarkable reminiscence of his dead wife:

> When my old wife lived, upon
> This day, she was both pantler, butler, cook;
> Both dame and servant; welcomed all, served all;
> Would sing her song, and dance her turn; now here
> At upper end o' th' table, now i' th' middle;
> On his shoulder, and his; her face o' fire
> With labor and the thing she took to quench it,
> She would to each one sip.   [IV.iv.55–62]

The shepherd's praise of his wife resembles Florizel's more formal praise of Perdita—in its rhythms, its repetitions, its emphasis on particular and multiple actions, and its reference to singing and dancing. Appreciating his wife's sexuality, he accepts Perdita's, encourages her romance and betrothal—"I think there is not half a kiss to choose / Who loves another best" (IV.iv.175–76). He rejoices in his son's fortune and, matter-of-factly noting his own barrenness, looks forward to the prospect of grandchildren, something other romance fathers do not do: "Come, boy, I am past moe children; but thy sons and daughters will be all gentlemen born" (V.ii.129).

The shepherd, like all the inhabitants of the Bohemian countryside, views youth as a period of wantonness, not innocence, and accepts this fact grumblingly. He contemplates with exasperated tolerance the age "between ten and three-and-twenty," occupied with "getting wenches with child, wronging the ancientry, stealing, fighting" (III.iii.58–63). He speaks from experience, it seems, for the clown tells him, "You're a made old man; if the sins of your youth are forgiven you" (III.iii.116–17). The "delicate burden" of Autolycus's ballad urges, "Jump her, and thump her" (IV.iv.194–95); chastity is temporary and unnatural in the fourth act of *The Winter's Tale*, and aggressive male sexuality is celebrated. It is implied, too, that it is better to be even the usurer's wife "brought to bed of twenty money-bags at a burden" (IV.iv.263–64) than to be the woman "turned into a cold fish for she would not exchange flesh with one that loved her" (279–81). "Red blood reigns" throughout the act, as in Autolycus's introductory song; all are caught in its pulsing rhythms, even—temporarily—Camillo and Polixenes, enthusiastic participants in revelry, who welcome the rough satyrs' dance by the "men of hair" (IV.iv.328). Sexuality is natural, grotesque, or humorous; phallic aggression and female passivity are trivialized: "Pins and poking-sticks of steel; / What maids lack from head to heel!" (IV.iv.227–28).

Autolycus's role as parodic double of Leontes is centrally responsible for transmuting into comedy the conflicts and motives of the first three acts.[33] Leontes' dangerous fantasies are translated into Autolycus's tall tales, and his cruel manipulative actions into comic turns. Leontes' delusion of deceit and infidelity on the part of those he deceives and harms becomes Autolycus's enactment of victimization (by himself) as he robs the clown. Leontes' revulsion from sexuality and fatherhood is incorporated comically into the ballads with their rejected lover, their grotesque childbirth, and their love triangle of "two maids wooing a man" (a cheerful reversal from the male perspective of the triangle of Leontes' imagination). Autolycus himself, unlike Leontes, unanxiously equates daffodils with doxies and natural instincts for thieving with those for tumbling in the hay. Leontes' need to take revenge against his family is reiterated and displaced in Autolycus's exaggerated descriptions to the shepherd and clown of the revenge Polixenes will inflict on them as a result of their kinship to Perdita. This episode recapitulates the dangers of family intimacy and emphasizes Autolycus's freedom as an outsider, unencumbered by social or familial ties. (He does give himself a wife in his autobiographical sketch, but we cannot know if she is authentic; maybe she is dead!). Autolycus "makes change his constancy, directionless his direction, role playing his role."[34] His merry marginality is a positive version of Leontes' isolation in paranoia and penance. In the last act, Autolycus's repentance and promise of incorporation into the social hierarchy when the shepherd and clown promise to be his "masters" and to prefer him to Florizel parallel Leontes' repentance and restoration to his family. All along, Autolycus's manipulations are relatively harmless and ultimately beneficial. Since he has no intimate connections with women in the play, neither the sexual aggression nor the sexual disgust revealed in his songs is ever enacted dramatically. The family into which he is absorbed at the play's end is an all-male one, a benign version of that envisioned in the opening scene.

Leontes' isolation in Sicily issues in a yet more fruitful conclusion. He has not simply been worn down by a winter of abstinence and penance, "naked, fasting, / Upon a barren mountain" (III.ii.209–10)—in effect, a bleaker form of the eternal summer of youth which he with Polixenes had longed for, equally changeless, sexless, endless. Instead he has been changed, regenerated. His transformation is apparent in his continuing acknowledgment of guilt, his chastened rhetoric, but most of all in his new apprehension of Hermione. She is seen no longer as a conventional abstraction, but as a unique woman—"no more such wives, therefore no wife" (V.i.56). He now honors her sexuality as "the sweet'st companion that e'er man / Bred his hopes out of" (V.i.11–12), and he longs for her kisses (and for her words as well): "Then, even now, / I might have looked upon my queen's full eyes, / Have taken treasure from her lips" (V.i.52–54). Leontes now longs to see and touch Hermione.[35] With Paulina's help, he is able to conceive of her as human, flawed, "soul-vexed" (59)—liable like himself to jealousy, anger, vengefulness, and fully capable of berating him on his choice of a new wife (11). Leontes' resuscitation of the image of a wife who is peerless, sexual, and human—"the sweet'st companion that e'er man / Bred his hopes out of" (V.i. 11–12)—prepares him to enter into a transformed relationship with Polixenes and Perdita and Florizel and makes possible the climactic recovery of Hermione herself.[36] The arrival of the children brings memories of the boyhood friendship— not of idyllic innocence but of "something wildly / By us performed before" (V.i.129–30). Leontes no longer sees himself and Polixenes as identical, but contrasts them throughout the scene and breaks with his friend to condone the children's elopement. When Florizel begs him, "Remember since you owed no more to Time / Than I do now; with thought of such affections / Step forth mine advocate" (217–20), Leontes can become "friend" (V.i.231) to the couple's love because of his own transformed attitudes toward sexual "affections." He can associate his own youthful desires with Florizel's—"I'd beg your precious mistress." But he can also, when jolted by Paulina, both explicitly acknowledge and renounce the incestuous component of the desires, voicing his admiration for the youthfully peerless Perdita but differentiating it from the longing he once felt—and still feels—for his wife: "I thought of her, / Even in these looks I made" (V.i.227–28).

Leontes' willingness to support the affections of the younger couple (made possible by his new apprehension of his own marriage) precipitates the multiple recognition scene. Its joy, flowing from the reunions of Leontes with Camillo, Perdita, Polixenes, and Florizel, is interrupted and qualified by the loss of Antigonus and the absence of Hermione. The only reported dialogue in the scene is Leontes' "Oh, thy mother, thy mother," an exclamation that interrupts the description of his reunion with Polixenes. The joyous reunions build to a sorrowful climax, Perdita's grief for her dead mother. The crucial absence which the joyous reunions emphasize, the narrators' emphasis on "delivery," and the description of Hermione's statue issue into the final scene. Psychologically, the scene is generated by Leontes' restored vision of Hermione, by his recovery of Perdita, and by the longing of the daughter, though blessed now with three fathers, a brother, and a beloved, to be united with the mother "who ended when I but begun" (V.iii.45). The scene is possible, too, because Hermione has not been "content to die" but has "desire[d]" her life to "see" Perdita a woman (I.i.43–45).

The final scene, like the preceding recognition scene, is communal; all of the characters need to recover Hermione. Paulina shapes the desires of the participants into a shared verbal ritual, so that their speech gradually imbues the statue with life—for them and for the play's audience. The statue, first an "it," becomes a "she" (V.ii.61–80). The onlookers' remarks move toward greater verbal certainty: from questions, to a possibility, to a fact qualified by a comparison (61–68). They recreate Hermione bit by bit, pointing first to fragmented physical attributes like "blood" and "hand" and "lip," and then invoking integrated processes like "motion" and "speech." Leontes' earlier reduction of Hermione to her basest aspects— "Mingling bloods" and "paddling palms"—is thus reversed.[37]

The final scene is symbolic—among so much else—of Leontes' acceptance of Hermione as fully his wife. As Othello, at the last, transformed the sleeping Desdemona into "monumental alabaster" (V.ii.5), so Leontes, at the first, wanted to possess a Hermione who was, in effect, a statue. He had distrusted her wit, her warmth, her blood ("You charge him too coldly," Hermione complained to Leontes, and his delusion erupted with the words, "Too hot, too hot" [I.ii.30, 108]). Now he explicitly longs for her "warm life," her "blood," her "breath," her speech (V.iii.35, 65, 79). His determination to kiss the statue signals Paulina that he is ready for reunion with the woman Hermione.

The moment of reunion is as painful, laborious, and exhilarating as the moment of birth. Both Hermione and Leontes must experience constriction, separation, and transformation.

Hermione, as she moves from being hated to being loved, must break out of her own entombed emotions, while Leontes must replace the image of Hermione with a living woman and love *her*. Both must begin the relationship over. Hence Paulina, acting as midwife, entices Hermione out of her numbness with her reference to "time" and her image of fulfillment:

> 'Tis time; descend; be stone no more; approach
> Strike all that look upon with marvel; come;
> I'll fill your grave up. [V.iii.99–101]

She compels Leontes to enter into a reversal of his original courtship, eschewing a repetition of the crabbedness whose memory had been one catalyst for the couples' separation:

> Do not shun her
> Until you see her die again, for then
> You kill her double. Nay, present your hand.
> When she was young, you wooed her; now, in age,
> Is she become the suitor? [V.iii.105–09]

The action repeats and reverses the inception of their nuptials, when Leontes was the wooer who waited "Three crabbed months" for Hermione to "open [her] white hand" (I.ii.102–04) to him, as he bitterly recounted at the onset of his jealousy. Now Hermione must "become the suitor" and embrace him. Leontes' acceptance of her new autonomy, his abandonment of possessiveness, is embodied in his presentation of his hand. The reunion is completed as he accepts Hermione's embrace, registering his concrete physical delight and marking the naturalness of this miraculous event: "Oh, she's warm! / If this be magic, let it be an art / Lawful as eating" (V.iii.109–11). This reunion, like those in the other romances, recalls, as it reverses, the original rupture. Pericles asks Thaisa, whom he had buried at sea, to "Come be buried / A second time within these arms" (V.ii.42–43). When Posthumus, who had ordered the murder of Imogen, throws her on the ground, failing to recognize her, Pisanio interprets, "You ne'er killed Imogen till now" (V.v.231). Alonso, when Ferdinand, whom he had believed dead, reappears, exclaims: "If this prove / A vision of the island, one dear son / Shall I twice lose" (V.i.175–77). The language and gestures of these moments acknowledge the source and the pain of separation and the possibility of its recurrence even as they undo and transcend loss. The gradual physical regeneration of the Hermione whom Leontes had "killed" dramatizes most explicitly and extensively the reversal of the process of destruction.[38]

But the reunion with Leontes is not the final, indeed, not the central one for Hermione. Her own renewal is completed only when she speaks to Perdita, bestowing on her the blessing the daughter wishes for and reassuming her own motherhood:

> You gods look down,
> And from your sacred vials pour your graces
> Upon my daughter's head! Tell me, mine own,
> Where hast thou been preserved? Where lived? How found
> Thy father's court? For thou shalt hear that I,
> Knowing by Paulina that the oracle
> Gave hope thou wast in being, have preserved
> Myself to see the issue.   [V.iii.121–28]

Leontes has been preserved and renewed by Paulina. Perdita has been preserved by time and nature and her foster family in the Bohemian countryside. But Hermione, like Paulina bereft of husband and future, has preserved herself to see both Perdita and "the issue" in a wider sense: the outcome, "Time's news," which is "known when 'tis brought forth" (IV.i.26–27).

The last—and unexpected—union in the play, complementing the restored marriage of Leontes and Hermione and the ratified betrothal of Perdita and Florizel, is that of Paulina and Camillo. This marriage is offered as final testimony to the equality and mutuality of Leontes and Paulina: "Thou shouldst a husband take by my consent, / As I by thine a wife. This is a match, / And made between 's by vows" (V.iii.136–38). Along with the reestablished friendship of Hermione and Polixenes, this match assures that all of the destructive motifs of the play are altered. Symbolically incestuous relationships are transmuted into reproductive ones, and male bonds, although subordinated to marriage, are not eliminated. The static friendship of Leontes and Polixenes can now be extended and fulfilled through the marriages of their children and of their counselors. The marriage of Perdita and Florizel eradicates the fantasized illegitimacy of Perdita rather than signaling incest. The betrothal of Camillo and Paulina evaporates two potentially problematic triangles—the "marriage" of Leontes with both Hermione and Paulina, and the rivalry of Polixenes and Leontes for Camillo's services (seen in III.ii). The remaining triangle—that of Leontes, Hermione, and Polixenes—is now made safe through Leontes' restored fidelity, through his acceptance of the "holy looks" of Hermione and Polixenes (V.iii.48), and through the betrothal of the children, which provides continuity and regeneration for all three relationships. Leontes is not forced to give up friendship or either of his wise counselors for marriage, and Polixenes is not excluded from the happy ending.

In its intricately worked out reconciliation of marriage, family, and friendship, the conclusion of *The Winter's Tale* differs both from the endings of tragedy in which triangles remain unresolved, and from the endings of comedy, in which a solitary male figure is often left out of the marriage celebrations. It more nearly resembles the problem comedies, in which the marriage offers to Diana and Isabella similarly divide the heroines from their doubles, eliminate triangles, and nudge everyone toward marriage. In *The Winter's Tale*, however, though equally surprised by this last-minute union, we are undismayed by it. Marriage here is not a punishment or a convention but a hard-earned fulfillment. The reunions and marriages in *The Winter's Tale* work symbolically, dramatically, and psychologically because the women who are crucial to them are accepted into the play as fully human figures "freed and enfranchised" (II.ii.60) from the rigid conceptions and imprisoning roles projected onto them by foolish men. In all the romances, men, also freed, learn as the women do in a "wide gap of time" (V.iii.154) to wait patiently, to suffer, to weep, to forgive, to nurture children, to bless others, and to regenerate themselves.

Notes

INTRODUCTION: WOOING, WEDDING, AND REPENTING

1 Leo Salingar, *Shakespeare and the Traditions of Comedy* (Cambridge: Cambridge University Press, 1974), pp. 302–05.

2 Michelle Rosaldo, "The Use and Abuse of Anthropology: Reflections on Feminism and Cross-Cultural Understanding," *Signs* 5 (1980): 400.

3 Ian Maclean, *The Renaissance Notion of Women* (Cambridge: Cambridge University Press, 1980), emphasizes the profoundly conservative effect of the dominant paradigm of marriage on Renaissance thinking about women. This paradigm, he argues (as well as vested interest in preserving it) is crucially responsible for the maintenance of unchanged views of women's inferiority throughout the period in the disciplines of theology (pp. 25–27), ethics and politics (pp. 65–67), and law (pp. 80–81); only in the area of medicine is there conceptual change, because there the absence of the paradigm of marriage "acts as a liberating force" (p. 45). "Marriage is an immovable obstacle to any improvement in the theoretical or real status of women in law, in theology, in moral and political philosophy" (p. 85).

4 T. E., *The Lawes Resolutions of Womens Rights; or The Lawes Provision for Women. A Methodicall Collection of such Statutes and Customes, with the Cases, Opinions, Arguments and points of Learning in the Law, as do properly concerne Women* (London: John Grove, 1632), p. 6.

5   Allison Heisch, "Queen Elizabeth I and the Persistence of Patriarchy," *Feminist Review* 4 (1980): 45–56.
6   Anna Jameson, *Characteristics of Women*, 2 vols. (London: Saunders & Otley, 1832); Mary Cowden Clarke, *The Girlhood of Shakespeare's Heroines*, 3 vols. (London: W. H. Smith and Son, 1850–55); Helena Faucit Martin, *On Some of Shakespeare's Female Characters* (London: Blackwood, 1885).
7   Irene Dash, *Wooing, Wedding, and Power: The Women in Shakespeare's Plays* (New York: Columbia University Press, 1981).
8   Coppélia Kahn, "*The Taming of the Shrew*: Shakespeare's Mirror of Marriage," in *The Authority of Experience*, ed. Arlyn Diamond and Lee Edwards (Amherst: University of Massachusetts Press, 1977), pp. 84–100; L. T. Fitz, "Egyptian Queens and Male Reviewers: Sexist Attitudes in *Antony and Cleopatra* Criticism," *Shakespeare Quarterly* 28 (1977): 297–316; S. N. Garner, "Shakespeare's Desdemona," *Shakespeare Studies* 9 (1976): 233–52.
9   Carole McKewin, "Counsels of Gall and Grace: Intimate Conversations between Women in Shakespeare's Plays," in *The Woman's Part: Feminist Criticism of Shakespeare*, ed. Carolyn Ruth Swift Lenz, Gayle Greene, and Carol Thomas Neely (Urbana: University of Illinois Press, 1980), pp. 117–32; Marilyn Williamson, "Doubling, Women's Anger, and Genre," *Women's Studies* 9 (1982): pp. 107–20; Madonne Miner, "Neither mother, wife, nor England's queene: The Roles of Women in *Richard III*," in Lenz et al., *Woman's Part*, pp. 35–55.
10   Joan Klein, "Lady Macbeth: 'Infirm of Purpose,'" in Lenz et al., pp. 240–55; Clara Claiborne Park, "As We Like It: How a Girl Can Be Smart and Still Popular," in ibid., pp. 100–16
11   Louis Adrian Montrose, "'The Place of a Brother': Social Process and Comic Form in *As You Like It*," *Shakespeare Quarterly* 32 (1982): 28–54
12   Madelon Gohlke, "'I wooed thee with my sword': Shakespeare's Tragic Paradigms," in Lenz et al., pp. 150–70; "'All that is spoke is marred': Language and Consciousness in *Othello*," *Women's Studies* 9 (1982): 157–76; "'And When I Love Thee Not': Women and the Psychic Integrity of the Tragic Hero," *The Hebrew University Studies in Literature* 8 (1980), 44-65. Coppélia Kahn, *Man's Estate: Masculine Identity in Shakespeare* (Berkeley: University of California Press, 1981).
13   Linda Bamber, *Comic Women, Tragic Men: A Study of Gender and Genre in Shakespeare* (Stanford: Stanford University Press, 1982).

14 Peter Erickson, *Patriarchal Structures in Shakespeare's Drama* (Berkeley: University of California Press, 1985).

15 Marianne Novy, *Love's Argument: Gender Relations in Shakespeare* (Chapel Hill: University of North Carolina Press, 1985).

16 In *All's Well That Ends Well* the conventions are less central, and they are inverted. The woman idealizes her beloved, and the man actually participates (by virtue of the bedtrick) in what he imagines to be infidelity.

17 Kahn, *Man's Estate*, discusses the significance of the horns and delineates cuckoldry's connections with misogyny, the double standard, and patriarchal marriage (pp. 119–22). She notes that while *cuckquean* is defined by the *OED* as a female cuckold, the word does not appear in Shakespeare (p. 120, n. 2).

18 Pearl Hogrefe, *Tudor Women: Commoners and Queens* (Ames: Iowa State University Press, 1975), and *Women of Action in Tudor England: Nine Biographical Sketches* (Ames: Iowa State University Press, 1977).

19 Juliet Dusinberre, *Shakespeare and the Nature of Women* (New York: Barnes and Noble, 1975), emphasizes the importance of these factors.

20 Carole Levin, "Queens and Claimants: Political Insecurity in Sixteenth-Century England," paper delivered to Newberry Library Conference, Changing Perspectives on Women in the Renaissance, May 1983, and Louis Adrian Montrose, "'Shaping Fantasies': Figurations of Gender and Power in Elizabethan Culture," *Representations* 2 (Spring 1983): 61–94, explore some social and literary responses to the anxieties of having a woman on the throne. See also Heisch, "Queen Elizabeth I and the Persistence of Patriarchy."

21 Margaret King, "Thwarted Ambitions: Six Learned Women of the Early Italian Renaissance," *Soundings* 76 (1976): 280–300; "The Religious Retreat of Isotta Nogarola (1418–1466)," *Signs* 3 (1978): 807–22; "Book-Lined Cells: Women and Humanism in the Early Italian Renaissance," in *Beyond Their Sex: Learned Women of the European Past*, ed. Patricia H. Labalme (New York: New York University Press, 1980), and other essays in this volume.

22 Kathleen Casey, "The Cheshire Cat: Reconstructing the Experience of Medieval Women," in *Liberating Women's History*, ed. Berenice A. Carroll (Urbana: University of Illinois Press, 1976). pp. 224–49.

23 Lawrence Stone, "The Rise of the Nuclear Family in Early Mod-

ern England," in *The Family in History*, ed. Charles E. Rosenberg (Philadelphia: University of Pennsylvania Press, 1975), pp. 13–57; *The Family, Sex and Marriage in England 1500–1800* (New York: Harper & Row, 1977), pp. 123–218. Stone discusses the period from 1530 to 1660 as the patriarchal stage in the evolution of the nuclear family.

24 *Certaine Sermons or Homilies,* facsimile reproduction of 1623 edition, ed. Mary Ellen Rickey and Thomas B. Stroup (Gainesville, Fla.: Scholars' Facsimiles & Reprints, 1968), p. 239.

25 Desiderius Erasmus, *A ryght frutefull Epystle in laude and prayse of matrymony,* trans. Richard Tavernour (London: R. Redman, 1530?), sigs. B3-B4^v.

26 Although attacks on the double standard were commonplace, it did not, of course, disappear, as Keith Thomas incisively demonstrates in "The Double Standard," *Journal of the History of Ideas* 20 (1959): 195–216.

27 Lawrence Stone, *Crisis of the Aristocracy 1558–1641* (Oxford: Clarendon Press, 1965), pp. 637–39, 643–45.

28 George Elliot Howard, *A History of Matrimonial Institutions* (Chicago: University of Chicago Press, 1904), 1:377–80. Cf. Henry Swinburne, *A treatise of Spousals* written in the reign of Elizabeth I and first published in 1686, p. 15 (quoted in Howard, p. 377–78).

29 Juan Luis Vives, *Instruction of a Christian Woman,* (1523) trans. Richard Hyrd (London: Thomas Berthelet, 1540), excerpted in *Vives and the Renascence Education of Women,* ed. Foster Watson (New York: Longmans, Green & Co., 1912), pp. 105–06.

30 *Lawes Resolutions,* p. 130.

31 Howard, *Institutions,* 2:71–85, and Thomas, "The Double Standard," 200–01.

32 Maclean, *Notion,* p. 15–19. Stephen Greenblatt, *Renaissance Self-Fashioning from More to Shakespeare* (Chicago: University of Chicago Press, 1980), pp. 246–50, discusses Renaissance anxieties about sexuality even within marriage and their implications for Othello's relationship with Desdemona and his belief in her infidelity.

33 Watson, *Vives,* pp. 94–95. Cf. Edmund Tilney, *A brief and pleasant discourse of duties in Mariage, called the Flower of Friendshippe* (London: Henrie Denham, 1568), sigs. E3^v–E4^v.

34 Rickey and Stroup, *Homilies,* p. 241.

35 Tilney, *Flower of Friendshippe,* sig. E7^v.

36 J. Moncado, "The Spanish Source of Edmund Tilney's 'Flower of

of Friendshippe,' " *Modern Language Review* 65 (1970): 241–47, and Linda Woodbridge, *Women and the English Renaissance: Literature and the Nature of Womankind, 1540–1620* (Urbana: University of Illinois Press, 1984), pp. 59–60. I am especially grateful to Valerie Wayne, who is currently preparing an edition of Tilney's *Flower of Friendshippe,* for allowing me to read a draft of her introduction that illuminated the dialogue and its contexts.

37 Woodbridge, *Women and the English Renaissance,* discusses the stock misogynist characters in the dialogues of the formal controversy on women (see her index), and includes a chapter on "The Stage Misogynist" (pp. 275–95).

38 ". . . reason doth confirme the same, the man being as he is, most apt for the soveraignetie being in goverement, not onely skill, and experience to be required, but also capacity to comprehende, wisdome to understand, strength to execute, solicitude to prosecute, pacience to suffer, meanes to sustaine, and above all a great courage to accomplishe, all which are commonly in a man, but in a woman verye rare" (sig. C1).

39 *Becoming Visible: Women in European History,* ed. Renate Bridenthal and Claudia Koonz (Boston: Houghton Mifflin, 1977), pp. 137–64.

40 I was especially struck by this phenomenon at the Newberry Library Conference, Changing Perspectives on Women in the Renaissance, May 1983. During papers, brief presentations of works in progress, and lengthy discussion periods, participants, agreeing that women did not have a Renaissance, emphasized the numerous restrictions placed on them; at the same time, their presentations created a rich and complex existence for Renaissance women. This effect was apparent, for example, in Janel Mueller's analysis of *The Book of Margery Kempe,* Carole Levin's explorations of the insecurities created by Queen Elizabeth's reign, Mary Lamb's exploding of the myth of the Countess of Pembroke's patronage and her explorations of the functions of this myth, John Hill's report on the evidence for an extensive body of songs written by Francesca Caccini, Elissa Weaver's analysis of the nature of Italian sixteenth-century convent theatre, Jane Schulenburg's examination of the conditions for female sainthood, and Tilde Sankovitch's discussion of Madelaine and Catherine Des Roches's awareness of the special problems of female authorship. For essays, see *Women in the Middle Ages and Renaissance,* ed. Mary Beth Rose (Syracuse: Syracuse University Press, 1986).

41 Lisa Jardine, *Still Harping on Daughters: Women and Drama in the Age of Shakespeare* (Totowa, N.J.: Barnes and Noble, 1983).

42 Although neither book deals with Shakespeare as extensively as their titles might suggest, both wish to make him a central example of their respective theses about the period. Jardine begins by declaring that her book was generated by irritation at feminist criticism of Shakespeare, Dusinberre devotes a brief final chapter to him, and both books contain numerous remarks about particular moments in the plays. Both authors, however, are often at their least persuasive when analyzing these moments, perhaps because their piecemeal discussions of isolated characters, speeches, and scenes fail to do justice to the rich and complicated meanings these acquire as part of a complex whole. Jardine's book is a better one than Dusinberre's, but this is at least in part because she has had the benefit of much research that Dusinberre did not have available to her, including the feminist criticism which she finds inadequate, but which, like Dusinberre's book itself, has raised the issues she addresses.

CHAPTER 1   BROKEN NUPTIALS IN SHAKESPEARE'S COMEDIES: MUCH ADO ABOUT NOTHING

1 *Shakespeare and the Traditions of Comedy* (Cambridge: Cambridge University Press, 1974), pp. 302–05.

2 Titania appears in Ovid and elsewhere, and Bottom's ass's head has precedents in many tales of miraculous transformations; but the conjunction of the two is unique. See Geoffrey Bullough, *Narrative and Dramatic Sources of Shakespeare* (New York: Columbia University Press, 1966), 1:371–73. All subsequent references to Bullough's edition will be indicated in the text.

3 Salingar, pp. 298–325, esp. 298–99 and 305.

4 C. L. Barber in *Shakespeare's Festive Comedy* (New York: Meridian, 1963) gives extended discussion to *Love's Labor's Lost, Midsummer Night's Dream, Merchant of Venice, As You Like It, Twelfth Night,* and *Henry IV.* Sherman Hawkins, in "The Two Worlds of Shakespearean Comedy," *Shakespeare Studies* 3 (1967): 62–80, distinguishes between *Comedy of Errors, Love's Labor's Lost, Much Ado About Nothing,* and *Twelfth Night,* closed-heart comedies of intrusion, and *Two Gentlemen of Verona, Midsummer Night's Dream, Merchant of Venice,* and *As You Like It,* green-world comedies of extrusion, holding that *Taming of the Shrew* and *Merry Wives of Windsor*

share characteristics of both groups. Leo Salingar, in *Shakespeare and the Traditions of Comedy*, distinguishes three groups of comedies: *Comedy of Errors, Taming of the Shrew, Merry Wives of Windsor*, and *Twelfth Night*, farcical comedies derived from classical or Italian learned comedies; *Two Gentlemen of Verona, Love's Labor's Lost, Midsummer Night's Dream*, and *As You Like It*, woodland comedies with sources in pastoral or romance literature; and *Merchant of Venice, Much Ado About Nothing, All's Well That Ends Well*, and *Measure for Measure*, problem comedies with Italian *novelle* as sources (pp. 298–305).

5 In "The Argument of Comedy," *English Institute Essays, 1948*, ed. D. A. Robertson, Jr. (New York: Columbia University Press, 1949), Frye's Shakespearean examples tend to assimilate Shakespeare to the New Comedy structure he outlines, although he distinguishes Shakespearean green-world comedy from the generic norm. Even in *A Natural Perspective* (New York: Columbia University Press, 1965), where Frye looks more specifically at the three ritual phases of Shakespearean comedy, he continues to emphasize the anticomic society that must be overcome (pp. 72–117).

6 Barber, in *Shakespeare's Festive Comedy*, focuses on the release of emotion and, in " 'Thou that beget'st him that did thee beget': Transformation in 'Pericles' and 'The Winter's Tale,' " *Shakespeare Survey* 22 (1969): 61, compares that release with the transformation of emotion required in the romances.

7 I am indebted to Richard P. Wheeler's *Shakespeare's Development and the Problem Comedies: Turn and Counter-Turn* (Berkeley: University of California Press, 1981), which places the festive comedies and the late romances in relation to the problem comedies. See especially pp. 12–19.

8 Marianne Novy, "Patriarchy and Play in *The Taming of the Shrew*," *English Literary Renaissance* 9 (1979): 264–80.

9 This and subsequent citations of Shakespeare, unless otherwise noted, are from *The Complete Signet Classic Shakespeare*, Sylvan Barnet, gen. ed. (New York: Harcourt Brace and Jovanovich, 1972).

10 Madelon Gohlke Sprengnether first called my attention to this virtue of Petruchio's.

11 John C. Bean, "Comic Structure and the Humanizing of Kate in *The Taming of the Shrew*," in *The Woman's Part: Feminist Criticism of Shakespeare* ed. Carolyn Ruth Swift Lenz, Gayle Greene, and Carol Thomas Neely (Urbana: University of Illinois Press, 1980),

pp. 65–78, argues that Kate's speech advocates an ideal of marriage which, like that of progressive humanists, is based on reciprocal obligations and benefits.

12   Like my own, other recent feminist analyses of the play have the effect of taming the taming. They emphasize, using a variety of analogies and approaches, Kate's and Petruchio's mutual sexual attraction, affection, and satisfaction while deemphasizing her coerced submission to him. Like Germaine Greer in *The Female Eunuch* (New York: McGraw-Hill, 1971; p. 206), most stress Petruchio's virtues and Kate's happy release rather than their inequality. Margaret Loftus Ranald, "The Manning of the Haggard; or *The Taming of the Shrew*," *Essays in Literature* (Western Illinois University) 1 (1974): 149–65, interprets Petruchio's falconry metaphor positively to emphasize the couple's intimacy and mutual dependence. Marianne Novy, in "Patriarchy and Play" (see n. 8 above), argues that Petruchio's and Kate's games create space within the patriarchy for the expression of spontaneous individuality. John Bean, in "Comic Structures and the Humanizing of Kate in *The Taming of the Shrew*" (see n. 11 above), focuses on their reciprocal love and obligations, a transformation, he argues, of the conventional misogyny embodied in the source/analogue play, *The Taming of A Shrew*. Martha Andresen-Thom, "Shrew Taming and other Rituals of Aggression: Baiting and Bonding on the Stage and in the Wild," *Women's Studies* 9, no. 2 (1982): 121–43, finds in the play, as in the ritualistic mating behavior of animals, the playful transformation of negative aggression into energetic cooperation. Coppélia Kahn's discussion of *Taming* in *Man's Estate: Masculine Identity in Shakespeare* (Berkeley: University of California Press, 1981), pp. 104–118 argues more radically that the final speech, advocating submission, dramatizes female power, that it mocks the myth of male supremacy to embody a contrary myth "that only a woman has the power to authenticate a man, by acknowledging him *her* master" (p. 117). These critics are all, I think, responding, sometimes explicitly, to conflicting impulses—to their profound abhorrence of male dominance and female submission and to their equally profound pleasure at the play's conclusion, a pleasure created by the comic movement of the whole. Both impulses must be acknowledged. Feminists cannot, without ignoring altogether the play's meaning and structure, fail to rejoice at the spirit, wit, and joy with which Kate accommodates herself to her wifely role. Within the world of the

play there are no preferable alternatives. But we cannot fail to note the radical asymmetry and inequality of the comic reconciliation and wish for Kate, as for ourselves, that choices were less limited, roles less rigid and unequal, accommodations more mutual and less coerced.

13 Future marriages cannot be assumed—indeed, the issue cannot be debated, since its resolution is "too long for a play." But they remain a possibility, and although the play fails to achieve this expected comic resolution, it does, I think, achieve dramatic harmony and closure through the seasonal songs in ways that are explicated by William Carroll, *The Great Feast of Language in "Love's Labour's Lost"* (Princeton, N.J.: Princeton University Press, 1976), pp. 206–26. In contrast, Peter Erickson, "The Failure of Relationship between Men and Women in *Love's Labor's Lost*," *Women's Studies* 9, no. 1 (1981): 65–81, finds the ending harsh and disharmonious because of the unresolved divisions between the men and the women which he analyzes.

14 A number of recent critics analyze how these two plays use dramatic structure to contain or resolve tensions within patriarchy and present a restored and benign version of it. See Ann Parten, "Re-establishing Sexual Order: The Ring Episode in *The Merchant of Venice*," *Women's Studies* 9, no. 2 (1982): 145–55; Louis Adrian Montrose, "'The Place of a Brother': Social Process and Comic Form in *As You Like It*," *Shakespeare Quarterly* 32 (1982): 28–54; Peter Erickson, "Sexual Politics and the Social Structure in *As You Like It*," *Massachusetts Review* 23 (Spring 1982): 65–83.

15 For photographs of this scene, see *Peter Brook's Production of William Shakespeare's "A Midsummer Night's Dream" for the Royal Shakespeare Company* (Chicago: The Dramatic Publishing Company, 1974), p. 103, and *The Complete Works of Shakespeare*, ed. David Bevington (Glenview, Ill.: Scott, Foresman & Company, 1980), between pp. 54 and 55.

16 Jan Lawson Hinely, "Expounding the Dream: Shaping Fantasies in *A Midsummer Night's Dream*," paper circulated to seminar on Gender and Genre in Shakespeare at International Shakespeare Congress, Stratford-upon-Avon, August 1981, shows how the sexual anxieties and frustrations of the lovers are parodied in the comically confused bawdy reference of the Pyramus and Thisbe play. Her essay traces the growth of the lovers toward acceptance of mature heterosexual love. In contrast, Shirley Nelson Garner, *A Midsummer Night's Dream*: 'Jack shall have Jill; / Nought shall

go ill,'" *Women's Studies* 9, no. 1 (1981): 47–64, emphasizes the cost to the women and the advantages to the men of the comic resolution.

17 *Much Ado*, first published in 1600 and probably written in 1598 or 1599 is around the seventh of the thirteen comedies stretching from *Comedy of Errors* (early 1590s) to *Measure for Measure* (1604). In the introduction to his collection, *Twentieth-Century Interpretations of Much Ado About Nothing* (Englewood Cliffs, N.J.: Prentice-Hall, 1969), Walter R. Davis speaks of the play's "unique transitional status": ". . . largely because of its treatment of evil in society, it forms a bridge between the two halves of Shakespeare's career as comedian" (p. 2).

18 Most critics reluctantly accept the Claudio/Hero story as the "main plot," although they literally or figuratively put the term in quotation marks and are quick to point out that Beatrice and Benedick overshadow this "plot," however "main" it is. See, for example, Graham Story, "The Success of *Much Ado About Nothing*," in Davis, *Twentieth Century Interpretations*, p. 14; John Crick, "Messina," in ibid., p. 33; and Elliott Krieger, "Social Relations and the Social Order in 'Much Ado About Nothing,'" *Shakespeare Survey* 32 (1979): 50, n. 3. James Smith, "*Much Ado About Nothing*: Notes from a Book in Preparation," *Scrutiny* 13 (1945–46): 242–57, whose claims seem to be somewhat misrepresented in Krieger's footnote, is one of the few critics who argues, as I will, that the two plots depend on each other and to explore psychological and dramatic interdependence as well as thematic relationships among the different parts of the play: Beatrice/Benedick, Claudio/Hero, Dogberry and the Watch, and Don John.

19 For giddiness, see Graham Story; for complacency, see John Crick; for deceptiveness of appearances, see Walter N. King, "Much Ado about *Something*," *Shakespeare Quarterly* 15 (1964): 143–55 , A. P. Rossiter, *Angel with Horns* (New York: Theatre Arts Books, 1961), pp. 65–81, and many others.

20 Pp. 6, 114, 222. In *The Whole Journey: Shakespeare's Power of Development* (Berkeley: University of California Press, forthcoming), Barber suggests that it is the "precariousness" of *Much Ado* that separates it from the festive comedies proper.

21 Sherman Hawkins, "Two Worlds of Shakespearean Comedy," pp. 65–73.

22 For Beatrice and Benedick, see *Natural Perspective*, p. 81; for Hero's rebirth, see ibid., pp. 83–84, and "Argument of Comedy," p. 69.

23 R. G. Hunter, *Shakespeare and the Comedy of Forgiveness* (New York: Columbia University Press, 1965), pp. 93–105.

24 Salingar, *Shakespeare and the Traditions of Comedy*, pp. 301–22, esp. 310–11 and 317–18.

25 A. P. Rossiter, *Angel with Horns*, p. 81.

26 Ibid., p. 74, and Barbara Everett, "*Much Ado About Nothing*," *The Critical Quarterly* 3 (1961): 322, both note the positive effects of the displacement of the Hero/Claudio story by the Beatrice/Benedick story. James Smith, in contrast, argues for the impact of Hero's broken nuptials on Beatrice and Benedick: "the tragic scenes of the repudiation of Hero and its immediate consequences would seem to be the centre of unity in *Much Ado*. Other sections of the play look to them for completion; themselves, they draw strength and significance from the other sections" (p. 253). Alexander Leggatt, in *Shakespeare's Comedies of Love* (London: Methuen, 1974), pp. 151–83, explores the interplay between naturalism and convention in the play and analyzes how the two plots and the two couples follow parallel movements into convention, with Claudio's and Hero's engendering that of Beatrice and Benedick. Another perspective on the interaction of the two plots is that of John Traugott, who, in "Creating a Rational Rinaldo: A Study in the Mixture of the Genres of Comedy and Romance in *Much Ado About Nothing*," *Genre* 15, nos. 31/2 (1982): 157–81, discusses the displacement of romance into comedy which enables the genres to transform each other: "it is this very doublemindedness of romance that invites its 'contamination' by comedy. Its grace will render comedy a new sort of triumph over a scurvy world, its violence and absurdities will have to endure laughter" (p. 158).

27 Kahn, *Man's Estate*, p.122.

28 Indeed, Shakespeare's bastards Falconbridge and Edmund, more than Don John, are characterized by their perverse drive and energy and by their need to assert their virility.

29 Barbara Everett, however, analyzes the play as a "clash" of masculine and feminine worlds in which "the women's world dominates" (p. 320).

30 Janice Hays, "Those 'soft and delicate desires': *Much Ado* and the

Distrust of Women," in Lenz et al., *The Woman's Part*, pp. 79–99, discusses in detail Claudio's fears of and defenses against sexual involvement.

31 Some critics insist on the conventional aspects of the courtship and marriage arrangements. See Nadine Page, "The Public Repudiation of Hero," *PMLA* 50 (1935): 739–44, and Charles T. Prouty, *The Sources of Much Ado About Nothing* (New Haven: Yale University Press, 1950), pp. 41–47. Other critics accuse Claudio of being a mere fortune hunter; he is termed "a brash and ambitious would-be sophisticate" by Bertram Evans, *Shakespeare's Comedies* (London: Oxford University Press, 1960), p. 67. But his concentration on the business arrangements seems to satisfy psychological needs even more than financial ones.

32 In contrast, Bandello's *novella* is explicit about the passionate desires of Claudio's prototype, Timbreo, for Fenicia: "The gentleman grew warmer every day and the more he gazed on her, the more he felt his desires to burn, and the fire increasing in his heart so much that he felt himself consumed with love for the beautiful maiden, he determined that he must have her at any cost" (Bullough, 2:113). As is common in Italian *novelle*, Timbreo woos Fenicia for his wife only after she refuses to be his mistress.

33 Editions commonly gloss "bachelors" in this speech as "male or female unmarried persons," claiming that the source of this meaning is the biblical passage, "For when they shall rise from the dead, they neither marry, nor are given in marriage; but are as angels which are in heaven" (Mark 12 : 25). But the *OED* cites this meaning (5) as rare and obsolete and gives only one reference (Ben Jonson: 1632). In all nineteen other Shakespearean uses, *bachelor* refers exclusively to unmarried men, as it must, for example, in "Such separation as may well be said, / Becomes a virtuous bachelor and a maid" (*MND*, II.i.59–60). When Beatrice claims that "Adam's sons are my brethren" (II.i. 60), hopes to join the bachelors in heaven, and wishes she were a man to "eat Claudio's heart out in the market place," she is testifying to the attractiveness of the world of male camaraderie, a world she would be excluded from after marriage.

34 Carole McKewin, "Counsels of Gall and Grace: Intimate Conversations between Women in Shakespeare's Plays," Lenz et al., *The Woman's Part*, pp. 117–32, explores the "unease" of this scene but does not see as its source Beatrice's and Hero's unacknowledged

identification with each other and Margaret's unacknowledged deception.

35 I was first led to consider the function of mock deaths and their combination of passive and aggressive elements by Kirby Farrell's paper, "Authority and Self-Effacement: Shakespeare's Imagination and Family Structure," presented to a special session, "Marriage and the Family in Shakespeare," at the annual meeting of the Modern Language Association, New York, 1978. See also his revision, "Self-Effacement and Autonomy in Shakespeare," *Shakespeare Studies* 16 (1983): 75–99, and his book, *Shakespeare's Creation* (Amherst: University of Massachusetts Press, 1975), chap. 6.

36 In contrast, in Bandello's tale Fenicia, following the pretended death, is merely sent off to the country with her aunt, uncle, cousin and sister, until she has grown up and changed enough so that she can return to be married under another name (Bullough, 2:121–22).

37 Marilyn Williamson, "Doubling, Women's Anger, and Genre," *Women's Studies* 9, no. 2 (1982): 107–19, discusses the use of female doubling in *Much Ado, Othello,* and *The Winter's Tale* that protects the heroine's docility by allowing her anger to be expressed and her chastity vindicated by a double who is typed as shrewish. See below, pp. 131–32 and 199–201, for further explorations of the relationship between the heroines and their defenders.

38 Maynard Mack, "The Jacobean Shakespeare: Some Observations on the Construction of the Tragedies," in Alvin B. Kernan, *Modern Shakespearean Criticism* (New York: Harcourt, Brace and World, 1970), pp. 344–45, discusses the transformations wrought or symbolized by the tragic heroes' journeys.

39 In the middle of the problem comedies, tragedies, and romances—between the last part of act 3 and the early part of act 5, but usually in act 4—many of the women undergo either a literal journey like that of the tragic heroes (Helen, Cressida, Cordelia, Imogen, Perdita) or a withdrawal through disguise (Imogen), madness (Ophelia, Lady Macbeth), mock death (Helen, Cleopatra, Imogen, Hermione), sexual death and assuming another's identity (Helen, Mariana), or actual death (Ophelia, Lady Macbeth, Portia). Cordelia is, of course, absent through most of the first three acts while Lear's love for her is being regenerated. Vo-

lumnia and Virgilia are absent from the fourth act of *Coriolanus*, which follows the protagonist in his banishment to Antium where he tries to escape his attachment to his mother but cannot. Desdemona, who is not granted any significant retreat from her predicament, does in act IV retreat to her bedroom with Emilia, where she confronts madness and death in the Willow Song. This withdrawal sometimes effects some transformation of the woman as well as transformed attitudes toward her by men. The most extreme and disturbing example of such a transformation is Cressida's unaccountable shift from being Troilus's faithful beloved in Troy in act 4, scene 4 to being a "daughter of the game" in the Greek camp in act 4, scene 5. Janet Adelman discusses her transformation in "'This Is and Is Not Cressida': The Characterization of Cressida," in *The (M)Other Tongue: Essays in Feminist, Psychoanalytic Interpretation*, ed. Shirley Garner, Madelon Gohlke, and Claire Kahane (Ithaca, N.Y.: Cornell University Press, 1984).

40 Traugott, "Creating a Rational Rinaldo" (see n. 26 above), analyzes in somewhat similar fashion the effect of the demand to kill Claudio: "Suddenly our expectations are derailed and they [Beatrice and Benedick] have stolen away the convention of service to the distressed lady, together with its man on horseback, its idealism, its grace, and incongruously incorporated it into the comic charades they concoct between themselves. The wit plot has absorbed the romance plot" (p. 164).

41 In the first scene of the play, Beatrice similarly deflated killing to eating, real battles to "merry wars" of wit, and Benedick from a "good soldier" to a "good soldier to a lady" (I.i.36–60).

42 The situation is quite different in Bandello's tale, in which Timbreo is effusively penitent and, after having taken his former beloved, Fenicia, as his wife without recognizing her, must prove his love by asserting that his love for Fenicia is greater than that for his new bride before she will reveal herself to him: "truly I loved her as much as a woman can be loved by a man, and if I love aeons of years I shall still love her, dead though she is" (Bullough, 2:130).

43 The vexing double substitution in which not only is Margaret to pretend to be Hero, but Borachio is to imitate Claudio (II.i.43–44), whether deliberate or a slip, foreshadows the problem plays in which the protagonist himself participates in the bedtricks with a substitute bride. At the end of *All's Well*, Ber-

tram, unlike Claudio here, does assert the identity of the "dead" Helen he married and the living Helen he slept with, affirming that, now pregnant, she is fully his wife, both the "name" and the "thing" (V.iii.308). Othello, too, at his death affirms the continuity between the actual woman he killed and the reidealized woman he loves: "I kissed thee ere I killed thee. No way but this / Killing myself to die upon a kiss" (V.ii.339–40). And in the ritualistic conclusion of *The Winter's Tale*, Leontes imbues the statue with life, integrating his image of a perfected Hermione with the flesh-and-blood woman: "Hermione was not so wrinkled, nothing / So aged as this seems" (V.iii.28–29).

44 Clara Claiborne Park, "As We Like It: How a Girl Can be Smart and Still Popular," in Lenz et al., *The Woman's Part*, pp. 100–16, discusses how the assertiveness of the heroines is curtailed.

CHAPTER 2   POWER AND VIRGINITY IN THE PROBLEM
COMEDIES:
ALL'S WELL THAT ENDS WELL

1 Frederick Boas, *Shakspere and His Predecessors* (London: John Murray, 1896), chapter 13, "The Problem-Plays." The hyphen was subsequently dropped from the term.

2 A. P. Rossiter, *Angel with Horns* (New York: Theatre Arts Books, 1974). Rossiter also finds that *II Henry IV* has affinities with the problem plays (pp. 55–57) and views *Much Ado About Nothing* as their immediate predecessor (p. 81).

3 Michael Jamieson, "The Problem Plays, 1920–1970: A Retrospect," *Shakespeare Survey* 25 (1972): 1–10, rpt. in *Aspects of Shakespeare's 'Problem Plays,'* ed. Kenneth Muir and Stanley Wells (Cambridge: Cambridge University Press, 1982), pp. 126–35, along with many others, seems almost forced into using the term against his will and concludes his discussion, "They are no longer Problem Plays, and no longer unpopular" (*Aspects*, p. 135).

4 E. K. Chambers, *Shakespeare: A Survey* (London: Sidgwick & Jackson, 1925), says of *All's Well*, *Troilus and Cressida*, and *Measure for Measure*: "They are all unpleasant plays, the utterances of a puzzled and disturbed spirit, full of questionings, sceptical of its own ideals, looking with new misgivings into the ambiguous shadows of a world over which a cloud has passed and made a goblin of the sun" (p. 210); J. Dover Wilson, *The Essential Shakespeare* (Cambridge: Cambridge University Press, 1935), declares of the prob-

lem comedies: "The note of them is all disillusion and cynicism, the air is cheerless and often unwholesome, the mirth witless, the bad characters contemptible or detestable, the good ones unattractive. Helena in *All's Well* is a most noble and admirable lady; yet everything she does sets our teeth on edge" (p. 116). While Wilson attributes the altered tone of the work to changes both in the spirit of the age and in Shakespeare's mood and temper, it is clear that his view of the plays is also influenced by the spirit of his own age. Of *Measure for Measure* he says, "The hatred of sentimentalism and romance, the savage determination to tear aside all veils, to expose reality in its crudity and hideousness, the self-laceration, weariness, discord, cynicism and disgust of our modern 'literature of negation' all belonged to Shakespeare about 1603; and he would well have understood Mr. T. S. Eliot's *The Waste Land . . .*" (p. 117).

5　W. W. Lawrence, *Shakespeare's Problem Comedies* (New York: Macmillan, 1931).

6　In *Studies in Shakespeare: British Academy Lectures*, ed. Peter Alexander (London: Oxford University Press, 1964).

7　E. M. W. Tillyard, *Shakespeare's Problem Plays* (Toronto: University of Toronto Press, 1950), pp. 1–2.

8　Rossiter, *Angel with Horns*, chaps. 5–10 and 3–4 passim.

9　Richard P. Wheeler, *Shakespeare's Development and the Problem Comedies: Turn and Counter-turn* (Berkeley: University of California Press, 1981), esp. pp. 1–12.

10　Dover Wilson talks about "the strain of sex-nausea in the plays after 1600" (*Essential Shakespeare*, p. 118); Rossiter emphasizes the importance of the "sex-theme" in the problem plays (*Angel with Horns*, p. 125); Wheeler explores the "anxious mistrust for the sexual dimension of living" that "pervades *All's Well* and *Measure for Measure*" (*Shakespeare's Development*, p. 19).

11　Muriel Bradbrook, in *Shakespeare and Elizabethan Poetry* (London: Chatto & Windus, 1951), pp. 162–70, summarizing her article, "Virtue Is the true Nobility," *Review of English Studies*, n.s. 1 (1950): 289–301, calls the heroine of *All's Well*, "Hellen," which she did not do in the original article. She explains, in n. 2, that "Her name is so spelt throughout the Folio text" (p. 264). The heroine of *All's Well* does indeed seem to be named "Hellen" or "Helen" (both spellings are used, apparently indiscriminately, throughout the Folio text). So she is named in 16 of the 17 references in the Folio text and in 9 of the 12 references in Folio stage directions. She is "Helena" only in the first stage direction, in the text of act 1, scene 1 (one reference, in prose, by the Countess), and (after intervening stage directions use "Helen") in two other stage directions, in act 2, scene 4, and act 2, scene 5. From this point on, the heroine is consistently "Helen" (or "Hellen") in both text and stage directions. The early indecision about Helen's name is perhaps not surprising in a text which has many puzzling features about names and speech prefixes, most notably a tendency for names to be established late: e.g. "Rinaldo" for "Steward" (III.iv.19), "Lavatch" for "Clown" (V.ii.1), and brothers "Dumaine" for First and Second Lords (IV.iii.187). In the first edition after the Folio, Nicolas Rowe, *The Works of Mr. William Shakespeare* (London: Jacob Tonson, 1709), the heroine's name is regularized as "Helena" in the Dramatis Personae, the text, and the stage directions. So she has been called in all subsequent editions. I call her Helen throughout, restoring her Folio name.

12   None has a mother except for the twins in *Comedy of Errors*, whose mother does not appear until the last minutes of the play; only they, Lucentio in *Taming*, and Proteus in *Two Gentlemen of Verona* have fathers, who play small and not very influential parts.

13   R. G. Hunter, *Shakespeare and the Comedy of Forgiveness* (New York: Columbia University Press, 1965), p. 109 and following. Hunter discusses the ways in which the play repeatedly disappoints the audience's expectations.

14   The spectrum of critical opinion on Helen ranges from the view that she is ambitious, scheming, unappealing (see, for example, Dover Wilson in n. 4 above and Clifford Leech, "The Theme of Ambition in *All's Well*," *English Literary History* 21 [1954]: 17–29) to the view that she is an admirable representative of virtue or heavenly grace (see, for example, G. Wilson Knight, *The Sovereign Flower* [New York: Macmillan, 1958], pp. 95–160). Joseph G. Price, *The Unfortunate Comedy: A Study of All's Well and Its Critics* (Toronto: University of Toronto Press, 1968), chapters 5, 6, and 7, traces the critical fortunes of the play and of its characters. G. K. Hunter, in his Arden edition (London: Methuen, 1959), implies that the divided opinion on Helen reflects the divided nature of her role (pp. xxx–xxxii).

15   The source is the ninth tale of the Third Day of Boccaccio's *Decameron*, translated and included by William Painter as Novel 38 in his *Palace of Pleasure* (1575). The tale is told by Neifile, who herself

has set the day's topic, tales of "Such persons as have acquired, by their diligence, something greatly wanted by them, or else recovered what they had lost." Geoffrey Bullough, *Narrative and Dramatic Sources of Shakespeare's Plays* (New York: Columbia University Press, 1968), 2:377. Bullough reprints Painter's translation of the tale; all subsequent references to the source will be to this edition and will be indicated in the text.

16 Arthur Kirsch, *Shakespeare and the Experience of Love* (Cambridge: Cambridge University Press, 1981), pp. 134–37, discusses the "creativeness as well as the procreativeness of [Helen's] erotic energy" (p. 135) and the paradoxes of her love. Kirsch's essay, which I first read when mine was already drafted, focuses on the theme of sexuality in the play and illuminates its paradoxical, tragicomical complexities, seeing the play, as I do, as a blend of realism and romance, sadness and wit. His detailed comparison of *All's Well* with Montaigne's essay "Upon Some Verses of Virgil" is especially useful.

17 Isabella's scene with Angelo in *Measure for Measure* (II.ii) has similar dynamics, a similar rhythm of advances and retreats, and a similar increase in its erotic energy as it proceeds, heightened by Lucio's suggestive urgings: "You are too cold" (lines 45, 56). But Isabella does not control the movement of the scene and engenders not a cure but a disease.

18 "The Counte he knew her wel and had already seen her, although she was faire, yet knowing her not to be of a stocke convenable to his nobility, skornefully said unto the king, 'Will you then (sir) give me a Phisition to wife?'" (Bullough, 2:391).

19 For a detailed discussion of ironic relationships among the tales of Boccaccio's Third Day, see Howard Cole, "Dramatic Interplay in the *Decameron*," in *The All's Well Story from Boccaccio to Shakespeare* (Urbana: University of Illinois Press, 1981), pp. 12–32.

20 Helen's death is announced by the First Lord in IV.iii.55–59. The beginning of the Lords' conversation has emphasized that Bertram has left for his assignation with Diana (lines 16, 30, 31, 36), and, at the end of the conversation, Bertram enters directly from it: "the last [of the sixteen completed businesses of the night] was the greatest, but that I have not ended yet" (96–97).

21 Rosalie Colie, *Shakespeare's Living Art* (Princeton, N.J.: Princeton University Press, 1974), chapter 3, passim. "One of the most pleasurable, for me, of Shakepeare's many talents is his 'unmetaphoring' of literary devices, his sinking of the conventions back

into what, he somehow persuades us, is 'reality,' his trick of making a verbal convention part of the scene, the action, or the psychology of the play itself" (p. 145).

22 The dates of both plays are conjectural. There is no external evidence for the date of *All's Well*. Although first published in the First Folio, it is usually assumed, on the basis of internal thematic and stylistic evidence, to have been written after *Hamlet* (1600–01) and before *Measure for Measure* (1603–04). The February 1603 *Stationers' Register* entry for *Troilus and Cressida* suggests that it was completed and acted in late 1602. See G. K. Hunter, Arden edition, *All's Well*, p. xviii–xxv, and Kenneth Palmer, Arden edition, *Troilus and Cressida* (London: Methuen, 1982), pp. 17–22.

23 Kirsch, *Shakespeare*, discusses the intricate relationship between the two: "But the erotic significance of [Bertram's] role is also indirectly represented through the subtly modulated character of Parolles, who at once intensifies the implications of Bertram's behavior and dilates our response to him" (p. 128).

24 W. W. Lawrence, *Shakespeare's Problem Comedies*, pp. 39–49.

25 This insight is Janet Adelman's.

26 Cf. the textual gloss on the speech in Hunter's Arden edition of the play, p. 132.

27 See Lawrence Stone, *Crisis of the Aristocracy 1558–1641* (Oxford: Clarendon Press, 1965), chap. 11, esp. pp. 594–612.

28 Michael Shapiro, " 'The Web of Our Life': Human Frailty and Mutual Redemption in *All's Well That Ends Well*," *Journal of English and Germanic Philology* 71 (1972): 522, similarly stresses the positive implications of Bertram's words.

29 In *Le Livre de Trois Chevalereux Comte d'Artois et de sa femme*, the reconciliation of husband and wife occurs before the child is born. See Lawrence, *Shakespeare's Problem Comedies*, pp. 46–47, for a summary of this romance.

30 John Arthos, "The Comedy of Generation," *Essays in Criticism* 5 (1955): 107–08. Barbara Everett, in her fine introduction to the Penguin edition of *All's Well* (Harmondsworth: Penguin, 1970), also sees the pregnancy as an aspect of the open-endedness of the play (pp. 38–39).

31 Northrop Frye points to one aspect of the older generation's dominance in his well-known statement that "The normal comic resolution is the surrender of the *senex* to the hero, never the reverse. Shakespeare has tried to reverse the pattern in *All's Well That Ends Well*, where the King of France forces Bertram to marry

Helena, and the critics have not stopped making faces over it" (*English Institute Essays 1948*, ed. D. A. Robertson, Jr. [New York: Columbia University Press, 1949], p. 59). The reversal in effect continues when the marriage is reestablished under the aegis of the King in the last scene.

32   Wheeler, *Shakespeare's Development*, pp. 12–13, similarly compares the two bedtricks.

33   The light Folio punctuation of this passage emphasizes the fluid, shifting syntactical function of "for your lovely sake," which is both a reason for the Duke to pardon Claudio and a reason for Isabella to marry him; if she marries him for her own sake, she will enable him, as Mariana did, to merge coercion and remedy, his "satisfaction" with her "benefit" (III.i.154–55).

34   Nancy Leonard, "Substitution in Shakespeare's Problem Comedies," *English Literary Renaissance* 9 (1979): 295, sees Mariana in this way and explores her crucial role in the play's substitutions.

35   Wheeler, *Shakespeare's Development*, discusses the "almost pervasive silence" that attends the four marriages in the last scene (pp. 126–27).

36   Meredith Skura, "New Interpretations for Interpretation in *Measure for Measure*," *Boundary 2*, no. 7 (Winter 1979): 51–53.

37   Wheeler, *Shakespeare's Development*, instructively explicates the psychological and dramatic ramifications of the two contrasted speeches (pp. 116–20).

38   Skura, "New Interpretations," p. 51.

39   Lucio's description to Isabella of Claudio's and Juliet's conception is, not entirely explicably, an exception to the negative views; unlike all the other references, this one sees procreation as positive, perhaps presenting it this way in politic deference to Isabella: "Your brother and his lover have embraced; / As those that feed grow full, as blossoming time / That from the seedness the bare fallow brings / To teeming foison, even so her plenteous womb / Expresseth his full tilth and husbandry" (I.iv.40–44).

40   In this passage, Isabella, in an extension of women's willingness to defend men by taking shame on themselves, is ready to project the shame of unfaithfulness onto her mother in order to protect her father's "blood" from the humiliation of a degenerate son. For a fine discussion of Isabella's anxieties about sexuality, see Janet Adelman, "Mortality and Mercy in *Measure for Measure*," in *The Shakespeare Plays: A Study Guide*, University Extension, The University of California, San Diego, and Coast Community College District (Delmar, Calif., 1978), pp. 110–11.

CHAPTER 3 WOMEN AND MEN IN *OTHELLO*

1   Leslie Fiedler, *The Stranger in Shakespeare* (New York: Stein and Day, 1972), p. 169. The three he refers to are Emilia, Bianca, and Barbary. His description of Desdemona after her marriage as "a passive, whimpering Griselda" (p. 142) suggests that his statistics might more accurately be put at four out of four.

2   F. R. Leavis, "Diabolic Intellect and the Noble Hero or the Sentimentalist's *Othello*," in *The Common Pursuit* (London: Chatto & Windus, 1952, pp. 136–59; *Coleridge's Shakespearean Criticism*, ed. Thomas M. Raysor (Cambridge, Mass.: Harvard University Press, 1930), 1: 121–25; A. C. Bradley, *Shakespearean Tragedy*, 2d ed. (London: Macmillan, 1964), pp. 175–242; H. Granville-Barker, *Prefaces to Shakespeare* (London: B. T. Batsford, 1958), 2: 3–149; G. Wilson Knight, *The Wheel of Fire* (1930: rpt. London: Oxford University Press, 1946), pp. 107–31; John Bayley, *The Characters of Love* (New York: Basic Books, 1960), pp. 125–201; Helen Gardner, "The Noble Moor," *Proceedings of the British Academy* 41 (1955): 189–205.

3   On Othello's music, see especially Knight, *Wheel of Fire*, pp. 107–18, and Bayley, *Characters of Love*, pp. 150–59. On Iago, see especially Bradley, *Shakespearean Tragedy*, pp. 207–37, and Knight, pp. 125–26.

4   T. S. Eliot, "Shakespeare and the Stoicism of Seneca," *Selected Essays* (New York: Harcourt Brace, 1950), pp. 110–11; A. P. Rossiter, *Angel with Horns* (New York: Theatre Arts, 1961), pp. 189–208; H. A. Mason, *Shakespeare's Tragedies of Love* (New York: Barnes & Noble, 1970), pp. 59–161; William Empson, "Honest in *Othello*," in *The Structure of Complex Words* (London: Chatto & Windus, 1951), pp. 218–49; Leo Kirschbaum, "The Modern Othello," *ELH* 11 (1944): 283–96.

5   *Othello*, Arden Shakespeare, ed. M. R. Ridley (Cambridge, Mass.: Harvard University Press, 1958), II.i.200. All *Othello* quotations are from this edition, for I find persuasive Ridley's arguments for using the 1622 Quarto rather than the First Folio as his copy text.

6   For such quotations, see Fiedler, *Stranger in Shakespeare*, p. 158, and Mason, *Shakespeare's Tragedies of Love*, pp. 75–76. On Iago's honesty, see Empson, "Honest in *Othello*," and Mason, p. 75.

7   Bradley, *Shakespearean Tragedy*, p. 179. See also Granville-Barker, *Prefaces*, p. 124; Knight, *Wheel of Fire*, pp. 119–20.

8   Mason, *Shakespeare's Tragedies of Love*, p. 147. See also Fiedler, *Stranger in Shakespeare*, passim.

9   Robert Dickes, "Desdemona: An Innocent Victim?" *American Imago* 27 (1970): 279–97; Fiedler, *Stranger in Shakespeare*, pp. 141–42; Richard Flatter, *The Moor of Venice* (London: William Heinemann, 1950), pp. 72–74; G. Bonnard, "Are Othello and Desdemona Innocent or Guilty?" *English Studies* 30 (1949): 175–84; Jan Kott, *Shakespeare Our Contemporary* (with three new essays), trans. Boleslaw Taborski (Garden City, N.Y.: Doubleday/Anchor, 1966), pp. 118–19.

10 Neglect of her is apparent even in R. B. Heilman's *Magic in the Web* (Lexington: University of Kentucky Press, 1956) and in Marvin Rosenberg's *The Masks of Othello* (Berkeley: University of California Press, 1961), books that seek for Desdemona a middle ground between passivity and aggressiveness and that frequently illuminate the details of the play. Recently a number of articles have focused on her and have argued, with subtle nuances of difference, for her assertiveness, sensuality, and innocence. See, for example, S. N. Garner, "Shakespeare's Desdemona," *Shakespeare Studies* 9 (1976): 233–52; W. A. Adamson, "Unpinned or Undone: Desdemona's Critics and the Problem of Sexual Innocence," *Shakespeare Studies* 13 (1980): 169–86; Ann Jennalie Cook, "The Design of Desdemona: Doubt Raised and Resolved," *Shakespeare Studies* 13 (1980): 187–96, and a number of other discussions cited in the latter two articles.

11 Kenneth Burke, "*Othello*: An Essay to Illustrate a Method," *Hudson Review* 4 (1951–52): 165–203; Arthur Kirsch, *Shakespeare and the Experience of Love* (Cambridge: Cambridge University Press, 1981), pp. 10–39; Stephen Greenblatt, *Renaissance Self-Fashioning from More to Shakespeare* (Chicago: University of Chicago Press, 1980), pp. 232–54; Stanley Cavell, *The Claim of Reason: Wittgenstein, Scepticism, Morality, and Tragedy* (Oxford: Clarendon Press, 1979), pp. 481–96; Edward Snow, "Sexual Anxiety and the Male Order of Things in *Othello*," *English Literary Renaissance* 10 (1980): 384–412; Richard P. Wheeler, "'And my loud crying still': The Sonnets, *The Merchant of Venice*, and *Othello*," in *Shakespeare's Rough Magic: Renaissance Essays for C. L. Barber*, ed. Peter Erickson and Coppélia Kahn (Newark: University of Delaware Press, 1985).

12 Burke, "*Othello*," p. 196.

13 See, for example, Cavell, "we need to ask not so much how Iago gained his power as how Desdemona lost hers" (486); Greenblatt, "Desdemona performs no such acts of defiance, but her erotic

submission, conjoined with Iago's murderous cunning, far more effectively, if unintentionally, subverts her husband's carefully fashioned identity" (244); and Snow, "The tragedy of the play, then, is the inability of Desdemona to escape or triumph over restraints and Oedipal prohibitions that domesticate woman to the conventional male order of things" (407). By downplaying the power of Iago or subsuming him as a part of Othello, these critics underestimate, I think, the role the fantasy of cuckoldry plays in Othello's destruction. It is this fantasy which calls out and makes deadly whatever anxieties Othello feels about Desdemona's sexuality, and the fantasy is not, I would argue, inevitable.

14 I do not mean to suggest that critics have not noted that love is a theme in the play. This theme is at the center of John Bayley's study of *Othello* in *The Characters of Love*. Helen Gardner emphasizes the play's concern with the union of romantic love and marriage in "The Noble Moor," as well as in her useful survey of criticism, " 'Othello': A Retrospect, 1900–67," in *Shakespeare Survey* 21 (1968): 1–11. Rosalie Colie, in "*Othello* and the Problematics of Love," in *Shakespeare's Living Art* (Princeton, N.J.: Princeton University Press, 1974), pp. 148–67, brilliantly sees *Othello* as an "unmetaphoring" and a reanimation of the conventions of Renaissance love lyrics. See above, chap. 2, n. 21.

15 The translation is Geoffrey Bullough's, in *Narrative and Dramatic Sources of Shakespeare* (London: Routledge & Kegan Paul, 1973), 7:239. Subsequent Italian quotations are from M. Giovanbattista Giraldi Cintio, *De Gli Hecatommithi* (Vinegia: G. Scotto, 1566), vol. 1. Translations are my own.

16 The play's resemblances to comedy have often been noted. Barbara Heliodora C. De Mendonça, in " 'Othello': A Tragedy Built on a Comic Structure," *Shakespeare Survey* 21 (1968): 31–38, and Richard Zacha, "Iago and the *Commedia dell'arte*," *Arlington Quarterly* 2 (Autumn 1969): 98–116, discuss the play's similarities of subject, plot, and character with the *commedia dell'arte*. Mason, *Tragedies of Love*, pp. 73–97, and Fiedler, *Stranger in Shakespeare*, pp. 43–55, show how the first act or the first two acts form a Shakespearean comedy in miniature. Susan Snyder, *The Comic Matrix of Shakespeare's Tragedies* (Princeton, N.J.: Princeton University Press, 1979), pp. 70–90, explores how *Othello* releases conflicts that are latent in Shakespeare's comic treatment of love.

17 See Alvin Kernan, Introduction to *Othello* in *The Complete Signet Classic Shakespeare*, and Fiedler, *Stranger in Shakespeare*.

18   Fiedler, *Stranger in Shakespeare*, p. 194.

19   See Winifred M. T. Nowottny's excellent discussion of the way in
      which the murder reconciles Othello's conflicts, "Justice and
      Love in *Othello*," *University of Toronto Quarterly* 21 (1951–52): esp.
      340–44. Kirsch, Snow, and Cavell all argue, for slightly different
      reasons, that Othello's murder of Desdemona resolves his con-
      flicts concerning her. Wheeler, "'and my loud crying still': The
      Sonnets, *The Merchant of Venice*, and *Othello*," shows how death
      functions in the play as a whole to resolve conflicts between
      "manly autonomy, female sexuality and nurturant femininity,"
      erasing the mutual exclusiveness of these values in earlier works
      (see n. 11 above).

20   Jane Adamson, *Othello as Tragedy: Some Problems of Judgment and
      Feeling* (Cambridge: Cambridge University Press, 1980), has a
      fine analysis of Iago's self-defensive strategies, his "lust for im-
      perviousness" (see p. 97 and chap. 3, passim).

21   Timothy Murray, in *"Othello*, An Index and Obscure Prologue to
      Foul Generic Thoughts," an unpublished paper circulated to the
      seminar on Gender and Genre in Shakespeare at the Second
      International Shakespeare Congress, Stratford-upon-Avon, Au-
      gust 1981, vigorously, if a bit improbably, argues for Bianca as the
      play's hero and thus establishes himself as a Bianca critic. "Her
      assertion of significational purity and independence threatens
      the patriarchal dependence on her presence as an engine for so-
      cial definitions through the dialectics of generic impurity. Bianca
      no longer honors the signs of either whore or virgin. She will not
      be bought, conquered, or penetrated for some hero's assertion of
      self" (p. 17). This reading fails, however, to take into account her
      compliance with Cassio's fantasies. A short version of this paper,
      "Othello's Foul Generic Thoughts," will appear in *Persons in
      Groups*, ed. Richard Trexler (Binghamton, N.Y.: Medieval/Re-
      naissance Text Society, 1985).

22   Adamson discusses in detail parallels and contrasts between
      Emilia and Desdemona (and Bianca) in chapter 7 and emphasizes
      Emilia's "range of attitudes and feelings," which encompasses
      those of Desdemona and Iago (245–46).

23   Rosalind, likewise, educates Orlando in the necessities of time,
      and Bianca stresses its importance to Cassio. She, like Rosalind, is
      more anxious about time than Desdemona, who is assured of fu-
      ture meetings with Othello. Compare Bianca's "What, keep a
      week away? seven days and nights?" and "I pray you bring me

on the way a little, / And say, if I should see you soon at night" (III.iv.171, 195–96) with Desdemona's "Why then to-morrow night, or Tuesday morn, / or Tuesday noon, or night, or Wednesday morn" (III.iii.61–62).

24 Kirsch, p. 32, Greenblatt, p. 251, and Snow, p. 389 (see n. 11 above) all analyze this passage as conveying "the ultimate horror of the play" (Kirsch, p. 32)—namely, Othello's association of Desdemona's sexuality and his own with guilt and shame and contamination.

25 David L. Jeffrey and Patrick Grant suggest, in "Reputation in *Othello*," *Shakespeare Studies* 6 (1970): 197–208, that Othello corrupts the ideal of reputation, desiring "bad fame" rather than "good fame," secular rather than heavenly glory. It seems difficult to determine whether the characters are to be viewed as debasing the ideal or whether it is the ideal itself which Shakespeare is questioning. At any rate, Curtis Brown Watson, in *Shakespeare and the Renaissance Concept of Honor* (Princeton, N.J.: Princeton University Press, 1960), pp. 209–11, 377–79, oversimplifies the relationship of the men in *Othello* to the ideals of honor and reputation. They are clearly not straightforward representatives of these ideals.

26 Similarly, in *Julius Caesar*, male bonds are established largely through alliances against mutual enemies. The conspirators are linked by their desire to destroy Caesar; Antony's love for Caesar finds its fullest expression when he defends his honor against those who murdered him, and the triumvirate is precariously held together by their desire to avenge Caesar's murder.

27 Coppélia Kahn, *Man's Estate: Masculine Identity in Shakespeaare* (Berkeley: University of California Press, 1981), pp. 140–46, discusses the nature and function of cuckoldry in the play. See also my discussions of cuckoldry above, pp. 5–7 and 41–42.

28 Editors have been unclear about the precise implications of *Roman* and *triumph*, but the latter perhaps contains a sexual innuendo, as in Sonnet 151: "My soul doth tell my body that he may / Triumph in love; flesh stays no farther reason, / But, rising at thy name, doth point out thee, / As his triumphant prize." *Scor'd* seems to mean not only "defaced," as it is usually glossed, but also to have its contemporary meaning of "outscored," perhaps with sexual undertones. There is no *OED* citation for this sense before 1882, but *score* in the sense of "to add up" is used punningly and bawdily in *All's Well That Ends Well*: "When he

swears oaths, bid him drop gold, and take it; / After he scores, he never pays the score. / Half won is match well made; match and well make it; / He ne'er pays after-debts, take it before" (IV.iii.228–31). The first *score* is glossed by Ribner, in *The Complete Works of Shakespeare*, ed. Irving Ribner and George Lyman Kittredge (Waltham, Mass.: Xerox College Publishing, 1971), p. 461, as "(*a*) obtains goods on credit, (*b*) hits the mark, as in archery," and perhaps some of the latter sense is present in the *Othello* passage too. Othello's reference to throwing Cassio's nose to an unseen dog has also puzzled editors. Plucking, tweaking, or cutting off the nose was an act of humiliation and revenge, and here Othello imagines himself getting back at Cassio for his "triumph." But *nose* appears frequently in the plays with bawdy implications—in Mercutio's Queen Mab speech, in the tavern scenes in *2 Henry IV*, in the banter between Charmian, Iras, and Alexas in *Antony and Cleopatra*, and in *Troilus and Cressida*, where Troilus is described by Helen as "In love, i' faith, to the very tip of the nose" (III.i.125)—and it seems likely that the bawdy sense is intended here, especially as the preceding line is "Now he tells how she pluck'd him to my chamber." It is perhaps possible that, on this level of meaning, the "dog" Othello does not see and to whom he will throw Cassio's "nose" is Desdemona. At any rate, sex and combat seem fused and confused here, as in Othello's other asides.

29 Madelon Gohlke, " 'I wooed thee with my sword': Shakespeare's Tragic Paradigms," in *The Woman's Part: Feminist Criticism of Shakespeare*, ed. Carolyn Ruth Swift Lenz, Gayle Greene, and Carol Thomas Neely (Urbana: University of Illinois Press, 1980), discusses the way in which men who make themselves vulnerable to women must destroy those women to regain their control and relieve their own sense of powerlessness (see especially pp. 155–56). See also Madelon Gohlke, " 'All that is spoke is marred': Language and Consciousness in *Othello*," *Women's Studies* 9 (1981–82): 157–76.

30 Carole McKewin, "Counsels of Gall and Grace: Intimate Conversations between Women in Shakespeare's Plays," in Lenz et al., *The Woman's Part*, pp. 128–29.

31 Dickes, "Desdemona, an Innocent Victim?" and Stephen Reid, "Desdemona's Guilt," *American Imago* 27 (1970): 279–97; 245–62. Adamson offers a sympathetic discussion of the defensive aspects of Desdemona's passivity, as she does of the men's, (pp.

235–58; see n. 20 above). Gayle Greene, "'This that you call love'" Sexual and Social Tragedy in *Othello*," *Journal of Women's Studies in Literature* 1 (1979): 16–32, sees this passivity as grounded in a social ideal of femininity; both see Desdemona as more consistently passive than I do.

32 Although Greene's discussion, which appeared after the original publication of mine, takes quite a different view of the women and the play, she likewise pinpoints this mutual misunderstanding as the source of the tragedy.

33 Critics also willfully reinterpret—and misinterpret—the handkerchief. G. R. Elliott asserts that Othello gave it to Desdemona "with the secret hope that it would hold her faithful to him, as faithful as his 'amiable . . . mother' (56, 59) was to his father until her death," and explains further in a footnote the basis of this assertion: "It is surely obvious that Othello's dying mother in bidding him to give the handkerchief to his future wife was concerned for the faithfulness, not of her son, but of that unknown woman," *Flaming Minister: A Study of Othello* (Durham, N.C.: Duke University Press, 1953), p. 146. David Kaula, in "Othello Possessed: Notes on Shakespeare's Use of Magic and Witchcraft," *Shakespeare Studies* 2 (1966), is relieved when Othello alters his story of the handkerchief's history: "Nevertheless, the fact that Othello's *father* now becomes the one who gave his mother the handkerchief converts it into a more plausible love token than the horrific thing contrived by the superannuated sibyl in her prophetic fury. In communication once more with the civilized representatives of the Venetian order, Othello, even though he has yet to suffer his awakening, is returning to a more normal view of love and marriage" (pp. 126–27). While I cannot accept this view of the handkerchief, much in the article is illuminating, especially the discussion (p. 125) of the implications of the augmented first syllable of "handkerchief," "hank," whose meanings include a "restraining or curbing hold; a power of check or restraint" (*OED* 4, fig. a).

A number of recent penetrating interpretations of the handkerchief are likewise limited, I think, by a tendency to focus only on its significance for Othello and for his psychology. Kenneth Burke finds it an emblem of the possessiveness of monogamistic (male) love (196–200). Arthur Kirsch emphasizes its connection with Othello's mother and her betrayal of their original merger; thus it easily becomes proof of Desdemona's subsequent betrayal and symbol of the infantile, dependent component of Othello's love (32–33). Edward Snow gives it a similar reading, and suggests as well that the second account of its history includes the element missing from the first, the Oedipal betrayal implicit as the son receives "the emblem of the father's sexual power from the mother" (404); this betrayal's force seems mitigated by the fact that Othello's mother is "dying" and by the handkerchief's history and function, which makes it explicitly an emblem of female, not male, sexual power. Stanley Cavell, focusing on the handkerchief's motif of spotted strawberries and disregarding its history, sees it (as do Snow and Lynda Boose, "Othello's Handkerchief: 'The Recognizance and Pledge of Love,'" *English Literary Renaissance*, 5 [1975]: 360–74) as the emblem of Desdemona's deflowering and Othello's anxieties about this moment (see n. 11 above). Timothy Murray (see n. 21 above) in contrast to these monovalent readings, stresses its plurisignification. He reads it as a free-floating signifier, given a new signification by each of its keepers. While it is true that it is read differently by different characters, and that each is eager to control its symbolism, I would argue that its description and function in the play give it a meaning which transcends that imposed by any of its particular interpreters; the handkerchief, like Desdemona, has an essence which is independent of the fantasies surrounding it.

34 Cf. *OED*, *make* (96c), where "to make up" is "to supply (deficiencies); to make complete," and (a) "To fill up what is wanting to," and *to be made up* is "to be completed in former growth," and other Shakespearean uses of "scarce made up" to mean not completely formed or completely human, as in Richard III's reference to himself as "Cheated of feature by dissembling Nature, / Deformed, unfinished, sent before my time / Into this breathing world scarce half made up" (I.i.19–21), and Belarius's contemptuous reference to Cloten's inadequacy in *Cymbeline*, "Being scarce made up, / I mean to man, he had not apprehension / Of roaring terrors" (IV.ii.109–11).

35 *Fordo* means "to put [a living being] out of existence" (*OED*, 1), "to kill, to ruin, to undo or bring to nought" (*OED* 1. 2. 3. 4. 5.); Shakespeare uses it with reference to suicide, as in *Hamlet*, V.i. 221, and *Lear*, V.iii.25 and 29. Iago, characteristically, places the agent of his fordoing outside of himself. Stephen Greenblatt illuminates how Iago fashions and destroys himself through his improvisational narratives: "The only termination possible in his case is not revelation but silence" (p. 238).

See Adamson, *Othello as Tragedy*, pp. 283–99, for an acute analysis of the ways in which Othello's rhetoric in the last scene protects him from guilt and pain.

37 See *Richard II*, III.iii.161; *II Henry VI*, III.ii.176; and *Macbeth*, IV.i.55, where *lodging* is used to describe the destruction of young corn on the brink of maturity (as it still is today in central Illinois). Ridley cites these parallels in his detailed and informative note on the word in the Arden edition (p. 197), demonstrating that Quarto's *lodging* is richer in meaning than Folio's more familiar *loading*.

38 Edward Snow argues, in a more thoroughgoing way than I would wish to, that "Repression pervades the entire world of *Othello*," that in it there is "neither transcendence nor catharsis" (pp. 384–85).

CHAPTER 4   GENDER AND GENRE IN
ANTONY AND CLEOPATRA

1 R. H. Case, Introduction, Arden Edition, *Antony and Cleopatra*, ed. M. R. Ridley (Cambridge, Mass.: Harvard University Press, 1954), pp. xxxiii–xxxiv; A. C. Bradley, *Oxford Lectures on Poetry* (London: MacMillan, 1909), pp. 281–84; A. P. Riemer, *A Reading of Shakespeare's Antony and Cleopatra* (Sydney: University of Australia Press, 1968), pp. 101–15; and Peter Erickson, "*Antony and Cleopatra* as an Experiment in Alternative Masculinity," in *Patriarchal Structures in Shakespeare's Drama* (Berkeley: University of California Press, 1985), see it as distinct from the major tragedies. Derek Traversi, *Shakespeare: The Roman Plays* (Stanford, Calif.: Stanford University Press, 1963), p. 79; and M. W. MacCallum, *Shakespeare's Roman Plays* (London: Macmillan, 1967), p. 341, classify it as a Roman play and a tragedy. Ernest Schanzer, *The Problem Plays of Shakespeare* (New York: Schocken Books, 1963), calls it a problem play and a tragedy (p. 183 and passim). Donald A. Stauffer, *Shakespeare's World of Images* (Bloomington: Indiana University Press, 1949), p. 247; Paula S. Berggren, "The Woman's Part: Female Sexuality as Power in Shakespeare's Plays," in *The Woman's Part: Feminist Criticism of Shakespeare*, ed. Carolyn Ruth Swift Lenz, Gayle Greene, and Carol Thomas Neely (Urbana: University of Illinois Press, 1980), pp. 25–27; Julian Markels, *The Pillar of the World* (Columbus: Ohio State University Press, 1968), p. 151; and Richard P. Wheeler, *Shakespeare's Development and the Problem Comedies* (Berkeley: University of California Press, 1981), p. 210—all suggest that the play is a tragedy with affinities to the

romances. Numerous critics have found the play a mixture of comedy and tragedy, beginning with Richard Brathwait: "Love's interview betwixt Cleopatra and Mark Antony, promised to itself as much secure freedom as fading fancy could tender; yet the last scene closed up all those comic passages with a tragic conclusion" (*The English Gentlewoman*, 1631, quoted in *Shakespeare: Antony and Cleopatra: A Casebook*, ed. John Russell Brown [London: Macmillan, 1968], p. 25). Janet Adelman, *The Common Liar: An Essay on Antony and Cleopatra* (New Haven and London: Yale University Press, 1973), has the best extended discussion of the play's mixture of tragedy and comedy (pp. 40–52). Also see Adelman, p. 190, n. 2, for a useful summary of views on the play's genre.

2 On regression, see Constance Brown Kuriyama, "The Mother of the World: A Psychoanalytic Interpretation of Shakespeare's *Antony and Cleopatra, English Literary Renaissance* 7 (1977): 324–51; on transcendence, see Murray M. Schwartz, "Shakespeare through Contemporary Psychoanalysis," in *Representing Shakespeare: New Psychoanalytic Essays*, ed. Murray M. Schwartz and Coppélia Kahn (Baltimore: Johns Hopkins University Press, 1980), p. 30, and Adelman, *Common Liar*, pp. 144–45, 149; on feminization, see Madelon Gohlke, " 'I wooed thee with my sword': Shakespeare's Tragic Paradigms," in *Representing Shakespeare*, pp. 177–78; on alternative manhood, see Peter Erickson, *Patriarchal Structures*.

3 But see Wheeler, *Shakespeare's Development*, pp. 12–19, for a general discussion of the relationship between psychological conflicts and the genres of comedy, problem comedy, and tragedy.

4 Like other critics who talk about gender in Shakespeare, I find it difficult to avoid either imposing on Shakespeare the most conventional and stereotyped presentation of gender roles or prescribing for him my own (supposedly) unstereotyped notions of what these roles could or should be. To discuss the issue at all is to find oneself relying on some sort of assumptions, usually unexamined ones, about gender roles and gender oppositions. Sherry B. Ortner's "Is Female to Male as Nature is to Culture?" in *Woman, Culture, and Society*, ed. Michelle Zimbalist Rosaldo and Louise Lamphere (Stanford, Calif.: Stanford University Press, 1974), pp. 67–88, is a clear and useful discussion of the assumptions on which universal sex-role divisions and universal second-class status for women rest. Women, Ortner argues, are always found to be closer to nature than men, are thought to occupy an

intermediate position between nature and culture as a result of their physiology, of the social roles which this physiology originally imposed on them, and of their psychic states resulting from both the physiology and the social roles. Some such assumptions about male/female differences are rooted in Shakespeare's culture as in our own, and there are, I am afraid, traces of them in my discussion.

5 Marianne Novy, "Shakespeare's Female Characters as Actors and Audience," in Lenz et al., *The Woman's Part*, pp. 256–70, explores in the tragedies the audiencelike responsiveness of the female characters to the male hero and the heroes' distrust of their acting. Edmund Tilney, *A brief and pleasant discourse of duties in Mariage, called the Flower of Friendshippe* (London: Henrie Denham, 1568), advocates for wives the conventional responsiveness to men's moods that Charmian urges and Cleopatra reverses; the husband's face must be the wife's "daylie looking glasse, wherein she ought to be always prying, to see when he is merie, when sad, when content, and when discontent, whereto she must always frame her owne countenance" (E5ᵛ).

6 Linda Bamber, *Comic Women, Tragic Men: A Study of Gender and Genre in Shakespeare* (Stanford, Calif: Stanford University Press, 1982), pp. 59–60, contrasts Cleopatra's secure identity with Antony's unfixed one.

7 Rosalie L. Colie, *Shakespeare's Living Art* (Princeton, N.J.: Princeton University Press, 1974), suggests that "Part of their tragedy lies in Antony's feeling himself dissolve when he is with her, and Cleopatra's feeling her 'nothingness' when he is not with her" (p. 189).

8 I am indebted to illuminating discussions of this elusive speech by Colie, *Shakespeare's Living Art*, p. 189, and Barbara L. Estrin, " 'Behind a dream': Cleopatra and Sonnet 129," *Women's Studies* 9 (1981–82): 181–82.

9 Harold C. Goddard, *The Meaning of Shakespeare* (Chicago: University of Chicago Press, 1960), 2: 185–92, delineates shrewdly the nature and the limits of Roman politics and of Octavius's power.

10 Whether Caesar genuinely wishes the marriage to cement the alliance or hopes that it will give him an excuse to break it, and whether he thinks the marriage will satisfy Octavia or consciously sacrifices her to political ends, its political function is clear. For discussions of Caesar's motives, see Goddard, *Meaning of Shakespeare*, 2:186, and Traversi, *The Roman Plays*, pp. 112–14.

11 More typically, Shakespeare's women transfer their loyalty deci-
    sively from their fathers (perhaps Caesar's being Octavia's
    brother rather than her father makes the difference) to their lov-
    ers, as do Hermia, Portia, Juliet, Desdemona, Imogen, Perdita.
    Lynda Boose, "The Father and the Bride in Shakespeare," *PMLA*
    97 (1982): 325–47, examines the ritual that accompanies this
    transfer. In *Antony and Cleopatra* the circumstances of the mar-
    riage prevent the ritual from being accomplished, and in some
    other plays the transfer is not complete. Cordelia returns to fight
    for the father who has banished her, and France, her husband,
    drops out of the play. Lady Macbeth, when confronting the
    sleeping Duncan, and Hermione during the crisis of her trial, are
    reminded of the powerful prior bond: "Had he not resembled /
    My father as he slept, I had done 't" (II.ii.12–13); "The Emperor
    of Russia was my father. / Oh that he were alive, and here be-
    holding / His daughter's trial!" (III.ii.117–19).

12 Although Octavia is not fully characterized in Plutarch, she is a
    stronger and more sympathetic figure there than in Shakespeare.
    She is not a timid girl, but a widow with children when she
    marries Antony. Her skillful negotiations effect a temporary rec-
    onciliation between Antony and Caesar (Bullough, 5: 282–83);
    Plutarch's Cleopatra fears that Octavia "would then be too
    stronge for her" and feigns that she is fading away from love to
    keep Antony with her (pp. 288–89); in Plutarch, when Anthony
    has returned to Eygpt, Octavia will not leave his house as Caesar
    orders her to, but continues to behave well toward him and to
    pacify Caesar (pp. 289–90). She has three children by Antony
    and cares for them as well as for his children by Fulvia and Cleo-
    patra; the last paragraph of Plutarch's *Life* details her marriage
    negotiations on behalf of all the children in her charge. Samuel
    Brandon's *Tragicomedie of the vertuous Octavia* emphasizes and
    magnifies Octavia's strength and integrity, suggested by Plu-
    tarch, and diminishes the role of Cleopatra, omitting, for exam-
    ple, her death. Not only does Shakespeare diminish Octavia's
    role, her strength, and her connection with Antony, but he
    makes Cleopatra more sympathetic and more human than she is
    in Plutarch, further increasing the contrast between them. L. T.
    Fitz, "Egyptian Queens and Male Reviewers: Sexist Attitudes in
    Antony and Cleopatra Criticism," *Shakespeare Quarterly* 28 (1977):
    310–13, discusses the departures from Plutarch in Shakespeare's
    characterization of Cleopatra.

13 In contrast, many of the versions of the story sympathetic to the lovers assume or specifically include the marriage of Antony to Cleopatra. In the tale of Cleopatra in Chaucer's *Legend of Good Women* (1386?), Antony is a charming courtly lover, and he and Cleopatra are married in a ceremony that the narrator coyly refuses to describe because of lack of time (lines 616–23), *The Works of Geoffrey Chaucer*, ed. F. N. Robinson, 2d ed. (Boston: Houghton Mifflin, 1957), p. 496. In Boccaccio's novel *Fiammetta* (1343), the heroine is consoled and ennobled by comparing herself with Cleopatra, lamenting over the body of her dead husband (*Amorous Fiammetta*, trans. Bartholomew Young [1587], ed. K. H. Josling [London: Mandrake Press, 1929], book 7, pp. 151–52, quoted in Marilyn L. Williamson, *"Infinite Variety": Antony and Cleopatra in Renaissance Drama and Earlier Tradition* [Mystic, Conn.: Lawrence Verry, 1974], p. 55). In Giraldi Cinthio's *Cleopatra* (1583), both Cleopatra and Antony refer to her as his wife (cf. I.iii, trans. in Bullough, 5:348). In Robert Garnier's *Marc-Antonie*, translated by the Countess of Pembroke as *The Tragedie of Antonie* (1595), Cleopatra mourns for Antony, recalling their "holy marriage" (line 1947, Bullough, 5:405), and in Samuel Daniel's *Tragedie of Cleopatra* (1599) her wifehood and motherhood are persistently emphasized in order to manifest her dignity and pathos—as in this dialogue with Charmion:

> CH.   Live for your sonnes. CL.   Nay for their father die.
> CH.   Hardharted mother! CL.   Wife, kindhearted, I.
> [LINES 555–56, Bullough, 5:372]

14 Schanzer, *Problem Plays*, p. 140, likewise sees a "temporary fusion of Love and Honour" at this point in the play (see n. 1 above).

15 The same word, *pants*, is used by Cassio in his prayer for Othello's safety, which, like Antony's welcome, celebrates the potential for a regenerative union of love and valor: "Great Jove, Othello guard, / And swell his sail with thine own pow'rful breath, / That he may bless this bay with his tall ship, / Make love's quick pants in Desdemona's arms, / Give renewed fire to our extincted spirits" (II.i.77–81, Signet edition, Folio text).

16 The question of who is actually to blame—and for what—is a vexed one. In Plutarch, Cleopatra is specifically blamed for both the strategy and the loss: "Cleopatra forced him to put all to the hazard of battel by sea: considering with her selfe how she might flie, and provide for her safetie, not to helpe him to winne the vic-

tory, but to flie more easily after the battel lost" (Bullough, 5:298).
In Shakespeare, the two seem to share responsibility for the defeat. Antony decides to fight at sea, although Cleopatra may incite in him the recklessness to take on this challenge: "By sea?
what else?" she agrees (III.vii.28). Cleopatra's flight is, as far as
we can tell, unpremeditated, and its motive unknown, but the responsibility for it is hers. Neither the sea battle nor her flight need
have resulted in defeat, however, had not Antony followed her.
In Plutarch, Antony, before Cleopatra's flight, was holding his
own; in Shakespeare, he may even have been winning: "vantage,
like a pair of twins appeared / Both as the same, or rather ours
the elder" (III.x.12–13). After her flight, he still might have won:
"Had our general / Been what he knew himself, it had gone well"
(III.x. 26–27). In neither Shakespeare nor Plutarch is there any
support for Antony's accusation that Cleopatra was responsible
for the defection of the Egyptian fleet in the third battle; in Plutarch she does not explicitly deny responsibility as she does in
Shakespeare (IV.xiv.122).

17 Madelon Gohlke, in " 'I wooed thee with my sword,' " (see n. 2
above) analyzes the tragic heroes' fictions of femininity, their
fears of feminization, and their association of heterosexuality
with violence. See especially her discussion of *Antony and Cleopatra* pp. 177–79, which anticipates and has influenced my interpretation of the play, although I emphasize more than she does
the positive consequences of Antony's union with Cleopatra. Her
discussion of the negative consequences is a useful corrective to
mine.

18 Related mocking exchanges between the friends about the
woman occur in *Much Ado About Nothing* and *Romeo and Juliet*. In
the comedy, Benedick jokingly speaks "as being a professed
tyrant to their sex," ambiguously mocking Hero to dissuade
Claudio from marriage: "Why, i'faith, methinks she's too low for
a high praise, too brown for a fair praise, and too little for a great
praise. Only this commendation I can afford her, that were she
other than she is, she were unhandsome, and being no other but
as she is, I do not like her. . . . Would you buy her, that you
inquire after her?" (I.i.165–75). When Claudio asks, "Can the
world buy such a jewel?" Benedick replies, "Yea, and a case to
put it into" (176–77). In a well known and far more bawdy varia-
tion on the conventional scene, Mercutio, outside Juliet's garden,

mocks and degrades Romeo's love for Rosaline—"O, Romeo, that she were, O that she were / An open et cetera, thou a pop'rin pear!" (II.i.37–38), while Romeo inside, hearing him, rejects Mercutio's innuendos and commits himself to a passion that Mercutio cannot comprehend or alter: "He jests at scars that never felt a wound" (II.ii.1).

19 Adelman, *Common Liar* (see n. 1 above), likewise sees Enobarbus as "the pivotal figure in the play" (p. 131). Caught between "measure and overflow" (p. 131), he moves from being a detached commentator to becoming a "central actor" (p. 33) in the tragedy, one whose death teaches us "the cost of scepticism" (p. 131).

20 Colie, *Shakespeare's Living Art*, p. 194.

21 Adelman, *Common Liar*, pp. 144–45, has a fine discussion of the crucial importance of "becoming" in the play.

22 Cf. Cleopatra's "and as I draw them up, / I'll think them every one an Antony" (II.v.13–14) with her "Help, friends below, let's draw him hither" (IV.xv.13); "But come, come, Antony— / Help me, my women we must draw thee up" (IV.xv.29–30).

23 Anne Barton, "*Nature's Piece 'gainst Fancy*": *The Divided Catastrophe in Antony and Cleopatra* (An Inaugural Lecture, Bedford College, University of London, 1973), argues that the fifth act and Cleopatra's death create a "new angle of vision," an "alteration of emphasis" (p. 4) that transforms our earlier attitudes toward Antony, toward his death, toward Cleopatra, and toward the nature of the play.

24 In Plutarch it is made clear from the start that Cleopatra intends to deceive Caesar but not whether she and Seleucus are in collusion. Brents Stirling, "Cleopatra's Scene with Seleucus: Plutarch, Daniel, and Shakespeare," *Shakespeare Quarterly* 15 (1964): 299–311, shows how Shakespeare deliberately withholds from the audience all knowledge of Cleopatra's motives and of the implications of the scene as it is being enacted.

25 Caesar's need to identify with Antony's valor and passion is suggested in his lament for "my brother, my competitor / In top of all design, my mate in empire, / Friend and companion in the front of war, / The arm of mine own body, and the heart / Where mine his thoughts did kindle" (V.i.42–46); the first three lines follow Plutarch closely, but the last two are Shakespeare's addition. (Cf. "Caesar . . . burst out with teares lamenting his hard and miser-

able fortune, that had bene his frend and brother in law, his equall in Empire, and companion with him in sundry great exploytes and battells" (Bullough, 5:310).

26   Philip J. Traci, *The Love Play of Antony and Cleopatra* (The Hague: Mouton, 1970), argues, overschematically, that the structure of the play is a metaphor for the love-act (pp. 153–60); but this notion does bring out the importance of the sustained eroticism of the final scene and the sense of consummation and release engendered by Cleopatra's death.

27   Barton, *Divided Catastrophe*, points out that this is the only tragedy in which we want a protagonist who is not a villain to die (p. 16).

28   Sigurd Burckhardt, *Shakespearean Meanings* (Princeton, N.J.: Princeton University Press, 1968), p. 280.

29   Joan Larsen Klein, "Lady Macbeth: Infirm of Purpose," Lenz et al., in *The Women's Part*, p. 243.

30   Wheeler, *Shakespeare's Development*, pp. 146–47 (see n. 1 above).

CHAPTER 5   INCEST AND ISSUE IN THE ROMANCES: *THE WINTER'S TALE*

1   On the manipulation of tone in the romances, see Barbara A. Mowat, *The Dramaturgy of Shakespeare's Romances* (Athens: University of Georgia Press, 1976), especially chapter 2, and Charles Frey, *Shakespeare's Vast Romance: A Study of The Winter's Tale* (Columbia: University of Missouri Press, 1980), especially the discussion of comic rhythms and "parodic liberation" (p. 149) in the pastoral scenes, pp. 138–53.

2   In George Wilkins, *The Painfull Adventures of Pericles Prince of Tyre* (1608), an analogue to the play, this perversion is made explicit: "Much perswasion, though to little reason, he used, as, that he was her father, whome shee was bound to obey, he was a King that had power to commaund, he was in love, and his love was resistlesse, and if resistlesse, therefore pittilesse, either to youth, blood, or beauty: In briefe, he was a tyrant and would execute his will." Geoffrey Bullough, *Narrative and Dramatic Sources of Shakespeare* (New York: Columbia University Press, 1977), 6:496. All subsequent references to sources will be to Bullough's volumes 6 and 8 and will be indicated in the text.

3   In my analysis, incest is characterized by isolation and collapse of the family and denial of time and difference. Although these

characteristics are derived from the plays, they are compatible with the analysis of the incest prohibition in Claude Lévi-Strauss, *The Elementary Structures of Kinship*, trans. J. H. Bell, J. R. von Sturmer, and R. Needham (Boston: Beacon Press, 1969), as that which prescribes the exchange of women in marriage and hence allows the creation of social bonds and assures social cohesion. Lévi-Strauss's discussion illuminates the possessiveness that characterizes incest in the plays: "incest, in the broadest sense of the word, consists in obtaining by oneself, and for oneself, instead of by another, and for another" (p. 489). I use *incestuous* in such an extended sense to refer to nonsexual but similarly possessive, exclusive, and static bonds between friends, fathers and children, siblings. The fantasy of incest that the romances manifest and overcome is acutely articulated by Lévi-Strauss as the dream "that one could gain without losing, enjoy without sharing," the myth "eternally denied to social man, of a world in which one might *keep to oneself*" (p. 497). The patriarchal underpinnings of this myth are as explicit in Lévi-Strauss as in Shakespeare. I am indebted in a general way to Stanley Cavell's discussion of the connections among incest, romance, marriage, and remarriage in *Pursuits of Happiness: The Hollywood Comedy of Remarriage* (Cambridge, Mass.: Harvard University Press, 1981). I am more particularly indebted to Cavell for insisting, during a party conversation, that one must think about incest to understand Shakespeare's romances. I was persuaded, against inclinations, that I should try to do so, and the first part of this chapter is the consequence of that effort.

4 P. Goolden, "Antiochus's Riddle in Gower and Shakespeare," *Review of English Studies*, n.s. 6 (1955): 246. I am indebted to Goolden's analysis of Shakespeare's alterations in the form of the riddle as well as to his painstaking and lucid untangling of the meaning of its various versions.

5 In Laurence Twine's *The Patterns of Painefull Adventures* (1594?), one of the play's sources, the daughter explicitly laments her loss of roles and hence of the names that designate them. When her nurse calls her "deare childe and Madam," she replies, "even nowe two noble names were lost within this chamber . . . [b]ecause . . . before marraige, through wicked villanie I am most shamefully defiled." When the nurse asks why she does not tell "the King your father," the lady replies, "Where is my father? For if you well understoode the matter, the name of Father is lost in

me, so that I can have no remedie now but death onely" (Bullough 6:427). Phyllis Gorfain, "Puzzle and Artifice: The Riddle as Metapoetry in 'Pericles,'" *Shakespeare Survey* 29 (1976): 11–20, notes that the riddle in *Pericles* is unanswerable. Her useful analysis of the anthropological and structural function of riddles shows how this riddle confounds the ordinary function of riddles, which is to permit challenges to power, to bring life from death, to serve as verbal reorderings that lead to social reorderings.

6 The rarity of older women in the plays, however, contrasts with the prevalence of widows and the attention paid to them in the Renaissance, which is apparent in the ubiquitousness of the maid/wife/widow paradigm, in the careful provisions made for widows in wills, and even in the fact that Shakespeare's own mother, wife, and one or both of his two daughters all outlived their husbands.

7 Although Shakespeare's company did have a limited number of boy actors available, and although the roles of mature women may have challenged their skills, his creation of Lady Macbeth, Cleopatra, and Volumnia in the years just before the romances suggests that he could count on his actors to meet this challenge and that he was not required to "kill" Thaisa and Hermione or double them with Marina and Perdita to save his company's limited resources.

8 Jeffrey Stern's "*Pericles* and the Pattern of Forgiveness," a paper circulated for the Shakespeare Section, Midwest Modern Language Association Annual Meeting, Indianapolis, 1979, sees the location of the birth and death as significant because it engenders a symbolic reactivation of Pericles' fears of incest when he must pass, with his pregnant wife (mother and child in one), beyond the safety of Simonides' kingdom.

9 Miranda's mother, for example, is made known to her only at the time when she becomes ready for marriage, and then only as a "piece of virtue" who guarantees Prospero's paternity (*Tp*, I.ii. 56–57).

10 Marianne Novy, in "Transformed Images of Manhood in the Romances," a chapter in *Love's Argument: Gender Relations in Shakespeare* (Chapel Hill: University of North Carolina Press, 1984), explores how the men in the romances take on a number of heretofore conventionally feminine roles and attributes, including that of nurturing children. I am indebted to her analysis of the romances throughout this chapter.

11   Hero, in *Much Ado About Nothing*, has a mother named Innogen, who exists only in a quarto stage direction (I.i), and a father who shares the name Leonatus with Imogen's husband; in both cases, the man's name seems quasi-ironic, since both men are roused from their somewhat anxious passivity to leonine fury only through their violent and mistaken repudiation of daughter and wife for infidelity.

12   Richard Wheeler, Shakespeare's Development and the Problem Comedies (Berkeley: University of California Press, 1981), pp. 75–91, argues, however, that incestuous impulses in the two relationships, which are not fully transformed in the action of this play, impede the comic resolution.

13   Janet Adelman's "Male Autonomy and Trust in Women in *Cymbeline*: The Family Plot and the Marriage Plot," a paper presented to a Special Session, "Feminist Criticism of Shakespeare," Modern Language Association Annual Meeting, New York, 1981, incisively shows how the displacement of the Imogen/Posthumus plot by the Cymbeline plot serves to establish male power and female powerlessness, the preconditions for trust in women. Similar displacements of the marriage plots seem to me to occur in all of the romances.

14   Murray M. Schwartz, "Between Fantasy and Imagination: A Psychological Exploration of *Cymbeline*," in *Psychoanalysis and Literary Process*, ed. Frederick Crews (Cambridge, Mass.: Winthrop Publishers, 1970), pp. 219–83, views the protective strategies of the retreat in a way that likewise implies its incestuous components: "The pastoral world is a symbolic context, protected from the victory of desublimated sexuality by conventional agreement, a place where problematic experience is granted controlled release in order to be mastered and ordered. Isolation, apparent self-sufficiency, ritualized and idealized action, exemplary performance, hierarchic stability—all contribute to this world's symbolic reality" (p. 253).

15   The BBC production of *Cymbeline* beautifully brought out the equally perverse eroticism of the two scenes through suggestive closeups of the inert body, through disturbingly erotic yet comic embraces of this body by Iachimo and Imogen, and through parallel composition of the individual shots and of the overall rhythms of the scenes.

16   Cf. Arthur Kirsch, *Shakespeare and the Experience of Love* (Cambridge: Cambridge University Press, 1981), for a discussion of how Posthumus's erotic conflicts and erotic guilt are projected

onto Cloten and exorcised through his death (pp. 151–60), and Schwartz, "Between Fantasy and Imagination," who analyzes the "unadulterable phallic aggression" (p. 222) represented by Cloten (pp. 222–26), the sublimated version of the same instincts in Iachimo (pp. 226–31), and Posthumus's "tense and precariously balanced combination of the two" (p. 231).

17 In both the ninth tale of the Second Day of Boccaccio's *Decameron* and in *Frederyke of Jennen*, the husbands forgive their wives and ask forgiveness from them only after the deceivers have confessed their deception in elaborate trial scenes before rulers who order them executed (Bullough, 8:62, 77).

18 Meredith Skura, "Interpreting Posthumus' Dream from Above and Below: Families, Psychoanalysts, and Literary Critics," in *Representing Shakespeare*, ed. Murray M. Schwartz and Coppélia Kahn (Baltimore: Johns Hopkins University Press, 1980), pp. 203–16, analyzes the important functions of this dream for Posthumus and for the play.

19 Charles Frey, " 'O sacred, shadowy, cold, and constant queen': Shakespeare's Imperiled and Chastening Daughters of Romance," in *The Woman's Part*, ed. Carolyn Ruth Swift Lenz, Gayle Greene, and Carol Thomas Neely (Urbana: University of Illinois Press, 1980), pp. 295–313, explores the importance of and the important limits placed on daughters in the romances, who, by choosing husbands in opposition to their fathers, assure patrilineal continuity.

20 Lynda E. Boose, "The Father and the Bride in Shakespeare," *PMLA* 97 (1982): 325–47, demonstrates how the wedding ceremony ritualizes both the father's bonds with and requisite separation from his daughter and explores how in the tragedies the violation of this ritual has destructive consequences while in the romances its completion engenders harmony.

21 The paucity of references to grandchildren in the romances—Antigonus wishes their elimination (II.i.148–49) and the old shepherd looks forward to them (V.ii.128–29)—seems curious given these plays' emphasis on the continuation of the family line, the birth of a granddaughter, Elizabeth Hall, to Shakespeare in 1608, and the careful provisions he made in his will to bequeath his estate to future male grandchildren or, in their absence, to Elizabeth. See Samuel Schoenbaum, *Shakespeare: A Compact Documentary Life* (Oxford: Oxford University Press, 1977), pp. 299–300, 304.

22 Harry Berger, Jr., "Miraculous Harp: A Reading of Shakespeare's *Tempest*," *Shakespeare Studies* 5 (1969): 253–83, cites Prospero's escapist desires and his refusal to take responsibility for them, as well as other impediments to Prospero's progress toward forgiveness and renunciation.

23 Frey, *Shakespeare's Vast Romance*, p. 120, sees this innuendo as providing hints of Leontes' jealousy (see n. 1 above).

24 See my article, "*The Winter's Tale*: The Triumph of Speech," *Studies in English Literature* 15 (1975): 324–27, for a detailed analysis of the intertwining of imagery, emotion, and rationalization in this speech.

25 Mowat, *Dramaturgy*, pp. 8–26, illuminates the blend of comic and tragic elements in the characterization of Leontes (see n. 12 above).

26 Cf. Murray M. Schwartz, "Leontes' Jealousy in *The Winter's Tale*," *American Imago* 30 (1973): 256. In this essay and its continuation, "*The Winter's Tale*: Loss and Transformation," *American Imago* 32 (1975): 145–99, Schwartz argues that *The Winter's Tale* is "a play about how this fantasy of perfect mutuality can be made to survive the impact of 'great difference' (I.i.3) and yet remain itself" (30:256). Schwartz's comprehensive, dense, penetrating discussion serves, more often than I can note, to clarify or amplify ideas I touch on briefly. His analysis of the friendship reveals that it is, like incest, possessive and time-denying. Mark Taylor, *Shakespeare's Darker Purpose: A Question of Incest* (New York: AMS Press, 1982), p. 44, also suggests some parallels between homoeroticism and incest which seem relevant to the romances, although the discussion unfortunately suggests a generalized bias against homosexuality.

27 C. L. Barber, "'Thou that beget'st him / that did thee beget': Transformation in 'Pericles' and 'The Winter's Tale,'" *Shakespeare Survey* 22 (1966): 59–67, following J. I. M. Stewart, *Character and Motive in Shakespeare* (London: Longmans, 1949), pp. 30–37, interprets Leontes' jealousy psychoanalytically as a projection onto Hermione of his affection for Polixenes and explores the transformation of this motif in the rest of the play. I take this motif to be secondary, not primary, and see the restorations of Perdita, Polixenes, and Hermione as parallel, not interdependent; for each to be achieved, Leontes must come to acknowledge the realities of time, change, and difference—including sexual difference.

28 Cf. Schwartz, "Loss and Transformation," pp. 154–55; Wheeler,

Shakespeare's Development, p. 217 (see n. 12 above); and Coppélia Kahn, *Man's Estate: Masculine Identity in Shakespeare* (Berkeley: University of California Press, 1981, pp. 216–17), for related readings of Mamillius's death.

29 In "Recognition in *The Winter's Tale*," in *Essays on Shakespeare and Elizabethan Drama in Honour of Hardin Craig*, ed. Richard Hosley (Columbia: University of Missouri Press, 1962), p. 238.

30 George Sandys, trans., *Ovid's Metamorphosis, Englished, Mythologized, and Represented in Figures* (1632), ed. Karl Hulley and Stanley T. Vandersall (Lincoln: University of Nebraska Press, 1970), bk. V, lines 478–85, p. 239.

31 Proserpina cannot return permanently to her mother because while in the underworld she had eaten seven pomegranate seeds, meaning, in Sandy's gloss, that she "lost her virginity, alluding to the marks thereof in that fruit: because a rape so consummated is no way repairable but by marriage" (p. 256).

32 E. M. W. Tillyard, *Shakespeare's Last Plays* (London: Chatto & Windus, 1938), p. 47.

33 Cf. discussions of Autolycus's parodic and mediating functions in Frey, *Vast Romance*, pp. 148–49, and Joan Hartwig, "Cloten, Autolycus, and Caliban: Bearers of Parodic Burdens," in *Shakespeare's Romances Reconsidered*, ed. Carol McGinnis Kay and Henry E. Jacobs (Lincoln: University of Nebraska Press, 1978), pp. 91–103.

34 Schwartz, "Loss and Transformation," p. 166 (see n. 26 above).

35 For a discussion of Leontes' restored vision, see my "Triumph of Speech," pp. 332–33, 337. For extended discussion of related uses of eye imagery and its connection with acknowledging and being acknowledged, see Stanley Cavell, "The Avoidance of Love: A Reading of *King Lear*," in *Must We Mean What We Say?* (Cambridge: Cambridge University Press, 1976). Compare, too, the dominant motif of perverted sight in *Cymbeline*: Iachimo's voyeurism, Cloten's obsession with clothes, Posthumus's failure to recognize the disguised Imogen, and Cymbeline's extraordinary self-justification for his failure to recognize the Queen's evil: "Mine eyes / Were not at fault, for she was beautiful" (V.v.62–63).

36 C. L. Barber in "Thou that beget'st" and Peter Erickson in "Patriarchal Structure in *The Winter's Tale*," *PMLA* 97 (1982): 819–29 both claim that it is the restoration of the friendship of Polixenes and Leontes which makes Hermione's recovery possible. Barber

argues that, because the destructive tie to Polixenes has been transferred into the betrothal of their children, reunion is possible; and Erikson suggests that "the male network is solid, and copious enough not only to withstand the impact of Hermione's return but to supply replacements for Mamillius and Antigonus" (p. 824). These views misread, I think, the dramatic and psychological progression of the last act and overemphasize the renewal of the friendship, which is only a happy grace note to the finale. We know by act 4, scene 2 that the friends are reconciled; their reunion is given less space in the narrated recognition scene than that of Camillo and Leontes. The renewed friendship is important to accomplish the transformation of all the motives of the first act but is not essential to the family reunions.

37 See my "Triumph of Speech," pp. 335–37, for an extended discussion of this process, summarized here (see n. 24 above).

38 Or, as Charles Frey succinctly remarks of Leontes, "He can come out the way he went in," *Shakespeare's Vast Romance*, p. 163. Wheeler, *Shakespeare's Development*, pp. 214–19, makes suggestive use of the developmental theory of D. W. Winnicott, in which objects (persons) must be symbolically destroyed before they can be restored with new autonomy "at the point in time and space of the initiation of their state of separateness" (*Playing and Reality* [New York: Basic Books, 1971], p. 97), to understand the dynamics of Leontes' reunion with Hermione and the larger structural pattern of the romances. The theory also provides a way to account for the reunions' remembrance of and reversal of the original moment of rupture.

Index

CAROL THOMAS NEELY is a professor of English and women's studies at the University of Illinois at Urbana-Champaign. She is the coeditor, with Carolyn Ruth Swift Lenz and Gayle Greene, of *The Woman's Part: Feminist Criticism of Shakespeare*. She is the author of numerous articles on Shakespeare and Renaissance culture, and is a past president of the Shakespeare Association of America. Professor Neely is currently at work on a study of women and madness in early modern England.